# TOMMY'S HONOUR

## THE EXTRAORDINARY STORY OF GOLF'S
## FOUNDING FATHER AND SON

### KEVIN COOK

HarperCollins*Publishers*

HarperCollins*Publishers*
1 London Bridge Street
London SE1 9GF

www.harpercollins.co.uk

First published by HarperCollins*Publishers* 2007
This paperback edition 2008

4

© Kevin Cook 2007

The author asserts the moral right to be
identified as the author of this work

A CIP catalogue record for this book is
available from the British Library

ISBN 978-0-00-727124-5

Printed and bound by CPI Group (UK) Ltd, Croydon, CR0 4YY

MIX
Paper from
responsible sources
FSC™ C007454

This book is produced from independently certified FSC™ paper
to ensure responsible forest management.

For more information visit: www.harpercollins.co.uk/green

2pm

# CONTENTS

Beneath the sod poor Tommy's laid,
Now bunkered fast for good and all;
A better golfer never played
A further or a surer ball.

A triple laurel round his brow,
The light of triumph in his eye;
He stands before us even now
As in the hour of victory.

Thrice belted knight of peerless skill,
Again we see him head the fray;
And memory loves to reckon still
The feats of Tommy in his day.

— from 'Elegy on Tom Morris, Jr'
*Chambers' Edinburgh Journal*, 1876

# PROLOGUE

## *'Wake, Tommy'*

THE WIND CAME off the North Sea, pushing sand and bits of straw over grass-covered dunes to the links. The wind smelled of seaweed. It hurried past the sandstone clubhouse and ran uphill to the Morris house, where it slipped under the door and stirred the embers of the previous night's fire.

Tom Morris gave his son a mild kick on the backside. 'Wake, Tommy.'

The boy twitched. He was thirteen and slept like a paving stone. After another kick he stretched and yawned. 'What time is it?'

'Tea time.'

His father, the early riser, had already rekindled the fire, boiled water and filled two cups. Tommy was stretching and rubbing his eyes as the old man put a cup and saucer in his hands. Outside, a cock crowed. Tommy sat up and sipped his black tea. It was bitter and scalding, hot enough to numb the tip of his tongue. Next came a chunk of oatcake, dropped onto the saucer as his father bustled past.

Tom Morris threw open the door to the street. His reddish-brown side-whiskers caught the day's first light. He was forty-three years old, with teeth the colour of pale ale and a dusting of white in his beard. He rubbed his callused, veiny hands together as the breeze tossed motes of ash around the room, dropping ash on the Championship Belt on the mantelpiece and on Mum's untouchable china dishes in their rack on the wall. 'Chilly,' he said. 'We'll have stingin' hands today. Stingin' hands.'

Tommy smiled. His father loved to say things twice, as if repeating something could double its import. 'Aye, aye,' he said, amusing himself. 'Stingin' hands.' His father didn't hear a word. He'd pulled on his cap and stepped into the wind, leaving the door flapping open behind him.

'Wait,' Tommy said. But the old man would not wait. Tommy gulped his tea, pulled his boots and jacket on, stuck the oatcake in a pocket and clattered out the door with his father's clubs under his arm.

His footfalls echoed down Golf Place, a double row of dark stone houses. No one else was awake. Any caddie or gentleman golfer who was up at this hour would be hung over, cradling his headache in his hands and wishing he had died at birth. The links were empty except for gulls, crows, rabbits, a mule tethered to a post by the stationmaster's garden, and Tom Morris, now joined by his panting son.

Tom examined his six clubs – driver, spoon, two niblicks, a rut iron and a wooden putter – and selected the driver. He took a pinch of damp sand from a wooden box by the teeing-ground and built a small sand-hill – a tee – for his ball to sit on. He took his stance and waggled his club at the ball as if to threaten it. 'Far and sure,' he said.

Tommy had heard the old motto a thousand times. He was supposed to repeat it, to say 'Far and sure' before the first swing, just as golfers had done on this spot for centuries. He was tempted to try something new, to blurt 'Long and strong', or 'High and mighty!' But he held back. His father might take offence, might turn into one of those stern Old Testament fathers he was starting to resemble. So Tommy mumbled 'far'n'sher' and watched the old man draw back the driver to start the slow, clockwork swing that all St Andrews golfers knew, laying the hickory shaft almost flat across his shoulders at the top, starting down slow as honey and then whipping the head of the club through the ball, which took off towards the white flag in the distance.

Tom squinted as he followed its flight. Nodding, he reached into his jacket for his pipe and pouch. He tapped a few tobacco leaves into the pipe's bowl, lit a match and breathed blue smoke. Mum detested that smoke but Tommy loved it, the sweet reek of his father. Tom stood five foot seven, a bit above average for a Scotsman of his time, but in Tommy's eyes he loomed larger. Tom Morris was the Champion Golfer of Scotland. He was the hero of St Andrews, the only man who could beat the golfing brutes of Mussel-burgh. He was the official keeper of these famous four miles of turf, the links of St Andrews. Beloved by all men – excepting jealous golf professionals, several red-coated gentlemen of the Royal & Ancient Golf Club, and the Musselburgh brutes – he was a pious churchman who was not above joking and drinking with foul-smelling caddies. Tom Morris was all these great things and one more: he was the one golfer Tommy was dying to beat.

Not to humble him, never that, but to be more like him. Not as a rival, but more like an equal. More like a man. Tommy was nearly as tall as his father, and suspected he would soon be stronger. And the more he grew, the more he believed that a boy needed to make his own name in the world. He needed to be more than his father's caddie.

With such thoughts in his head and the scent of tobacco in his nose, Tommy took the driver from his father's hand. He took a pinch of sand from the box, knelt to make a sand tee for his ball and then stood tall, waving the driver back and forth. His swing was short and fast: bang! Tommy's drives didn't always go straight, but a few went further than his father's. This one sailed past the other ball before it bounced near

Swilcan Burn, the brook that curled past the putting-green.

Tommy was thrilled. How many lads could hit a ball so far? How many grown men could?

His father was less impressed. Long or short didn't matter so much to Tom Morris. Position mattered. Tommy's drive was long, but too far to the left. Tom checked his pocket-watch as he set off towards the green. A minute later he was hitting again. Without a word he took the wooden niblick from Tommy and slapped a low approach the wind could not catch. His ball cleared the burn by a safe five yards and rolled to the back of the green.

Tommy faced a harder shot. There was no easy play from the left side. The only way to stop the ball near the hole would be a high, soft pitch, the opposite of the usual approach. But no one attempted such shots with the shallow-faced clubs of the day. Tommy had tried hitting shots from flat ground with the rut iron, a lofted club made for lifting a ball out of cart or wheelbarrow ruts. He found that he could make the ball drop and stop. Not every time – you had to strike it just right or you'd foozle the shot. But when it worked, the ball came down like a snowflake.

He waggled the rut iron. His father looked surprised – Tommy liked seeing that. He drew the club back, keeping his hands high, then yanked them straight down, chopping the rut iron's heavy head into the turf. He grunted; dirt flew.

The ball squirted along the ground, bouncing two or three times before it splished into the burn. He dropped the rut iron. Damned useless stick. He lost the hole.

His father moved to the second teeing-ground a few yards away. There was no sandbox here; you fished a bit of sand from the bottom of the hole on the first green. Tom Morris fashioned his sand tee, then pulled his driver back over his shoulder – *tick* – and whipped it smoothly to the ball – *tock*. But this ball flew low. It was a 'scalded cat', a near-miss that skipped along the ground. On dry days a scalded cat would run out of sight, but this one kicked up dew and stopped only 120 yards out.

Tommy took his pinch of sand from the bottom of the first hole and made a perch for his ball. His father watched him take his stance. Was he aiming for Cheape's Bunker? No sane golfer tried to clear that crater, not without a gale at his back, and the wind was blowing across the fairway. Tom shook his head – the boy was his own worst enemy.

But Tommy had a plan, and a picture in his mind. He remembered all the rounds he had played with his father, not the friendly foursomes but the singles, one against one. They were all losses. At home the old man was kind, even tender. He tucked Tommy into bed every night and they prayed together. *I pray the Lord my soul to keep.* But there was no kindness on the links, where Tommy was beaten again and again, leaving him to dream of the day he would win at last. A day when he told the ball to duck into the hole and down it went. A day when he willed the ball to curve in flight and it curved. Now he used the dream to picture his next shot. Pulling the driver back with his right elbow high, he brought it down and sent his drive on a beeline for Cheape's Bunker. In mid-flight the ball curved to the right as if it knew where to go.

Sheer willpower may have helped, but so did something more tangible: the spin Tommy had applied with a swing that went from high and away from his body to low and closer, towards his left foot. That sidespin gave the ball a gentle arc from left to right, and his drive landed safely to the right of the bunker, leaving him a clear shot to the green.

'Well played,' his father said.

Praise from Tom Morris! That alone made this a good day. And it might get better yet, for Tommy had a secret: he was learning to make the ball curve at will.

They played fast, as always, with Tom checking his pocket-watch. He hated spending more than two hours to play eighteen holes. As he marched down the fairway he would reach over and take a club from Tommy, who carried the clubs under his armpit. Within seconds of reaching his ball, Tom began his clockwork swing and dispatched the ball on a low, straight line. He knew every cranny of the links and always took the safe route, trusting opponents to make more mistakes than he did.

Tommy played a bolder game. He was strong – the only boy his age in town who could topple a full-grown cow, not that his father would allow mischief like cow-tipping if he knew of it. On the links, Tommy swung hard and took chances. If a high-risk shot failed, he would try again. And again. He was more than fearless. He was a joyful golfer, a boy who could laugh at a terrible shot and swing harder at the next.

His ball had found a level lie near Cheape's Bunker. The ball was a dull white gutty, made of gutta percha, the sap of a gum tree in Malaysia, a far corner of Queen Victoria's vast empire. Hard as rock, it made a loud click at impact, like a billiard ball hitting another. This one clicked and climbed like a rocket as he slammed it towards the putting-green. With a chip and a putt, he won the second hole. The match was even, one hole apiece. This was match play, the usual way of keeping score. Total strokes didn't matter; each hole was a separate contest, and whoever won the most holes won the day.

They halved the next two as the wind picked up, humming in their ears. Neither golfer spoke much. Tommy won the fifth hole when his father left a three-pace putt a yard short. Everyone knew how Tom Morris struggled with short putts. 'You'd be a fine putter, father,' Tommy needled, 'if the hole was always a yard closer.'

Tom smiled. The boy had spirit. But the boy was a long way from winning the day. In fact this was golf the way Tom liked it. Out-driven and outplayed for five holes, he was only one behind with miles to go.

Clouds turned red as the sun climbed over the sea. When a low cloud began drizzling, Tommy reached into a jacket pocket where he kept a lump of pine tar to aid his grip. He found the tar as well as a slick, blackened oatcake; the breakfast he had stuck in the wrong pocket. He tossed the oatcake over his shoulder for the crows to gag on.

At the sixth hole, called Heathery due to its rough, weedy putting-green, both players lay two and had thoughts of chipping in for three. Tommy often joked that this green was more brown than green. In spots you could see bits of the seashells that gave the hole its traditional name, Hole o' Shell. On a windless day you could hear shells crunch under your boots. Putts didn't roll here, they bounced. Tom had no trouble bump-and-running his way to a four, while Tommy two-putted for a frustrating five, the same five any club man could make with four gouty swings and a lucky putt.

The High Hole, the seventh, was where Tom loved to tell of the Great Storm of 1860. Waving his arm towards the beach, he re-launched the tale of Captain Maitland-Dougall, recalling the day when the captain stood poised to compete for the medals of the Royal & Ancient Golf Club. But a tempest rose up! Winds and five-yard waves capsized a ship in the bay. Ten men dragged the town's lifeboat across the links to the raging surf, but who would lead them? Captain Maitland-Dougall! Dropping his clubs, he left his fellow golfers behind and leaped into the lifeboat, taking the stroke oar himself. A dozen sailors were saved that day, many pulled from the maelstrom by Maitland-Dougall himself. When the captain had rowed the lifeboat safely to shore, he returned to the links. Wet as an otter, his arms like lead weights, he took up his clubs and won the gold medal with a score of 112.

Finishing his story, Tom Morris looked as proud as if his own niblick were the stroke oar.

Tommy was, as ever, amazed by this story. A hundred and twelve? That was worse than straight sixes. He was no admirer of his father's bosses, the club men in their red golfing jackets, calling themselves Captain this and Major that, wagering tens and scores of pounds and then swinging and missing. 'God save Captain Maitland-Dougall,' he said, still shaking his head at a winning score of 112.

Tommy won the High Hole but lost the eighth when his father rolled in a putt for a deuce (and tipped his cap). The eighth, ninth, tenth and eleventh holes were where the course reached the top of its shepherd's-crook shape and doubled back towards town. On the evil eleventh, Tommy's tee shot met a sudden gust of wind, struck the face of the Hill Bunker and slid straight down. No one could save three from there. But his father took three putts (and Tommy tipped his cap). They halved the hole. The boy was still two holes ahead.

From the twelfth teeing-ground they could see the town's old towers. To the west was the Eden Brae, a grassy slope that leaned down to the mudflats where the River Eden fed into the sea. Fisher-women toiled down there, moving through acres of mussel-scalps a hundred yards out, gathering mussels for their men to use as bait. A wrack-picker shoved a wheelbarrow along the sand, heading for the corner where the tides brought great tangles of wrack – seaweed – that would fertilize gardens all over town. As a rule, the golfer and the wrack-picker eyed each other warily, each thinking the other a fool for doing the world's dullest chore. But like everyone in town, this straggle-bearded wrack-gatherer knew Tom Morris. He looked up and waved.

Tom waved back. He took a deep, bracing breath of salt air and turned from the brae to the work at hand. He tossed a blade of grass to gauge the wind, then hit a modest drive, straight as a telegraph wire. It was easy to spend strokes on the way in. He spent carefully, tacking his way through the next three holes, giving Tommy every chance to stumble. Which Tommy did on the long fourteenth, hitting a spoon that rolled into Hell Bunker. Three swings later he rose from Hell with his face pink, hot with shame. His advantage cut to one hole, he was dying to make up for his blunder. And so, after a clean four on the fifteenth hole, he did exactly what his father expected him to do at the sixteenth: he took the bold line off the tee, smacking his drive up the right side along the railway tracks. It was the wrong play. You could make three that way – or seven or eight. But sometimes the wrong play works. Tommy's drive landed 200 yards out, hopped to the right and stopped just shy of the tracks. Safe by the length of a thumb. From there he hit a spoon to two-putt distance and the hole was his. That made him dormy: leading by two holes with two to play, he could not lose. His father's only hope was to win both of the last two holes to salvage a half, a draw.

Tommy had the honour at the Road Hole. He knocked his drive over the railway sheds, but turned his wrists a hair too soon. The ball hooked into knee-high grass. Three swings later he lay four in the greenside bunker, with Tom lying three on the edge of the green. Tommy scraped out of the sand and now lay five, forty feet from the flag. He shrugged and picked up his ball, conceding the hole. He was one hole up with one to play.

The Home Hole was short, less than 300 yards. Tom's drive wasn't long, but it was straight. By now there were golfers milling around the clubhouse – club members in red jackets. A few spectators, early-rising townsmen, stood near a mudpile behind the Home green. Two shovels jutted up from the mudpile, which was roped off with wood stakes and fishing line. Tom was building a new green up there, above and behind the current one. To reach it, future golfers would have to play over or through the hollow where the green was now. He had been casting about for a name for that hollow, a memorable name to fit with the old reliable Hell Bunker and Elysian Fields – 'Shady Acre' or 'Slough of Despond', something like that.

Teeing up, Tommy spat on his fingers. If he won or halved the last hole, he would carry the day. He took his stance and gave the ball a swat. His drive climbed towards the clouds over the town, blue-grey clouds split by shafts of sunlight. He lost sight of the ball, but the spectators watched it bounce thirty yards past his father's. Tommy heard shouts and clapping as he crossed the old stone bridge over the Swilcan Burn, and he couldn't help himself – he waved.

All this time, Tom Morris was busy playing golf. He bumped his ball to the hollow, just hard enough to send it running towards the flag. Would it fall for a deuce? There was new applause, then a groan as the ball slipped past the hole. Still, Tom's three was a sure thing. Tommy had two strokes left to win the match.

He had thirty yards to the flag: a twenty-yard bump and ten yards of roll. But there was a patch of ankle-high grass just short of the green. He would have to clear that grass by an inch or two.

As he circled his ball, studying his lie, a pair of

red-coated club men came to stand behind him. 'I'd putt it,' one said.

Tommy's chip cleared the ankle-high grass, but by too much. It ran three paces past the hole. The red-coats were quiet. The whole town was quiet. Except for Tom Morris, who nodded at the ball and said, 'You're still away, son.'

The putt was uphill. It would go left, but if he aimed for the right-hand edge of the hole and hit it hard, it would fall. Tommy drew back his putter and rapped the ball, hard.

In it went. The redcoats whooped. Tom Morris nodded again. He walked past the hole and offered a handshake and, in that moment, Tommy was so happy that he didn't want to blink. He didn't want to move from this spot. He leaned back and flung his putter straight up at the sky. The club rose, turning like the wheels in God's pocket-watch.

# ONE

## *Born in Scotland*

THE GAME THE Morrises played was already ancient. It was in the kingdom of Fife on Scotland's east coast, the place where medieval shepherds used their crooks to knock stones at rabbit holes. They were at it within a century or two of King Macbeth's death in 1057. In time, the shepherds' sons and their sons' sons whittled balls of wood to whack around the links, coastal wastelands where no trees or crops grew. They dug holes in flat places and planted sticks in the holes – targets for a game they called 'gowf' or 'golfe'. Over the centuries the game would be called many other things, some printable, including 'this human frustration', 'a good walk spoiled' and 'a weird combination of snooker and karate'.

Other countries had similar sports. One was *chole*, a Flemish pastime in which a team of players got three swings to advance a ball towards a goal that might be half a mile away. Then the opponents played defence, hitting the ball towards the nearest bog. The Dutch played a golflike game on ice, and it is fashionable in some circles to say that golf began in Holland. But if you ask a Scotsman if he owes his national game to some Amsterdammers on ice skates, he may shoot back, 'That's not golf.' In fact, the Scots' claim to the sport is simple and correct: they invented the game with the hole in the ground.

But they borrowed its name. 'Golf' is probably a corruption of *kolf*, a Dutch word for club. And as the game spread it corrupted its players – or so thought Scotland's King James II, who banned it. The king was sick of seeing his soldiers wasting time on the links, neglecting their archery practice. No wee wooden ball would pierce armour and kill the damned English. In 1457, in the first recorded reference to the game, King James II decreed that 'the golfe be utterly cryit doune and not usit'. Golfers ignored him.

His grandson, James IV, kept up the family tradition by calling the game 'ridiculous ... requiring neither strength nor skill'. Then he tried playing it. During a lull between wars with England, the young monarch emerged from Holyrood Palace with a brand-new driver in his hand. He greeted several lords and ladies gathered to mark the occasion, stepped up to the ball and – whiff! He missed. He tried again, whiffed again, threw down his club and stalked back to the palace. That might have been the end of royal golf, but to his credit James IV practised in secret until he could lace his drives more than fifty yards. He became the first royal golf nut and the first royal golf gambler. In 1504, after the king lost a two-guinea bet to the Earl of Bothwell, the debt was added to the nation's tax bill.

A love of golf often passes from father to son. In the middle of the sixteenth century it went from father to son to daughter. Mary Stuart, better known as Mary Queen of Scots, was the only child of King James V, the golfing son of James IV. Mary ascended to the throne after her father died in 1542. She was six days old. When the news reached London, the gluttonous wife-killer Henry VIII, a tennis player, saw a chance to expand his empire. In a series of invasions called the 'rough wooing', he tried to force a royal marriage between his son, Prince Edward, and Scotland's child queen. Mary was shipped to safety in France, where she grew into a striking beauty, six feet tall. Upon returning to Scotland the seventeen-year-old queen took up the national game and gave it a new word: she called the boy who lugged her clubs a *cadet*, which the Scots heard as 'caddie'. Mary went on to be a golfing widow, hitting the links the same week her husband, Lord Darnley, was murdered. That *faux pas* gave her cousin, England's Queen Elizabeth, an excuse to charge her with crimes against God, nature and good government. Mary Queen of Scots went on to lose a few more golf balls in Scotland and later, in England, her head.

By then a dozen generations of golfers had walked the four-mile loop of the links at St Andrews, over Swilcan Burn to the mouth of the River Eden and then back towards town, aiming for rooftops and the crumbling twelfth-century cathedral where ghosts were said to guard the remains of St Andrew, supposedly brought here by a monk in the year 345: three of the Apostle's finger bones, an arm bone, a tooth and a kneecap. No man designed the golf course west of the town. The course was an accident. The fairways were narrow paths through thickets of scrub: thorny whin bushes, which the rest of the world called gorse, as well as heather, nettles, brambles, ground elder, dogtail, cocksfoot and chickweed. The putting-greens were clearings where players' boots and the nibblings of rabbits and sheep kept the grass down. During storms the sheep huddled behind hillocks, where they scuffed and nibbled the grass and clover to the roots, leaving bare spots that eroded into sand bunkers. Other bunkers were carved by golfers slashing the turf in hollows where bad shots collected.

Golfers and sheep vied for space on the links with fishermen drying their nets, women beating rugs or bleaching clothes, dogs chasing rabbits, cows and goats grazing, larks darting in and out of the whins, children playing hide and seek, and even the occasional citizen soldier doing his duty by old James II, practising his archery. Still, it was a golf town. In the seventeenth-century sermons of Robert Blair, minister of the town church, Reverend Blair likened the bond between God and the Church of Scotland to that of shaft and club-head. Remote, wind-blistered St Andrews may have been shrinking as Edinburgh, Glasgow and Dundee grew, but the town's sway in golf never shrank. Courses in Perth, Edinburgh, Kirkcaldy, Montrose and Musselburgh ranged from five to twenty-five holes, but after St Andrews rejiggered its twenty-two-hole course to make it tougher, the 'St Andrews standard' of eighteen became everyone's standard. Scottish sportsmen played the game by thirteen rules adopted in 1754 by the Society of St Andrews Golfers. Some of those rules sound reasonable enough today ('If a ball is stop'd by any person, horse, dog or any thing else, the ball so stop'd must be played where it lyes'), while others sound puzzling ('Your tee must be upon the ground'). One timeless feature of the game was already clear to a St Andrews writer: 'How in the evening each dilates on his own wonderful strokes, and the singular chances that befell him – all under the pleasurable delusion that every listener is as interested in his game as he himself is.'

The men who made the rules and played most of the golf were gentlemen: well-to-do landowners who didn't need to work. The game was technically open to all and the St Andrews links, like most links, occupied public land. But few working men could afford to play in an age when whole families, including both parents as well as children as young as five or six, toiled six days a week to earn what a gentleman spent to buy a single golf ball.

Golf evolved as a rich man's game partly because the feathery balls of the 1700s and early 1800s, leather pouches packed tight with goose feathers, were expensive. Men who could afford them saw golf as a healthy outdoor pastime like fox hunting. They met in town halls and taverns to drink, joke, argue and arrange challenge matches, and as the game grew they formed local clubs and played for trophies. In 1744, after tabling discussions of taxes, prostitution and the latest cholera outbreak, Edinburgh's town council approved the purchase of a silver cup, to be played for each year by the Honourable Company of Edinburgh Golfers. That move seemed to establish the gentlemen of the capital, who played in satin breeches and silk-lined jackets, as the game's ruling body. But the golfers of Fife would have something to say about that.

The 'twenty-two noblemen and gentlemen' of the Society of St Andrews Golfers played in red hunting jackets, a look borrowed from the Fife Fox and Hounds Club. Some wore hiking boots that had tacks driven through the soles – the first golf spikes. After forming the Society of St Andrews Golfers in 1754 they commissioned a trophy of their own, a silver golf club. They also played for gold and silver medals, and these medal competitions led to a new way of keeping score. Since a round robin of one-on-one matches could take forever, the society came up with a different format: '[W]hoever puts in the ball at the fewest strokes ... shall be declared and sustained victor.' The new style was called medal play. In time it would eclipse the old way of playing. Medal play is what Tiger Woods, Phil Mickelson and almost everyone else in modern golf play ninety percent of the time. Often called stroke play, it is the modern way to play golf: whoever takes the fewest strokes wins. But for more than a century, it was a sideshow. Golf was a match-play game between players who challenged each other to man-to-man contests (singles) or two-man battles (foursomes). In match play, you can take ten swings in a bunker or even pick up your ball and surrender; you lose only that one hole. Whoever wins the most *holes* wins the match.

'Challenge matches are the life of golf,' Andra Kirkaldy of St Andrews would write, looking back on the game as it was played in his youth. 'Man against man, pocket against pocket, in deadly earnest is the thing.'

Stroke play might win you the honour of a club medal once or twice a year, but the rest of the calendar was for match play. That meant bets and more bets. Many wagers were for a few shillings, but there were plenty of five- and ten-pound matches. Some gentlemen thought nothing of playing for fifty pounds – more than enough to buy a fine pony like the one Sir John Low rode around the links, dismounting when it was his turn to hit. Fifty pounds was more than most men earned in a year. In Scotland in 1820 the average annual income was less than fifteen pounds, a sum Sir John might bet on one putt.

Some matches were for territorial pride as well as cash. In 1681 a pair of English noblemen told the Duke of York that golf began in England. Any Scot who claimed otherwise, they said, was a liar! The duke, a Scotsman who would be king of both countries, agreed to a challenge match to settle the matter. For his partner he chose John Patersone, a cobbler who was said to be the best golfer in Edinburgh. The shoemaker arrived with his clubs tucked under his arm, trembling to be in such exalted company. After the other men hit their tee shots, he steeled himself, swung from the heels and belted a drive that dropped their jaws. With Patersone leading the way, the Scots routed the English pair. The duke was so pleased he split his winnings with Patersone, who used the money to build a house on Edinburgh's Royal Mile, a fine stone house with the old golf motto etched above the front door: *Far and Sure*.

By the 1800s, with seven golf societies scattered through Scotland and England, the game was respectable enough to seek royal patronage. In 1833, the officers of the upstart Perth Golfing Society irked golfers in Edinburgh and St Andrews by jumping the queue, securing the sponsorship of King William IV. The Perth club became Royal Perth, despite being only nine years old while Edinburgh's Honourable

Company was eighty-nine years old and the Society of St Andrews Golfers seventy-nine. *Royal Perth!* The sound of it soured all the claret in St Andrews. In 1834 a politically connected R&A member, Colonel John Murray Belshes, wrote to the king urging him to restore the old town's prestige. When the monarch ignored his plea, Belshes reminded King William that among his many titles was one that warmed the hearts of St Andreans, for His Majesty was also the Duke of St Andrews. How fallible he would appear if he forgot the town that was part of his birthright!

With the speed of the latest laboratory fluid, electricity, the king gave his patronage to the Society of St Andrews Golfers, which got a new name, including two words to remind Royal Perth of its youth: the Royal & Ancient Golf Club of St Andrews. Three summers later, King William sent the club 'a Gold Medal, with Green Ribband ... which His Majesty wishes should be challenged and played for annually'. The Royal & Ancient had taken a step towards its destiny as ruling body of a game that would be played not only on rough town greens but all over the world, and not only for crowns and shillings and the occasional fifty pounds, but for millions.

For the moment, though, golf still belonged to three or four hundred men in hunting jackets. Like the hunt, golf was a pursuit for prosperous fellows who wanted to stretch their muscles a bit before they fell into overstuffed chairs in chandeliered rooms to eat duck, pheasant, mutton and beef and drink claret and gin while they smoked and told stories. As some writers had already noted, the game was an abstract form of the primordial hunt: a pack of men journeys into perilous land, avoiding dangers, tracking first one target and then another, getting home safely by nightfall to gather by the fire.

Golf also shared something important with cock-fighting and bare-knuckle boxing: it was easy to bet on. Every morning but Sunday the gentleman golfers of St Andrews would meet near the first teeing-ground to arrange their singles and foursomes matches, haggling over odds and strokes given. Starting in the hour before noon they slapped their first shots towards the railway station and marched after them, their caddies following a few respectful steps behind. The caddies were a threadbare lot, boys as young as seven jostling for work beside toothless men of eighty. They called the golfer 'Mister' unless he held a still-more-exalted title such as Captain or Major. The occasional golfer of high rank, like the sports-mad Earl of Eglinton, was called 'M'lord'. Caddies were addressed by their first names, befitting their low rank. They were lucky to get a shilling per round, and lucky if their gentlemen didn't smack them as well as the ball. A golfer who got bad advice from his caddie, or who detected laziness or cheek in him, was within his rights to backhand the caddie full in the face, or to take a club and whip him with it. Like the vast and growing empire some of them had served in India, Africa or the Holy Land, the men of the Royal & Ancient Golf Club held firm to the belief that they ruled by right with God's approval. Never mind that revolt was in the air from teeming India to bloody Europe to distant America, or that the land these country gentlemen ruled was literally being turned upside-down, with farmland torn into quarries and mines as the Industrial Revolution gained steam by the hour. Scotland's gentleman golfers could escape the cities' sooty air, blast furnaces and hungry rabble by spending the day on the links. If the rest of the world was hurtling forward at breakneck speed, they told themselves, at least the old game was safe from revolution.

They were wrong.

Here is the Royal & Ancient golfer in 1830: dressed in a tan golfing frock, matching breeches, silk-lined waistcoat and red jacket, with a high collar and a black top hat, he crosses muddy North Street on his way to the links. His pink nose, with ruby veins hinting at rivers of claret and gin, wrinkles at the scent of piss and dung. The gutter steams with the empty-ings of chanty-pots. Pigs snuffle weeds in the rutted, unpaved street. The golfer dodges horses pulling coaches, donkeys pulling carts, ducks, chickens. Now a cork comes flying through the air, just missing him.

The cork, punctured with short nails to give it weight, lands with a plunk. He turns to see who hit it – a boy of eight or nine, trying to hide a cut-down golf club behind his back.

'Sillybodkins,' the golfer says. He smiles. He'd played that game himself on this very street, long ago.

Sillybodkins was the pretend golf of boys who cadged broken or discarded clubs and knocked corks up and down St Andrews' streets, aiming for targets of opportunity: lampposts, doorways, sleeping dogs. Real golf balls were impossibly expensive, but claret and champagne corks were plentiful; a properly weighted cork might carry a hundred yards. It might go further than that if struck by nine-year-old Tom Morris, the sillybodkins king of North Street.

Tom Morris was born in 1821, the year a member of the Royal & Ancient Golf Club bought the town's links. Ordinary men like John Morris, Tom's father, were allowed on the course when the R&A men weren't playing. John got in an occasional round with a second-hand ball, but he had little time for golf. He worked six days a week as a hand-loom weaver, doubling as a postman when the weaving trade went slack. He spent Sundays reading the Bible and shepherding his wife and seven children to morning and afternoon services at the town's church.

Tom was the family's second-youngest child. Born in a time when disease killed one in five children by the age of three, he had a life expectancy of forty-one. He ran the streets barefoot but didn't go hungry. He got enough schooling to read, sign his name and do simple sums, but what he loved was golf and, to his everlasting delight, golf's holy land was two clouts of a cork from North Street.

In its medieval heyday, St Andrews had been the centre of Scottish Catholicism. The legendary bones of St Andrew, housed in St Andrews Cathedral according to the old story, brought Catholic pilgrims from all over Europe. But after Scotland became a Protestant country in 1560, the town began a long decline. St Andrews' population fell from a high of about 14,000 in the early 1500s to 2,854 in 1793. In Tom's youth there were no more than 4,000 souls in a town whose landmarks were the towers of a ruined cathedral, a crumbling castle and the busy links. Many St Andreans still lived in wooden houses with thatched roofs, covered with sod from the links, dried sod that periodically caught fire and burned down three or four houses. Each day a runner jogged eleven miles from nearby Crail, toting the daily mail for Tom's father and other postmen to distribute. The first regular stagecoach service, going twice a week to Dundee and once a week to Cupar, began when Tom was seven.

As a boy he never expected to roam much past Dundee. He was sure to be a weaver, sitting at a loom all day, and perhaps a part-time postman, too. But

Tom's head was full of golf. He could take dead aim at a lamppost and hit it from ten paces. On the links he moved through the whins and tall grass like a hound, sniffing out lost balls. Each feathery ball was a treasure, even a misshapen, waterlogged one. He would play a few holes in the morning, before the redcoats came out, or at dusk when they were done, or race out between foursomes to hit a ball and chase it to the putting-green.

In 1835, Tom's schooling ended. He was fourteen. His father lacked the money and social standing to send his sons to university; it was time for Tom to apprentice himself to a tradesman. Through a family connection, John arranged a meeting with Allan Robertson, the golf-ball maker who caddied for R&A worthies and even partnered them in foursomes. A short, bull-necked fellow who sported filigreed waistcoats and bright-coloured caps, Robertson was the first man to parlay caddying, ball-making and playing into something like a fulltime job. If his trade was a bit disreputable, at least it offered steady work. Tom's mother might fret about her son working for a man who consorted with gamblers, drunkards, cheats and low-livers, but what could she say? Her husband was all for it. John Morris contracted his son to Allan Robertson for a term of four years as apprentice, to be followed by five years as Robertson's journeyman. On the morning his boyhood ended, fourteen-year-old Tom gathered his few belongings, left his parents' house and walked a quarter of a mile to a stone cottage that would be his new home.

Allan Robertson would prove easy to know, if not always easy to work for. Loud, cocky, full of mirth and wrath that could switch places in a blink, he was a grinning, muscular elf. Not quite five and a half feet tall, he had mutton-chop side-whiskers, an off-kilter smile and the wrists and arms of a blacksmith. His strength and pickpocket's touch, helped make him the best golfer of his generation. In an era when anyone who made it around the links in 100 strokes had something to celebrate, the pint-sized Robertson often broke 100 and once shot 87. Still, he was not a golfer by trade. No such career existed. So Robertson made and sold golf balls and caddied for the gentlemen of the R&A. As the town's keenest eye for golf talent, he also set the club members' handicaps and played matchmaker, pairing them up in fair, interesting or mischievous ways.

Tom worked in Robertson's golf-ball factory – a grand term for the kitchen in his little stone cottage at the corner of Golf Place and Links Road. The cramped kitchen had a floor of wood planks. A pot kept water boiling over the fire. A sturdy worktable sat under an oil lamp that cast a wan yellow light specked with feather dust. Three men worked here: Allan Robertson, his cousin Lang Willie Robertson, and Tom Morris. Allan and Lang Willie were Tom's teachers in ball-making, a craft that was equal parts science and upholstery.

To make a feather ball, you start with a wide strip of cowhide. Take a straight razor and cut three thin sections of hide, then soften the sections in water and alum. Trim the largest piece to the shape of an hourglass; this will be the middle of the ball. The other two pieces should be round. They are for the top and bottom. Sew the pieces together with waxed thread, forming a ball with a small hole at one end. Turn the ball inside-out so that the stitches are hidden on the inside. Now you're ready for the gruntwork.

After boiling enough goosefeathers to fill the standard measuring device – a top hat – pull a thick leather cuff over the hand that will hold the empty ball. Grab a handful of boiled goosedown, soft as warm sand, and use a finger-length poker to push the down through the hole into the ball. Repeat until you need a short, T-shaped iron awl to stuff more and more feathers through that little hole. After twenty minutes of this, the short awl will no longer be of any use. To drive one last handful of down into the jam-packed, unyielding ball, you need to wear a wood-and-leather harness. The harness straps around your chest. It has buckles up the side, a wooden panel in front and a slot. Place the butt end of a long awl into the slot and lean forward with all your weight at the crux of your ribcage, forcing the last feathers through the hole. When the top hat is empty and the ball is finally full, sew the hole shut as fast as you can.

The last stage of ball-stuffing was dangerous. If the awl slipped, the ball-maker could break a rib or impale himself. Lang Willie Robertson liked to tell the story about a ball-maker who pushed so hard that his workbench split in two, sending him tumbling forward in a whirl of awls, calipers, paint, waxed thread and knitting needles as the ball bounced away, squirting feathers. As Allan's cousin and assistant, Lang Willie outranked Tom in the Robertson kitchen, but he never acted superior. Six foot two, with rheumy eyes and whisky breath, he was older than Allan – almost forty. Lang Willie told the new apprentice all about the Robertsons, including a forebear who caddied for decades and 'died in harness', dropping dead in a clatter of clubs on the Burn Hole. That caddie left behind a son, David Robertson – Allan's father, Lang Willie's uncle – a caddie and golf hustler immortalized in a poem called 'Golfiana': 'Davie, oldest of the cads/Gives half-one to unsuspicious lads/When he might give them two or even more/ And win, perhaps, three matches out of four!' David Robertson sold golf equipment, too. That sideline came about when a club-maker from Musselburgh grew weary of taking a ship across the Firth of Forth to Kirkaldy, then shouldering his wares and hiking twenty miles to St Andrews. To spare himself the trek, the club-maker hired David Robertson as his salesman in the old town. Both men prospered, and upon his death David left his son, Allan, an estate worth ninety-two pounds, including two pounds' worth of feathery golf balls.

Allan's kitchen crew made or repaired an occasional club, but the trade was mainly featheries. The feather ball had been standard since the 1600s. It was expensive – up to two shillings and sixpence each, enough to buy a new driver – because making the thing was so difficult. Even after you stuffed a ball and sewed it shut, there was work to do. You gave it a light knocking with a thin-headed hammer to even out any bumps. You gave it three coats of white paint and a stamp that showed who made it. (Balls from Allan's kitchen were stamped simply ALLAN.) Then you put the ball aside for two days. As it dried, the feathers inside expanded, pushing the cover to its limit. A feathery might sound soft, but a new one was like hardwood – hard enough to kill a man. Tom knew of two people who had died after being felled by flying golf balls, a schoolboy hit on the head and a grown man struck in the chest.

Feathery balls were so precious that one of Allan's rivals, the Musselburgh ball-maker Douglas Gourlay, put one in the collection plate at the Episcopal Church in Bruntsfield one Sunday. If you were to find that ball today, you could sell it for thousands of pounds.

A skilled ball-maker could stuff, sew, paint and stamp three balls in a day. An adept could make four.

Allowing for misfortune (torn leather, bruised ribs, needle-pricked fingers), three men could make fifty or more featheries in a week, enough for Allan to keep up his household, pay Lang Willie and feed apprentice Tom, who worked for room, board and training. One year Allan Robertson's kitchen-table factory produced 2,456 balls. All the while Allan barked at Lang Willie and Tom to work harder, faster. Laggards and dullards, he called them. Or worse, *Irish* laggards and dullards, which only amused Lang Willie and Tom, neither of whom had been much closer to Ireland than the Eden Brae at the end of the links.

Lang Willie, sitting with his endless legs bent under him, made the time pass with jokes, like the one about the caddie who died and found himself back on the links, at the bottom of a ladder that stretched into the clouds. 'Greetings, my son,' said St Peter, handing the man a piece of chalk. The saint informed the caddie that as he climbed to heaven he must write his sins on the ladder, one per rung. So up the caddie went. 'Took the Lord's name in vain. *Step*,' said Lang Willie, narrating the ascent. 'Impure thoughts. *Step*,' he said. 'Drank to excess. *Step. Step. Step. Step.*' This went on until the man was miles above the earth. And then, to his astonishment, he saw another caddie – his own long-dead grandfather – climbing down the ladder out of the clouds. When asked why, his grandfather cried: 'More chalk!'

Tom learned more than ball-making and old stories

in Allan's house. He learned that a man can have multiple aims. Tom, like his father, was a straightforward character, striving to serve God and family by working hard, speaking plainly and deceiving no one. But the more he knew of ball-making the more clearly he saw that it took no great skill to stuff and sew golf balls. Why then should the great Robertson have chosen Tom Morris to be his apprentice? They weren't cousins. Allan had always been cordial to Tom's father, but the men were not friends. Of all the lads who could use a leg up into a thriving trade, why Tom?

From the week Tom went to live in the Robertson cottage, fifty paces from the links, Allan schooled him in the game as well as the trade: how to grip the club for more control, how to hit shots high or low to suit the weather, how to flip the ball out of sand. On summer evenings when the sun stayed up past ten o'clock, they played match after match of two or three or nine holes, with Allan giving Tom strokes and beating him anyway. There was always a bet. Playing without betting, Allan said, was 'no' golf'. After Tom had lost the few pennies Allan had given him that week, they played for plucks – winner gets to keep one of the loser's clubs. This made no sense, since both of them played with Allan's clubs, but the boss didn't mind as long as he won. Tom didn't mind, either. He welcomed any chance to leave the sweaty kitchen for the great green links. Boss and apprentice spent long hours out there, hours of thunder and wind, much of which came from Allan's mouth. He loved to sound off on things he had read in the *Scotsman* and *Chambers' Edinburgh Journal*, from politics and art to the price of good leather. Tom, straining to hear as the wind blew the words down the fairway, gathered that good leather cost too much, that India was a powderkeg, that Lord Palmerston was not to be trusted, and that some mad Englishman had dug up a Grecian Venus that had no arms.

Tom listened harder when the subject was golf. He heard about the weaknesses of gentlemen like Sir David Baird, who might be the R&A's best ball-striker, but who could not play in rain. Monsieur Messieux, the Frenchman, could hit the ball a mile, but was *merde* on the putting-green. There were other secrets: an invisible break on the eighth green; a spot to the right of the twelfth green that would kick a ball straight left. Each night, lying on his straw mattress, Tom pictured the golf course in his mind's eye, as if from above, and imagined different ways to play each hole. He would leave the window open a few inches even on cold nights, to test his strength while he slept. The chill never woke him. He slept like a stone. When he woke he was alert right away but kept his eyes shut for a moment as he prayed, smelling salt air redolent of sand, mud and turf . . . the scent of the links.

By his sixteenth birthday, Tom Morris could have beaten most of the gentleman golfers. 'Don't let 'em know,' Allan said. 'They'll find out soon enough.' Tom caddied for many of the club members, and when his advice and encouragement helped his man win a bet, Tom might get more than the usual shilling at the end of the round. He might find a crown in his palm. One day it was a five-pound note! On that day he was wealthy. He could give half to his parents, buy a pair of warm socks, dine at the Golf Inn and still have enough to tithe to the church on Sunday morning.

In 1839, after four years of apprenticeship, Tom began his five-year term as a journeyman, living in rented rooms nearby but still working in Allan's kitchen. He now stood two inches taller than Allan (though half a foot less than Lang Willie) and was ten to twenty yards longer off the tee. He could not help shaking his head at the get-ups his employer wore, including a different colour of waistcoat and cap for every day of the week. Sepia photos would preserve Allan Robertson in tasteful black and tan, but that dark cap was likely to be purple, matching his tie, while the waistcoat under his red jacket might be orange or lime green. Watching this peacock bustle to the first teeing-ground, Tom knew that plain brown tweed was right for him.

Allan's red jacket might have seemed lacking in tact, too forward for a commoner, had he not been known and liked by the gentlemen. If his colourful clothes out-sparkled theirs, if his quoting of Homer or Shakespeare overreached, he knew his place. It was Allan who knelt to tee up his master's ball. Scotland's best golfer then waited at a respectful distance while the man topped his ball or sliced it into the whins.

When club members played matches, Allan, Tom, Lang Willie and the other caddies carried their clubs. Sometimes a club man hired a caddie to lug his clubs and be his partner against another member-caddie pair in foursomes – each two-man team playing a single ball, taking turns at hitting it. If the gentleman drove off the tee, the caddie hit the next shot, and so on. At the end of the round the caddie on the losing side got the usual fee, but the one who helped his man win could expect a bonus. Tom earned most of his money this way. If his team won he'd get silver in his palm and eat meat and potatoes that night at the Golf Inn, the Cross Keys or the Black Bull. If not, it was porridge in Allan's kitchen.

Soon Tom was playing matches of a different kind. Two caddies would play two others for a small bet, or two caddies would team against a pair of club members, giving the gentlemen strokes. Tom found himself getting released from work to play as Allan's partner. He relished those matches, not only for the golf, but also for the fun of seeing his boss in action. Allan was a born performer, fully in character from the moment he reached the teeing-ground, giving a little bow and doffing his cap to the gentlemen. Tom liked to watch him rehearse his swing as if he needed practice. Allan might make a clumsy practice swipe, digging up turf, then wince and say his back ached. That could be worth a stroke as the match was arranged.

Once the teams and strokes were set, Allan waited for any gentlemen in the group to hit. Then he stepped forward to tee up his own ball. He spat in his hands, rubbed them together. A quick waggle triggered his swing, the clubhead gliding in a perfect circle around his small, bullish frame. His clubs had quirky names – his flat-bladed bunker iron, a forerunner of the sand wedge, was called the Frying Pan; another club was the Doctor; another was Sir David Baird, named after the R&A medalist who gave it to him. He held them all high on the handle, a fingery grip that helped him flip the clubface open or closed at the last instant. No golfer had better touch, or more tricks.

Tom called Allan 'the cunningest player'. It was a polite way of saying that he was a hustler. If an opponent had the honour in a singles match, Allan would mutter aloud about the wind, even if there was no wind. If Allan had the honour he might pretend to swing all-out, grunting for effect, but hold off a bit at impact so that his ball stopped just short of a bunker. The opponent, believing the trap was out of range, would drive straight into it – and end up smiling as Allan praised his Herculean power. When teamed with a weak club member in an alternate-shot foursomes match, Allan had other ways to work the angles: if his partner faced a long carry over a hazard, he would make the man swallow his pride and putt their ball to the hazard's brink, making Allan's next shot easier. Sometimes he told a partner to swing and miss on purpose. 'Well done, sir,' he'd say, then step up and hit the ball past all trouble to the flag.

As Allan's journeyman, Tom was less than a junior partner but better than a cousin, having long since surpassed Lang Willie at work by being more efficient and much easier to wake up in the morning. It was the same on the links, where Lang Willie played but was so loosely strung together that his golf swing reminded Tom of a man falling down stairs. Lang Willie knew he was no golfer. He joked that when he swung, his elbows kept trying to switch places with his knees. Meanwhile, Tom kept improving. By the time he turned twenty, Tom was the second-best golfer in St Andrews. After years of getting strokes from Allan – nine strokes at first, then six, four and finally two – they played even. In 1842, when club members put up a few pounds to sponsor a tournament for the caddies (all caddies but Allan, barred because he was thought to be unbeatable), Tom took home the purse.

Allan Robertson became the town's hero in 1843 when he beat Willie Dunn, the long-hitting champion from Musselburgh. The match was a novel idea:

more than a week of single combat between the best players from towns whose golfers couldn't stand each other. Musselburgh was the golf hub of the south side of the Firth of Forth, the Edinburgh side, while St Andrews was the game's cradle, and Robertson its saviour. With grit, clutch putting and a trick or two, Allan edged Dunn over twenty rounds while dozens of bettors, newspaper reporters and other spectators walked along with the players.

It was in this heady time that Tom won his first match against Allan. They played for a short-waisted red jacket offered as a prize by an R&A member. There were no spectators or reporters that day, but Tom felt like shouting when he sank the winning putt. Allan shrugged and said he hadn't been trying because he didn't like the jacket: 'The wee coatie would fit Tom better,' he said. But Tom knew something had changed that day. He had stepped up a rung.

Over the next year Allan began giving him a small share of his golf-ball sales and a growing share of the bets they won as foursomes partners. Before that, the boss had put up their portion of the stakes when he and Tom played a money match. Allan covered any losses and, fittingly, kept almost all of what they won. If Tom played well, the boss might give him ten per-cent; if not, a token penny told him what losers were worth. But now they were sharing risk and reward, with Allan haggling over odds and strokes at the first tee and Tom surprising rivals with his maturing game.

And here was the answer to the question Tom had turned over in his head since he was fourteen: why had the great Robertson chosen Tom Morris as his apprentice? Because he had seen him swing. The game's keenest eye had watched a boy knocking spoon shots down an open fairway, sometimes with a cracked feathery, sometimes with a cork. That eye had spotted Tom's talent. Allan, who did nothing without a reason that served Allan, had needed a reliable foursomes partner. Now he had one.

Lying on his cot late at night, with the cold wind on his face, Tom may have wondered what God thought of all this. Here he was, still a journeyman, earning more money than his father ever had, most of it in wagers. Of course his luck could vanish in a breath – a broken leg, a plague of cholera, a new golfer who could beat him and Allan both. But for now he had every reason to be cautiously happy. If not yet prosperous, he was settled enough to think about settling down. If not fully respectable, he was close enough to smell the roast beef in Captain Broughton's house.

Captain Broughton, one of the R&A's leading players, lived in a columned mansion at 91 North Street. The beef in the captain's kitchen was clean and bloody, not tinged with pepper, ginger and charcoal like the rank meat in alehouses and inns and Allan's kitchen. Tom shut his eyes and breathed its scent into his nostrils. A working man like him could not set foot anywhere but in the kitchen of such a house, nor would he want to. In the hush of the parlour, with its grand piano, gold-framed mirror and leather-trimmed chairs around a table so perfectly polished that it shone like the mirror, he would have felt like a thief, a trespasser. It was better to stay in the kitchen, picking a scrap of fat off a platter of beef carried by Nancy Bayne, the maid.

Five years older than Tom, Nancy was one of four servants in the captain's house. Along with another maid and a housekeeper who outranked the maids, she scrubbed, polished, dusted and cooked from six in the morning till after dark – all under the stern eye of the captain's governess. Nancy was no beauty but rather a strong, sensible girl, a 'pattern girl' in the popular phrase. She knew her role in society's pattern and played it with vigour and good humour. She already had a suitor, but when Tom Morris entered the picture the other fellow had no chance. Tom was a favourite of Captain Broughton. He caddied for the captain and sometimes partnered him in foursomes matches. Tom was Nancy's favourite, too. He had a pleasing enough face, with neatly trimmed whiskers. His boots were almost new, and he took care to kick the dirt off them before he came into the captain's kitchen. Tom had a jacket with no frays at the sleeve or elbow, and a pocket-watch with a silver chain. He had a kind eye and a bit of a spark to him, asking about Nancy's day, offering a handshake when he took his leave. She was pleased to note that his hands were more callused than hers.

For Tom, even courtship was affected by golf. One day on the High Hole, he and Captain Broughton were playing a crown-and-shillings game – a crown on the match, a shilling per hole – when Tom found his ball buried in a bunker. He swung twice with no luck.

'Pick it up,' the captain said.

Tom said, 'No, I might hole it.'

'Ha! If you do, I'll give you fifty pounds.'

'Done.'

Tom's biographer W.W. Tulloch told the story sixty years later. According to Tulloch, Tom 'had another shot at it, eye on ball and perhaps on the fair Nancy. By some million-to-one chance the ball did actually go into the hole. "That will make a nice nest-egg for me to put in the bank," said the young fellow.' But the next day, when the captain brought the money, Tom surprised him by turning it down. There was no debt, he said – he had been joking.

Tom Morris married Nancy Bayne on 21 June 1844. The vows were read by the Reverend Principal Haldane of Holy Trinity church, who had christened baby Tom twenty-three years before. After the vows Captain Broughton, who had given the bride and groom a wedding gift of fifty pounds, led toasts to his favourite caddie and his former maid, who would do her scrubbing, dusting and cooking for Tom Morris from that day on.

Life was moving faster. In a year Nancy was pregnant, though no one in that time and place would use such an indelicate word. People said she was in 'a family way', or 'no longer unwell', meaning that her monthly flow of blood had ceased.

In the summer of 1846 Nancy reached the last stage of being no longer unwell – her confinement, when her husband was banished to a far room while women from both their families and then at last a midwife clustered around Nancy as she howled in her labour. Soon the midwife showed Tom the glad result: a healthy son. He and Nancy named the baby Thomas Morris Junior and called him Wee Tom.

If the child was meant to be a golfer, he was born at a good time. After Allan Robertson's grand battle with Willie Dunn, other professionals began making their names in the game. Dunn and his brother Jamie were Musselburgh's champions. Bob Andrew was Perth's. Amateur competitions at the R&A and other clubs were still the main events on golf's calendar, but people had now seen enough of the 'cracks', as crack-shot caddies were called, to know that amateur medalists were not in their league. Golf talk revolved around the cracks: who was the best of them? Could Dunn win a rematch against Robertson? Which town could field the best foursomes duo? By the middle of the century bettors from various clubs were risking weighty sums to find out. To their surprise, hundreds and even thousands of ordinary citizens were also excited about this new craze, the professional golf match. Soon a great foursomes match was arranged: a duel between the Dunns of Musselburgh and those two noted sticks from St Andrews, Allan Robertson and Tom Morris.

Sportsmen on both sides of the Forth pooled their cash. Each side came up with £200, which meant that the cracks would play for the staggering sum of £400. It wasn't the players' money; they would perform for the benefit of the bettors who put up the stakes. Still, news of the record-setting stakes catalyzed a reaction that fed on itself – more crucial than the prize money was its power to keep people talking about it, to keep the small but growing world of golf abuzz for weeks before the match. This was hype Victorian style. News may have travelled at a walking pace, in weekly newspapers and by word of mouth, but as the match approached it seemed half of Scotland knew about it. The players made bets of their own (they would get a piece of the £400 – ten percent was customary – if they won), and polished their clubs as the first day of play dawned clear and cool. The format was two out of three, with three matches of thirty-six holes each, to be played first at Musselburgh, then at St Andrews and finally on the supposedly neutral links at North Berwick, near Edinburgh. Everyone expected Allan Robertson and Willie Dunn to play stellar golf.

Everyone knew that Jamie Dunn, Willie's identical twin, was nearly his brother's equal. The question mark was young Morris, who had never played in front of spectators and reporters.

Allan liked to joke about the Dunns: 'Keep your eye on 'em, or Willie might hit every shot.' The tall twins often dressed alike, but at Musselburgh they did their opponents and spectators a favour by wearing different ties, Willie's blue and Jamie's grey. They went on to play identically well, out-driving the St Andrews duo, alternating shots with dead aim. To the cheers of their home-course supporters, the twins routed Allan and Tom. The day's scheduled thirty-six holes ended after only twenty-four, the Dunns leading by thirteen holes with twelve to play. It was a bitter defeat for the St Andreans. Matters worsened a week later at St Andrews, where the ballyhooed showdown looked to be a mismatch. Allan kept missing putts – 'funking', it was called, meaning choking. Then, late in the day, the twins faltered. Tom led a rally over the last nine holes and he and Allan squeaked by with a victory on the Home Hole. Now the sides were dead even. Had the contest been scored by holes rather than courses, Tom and Allan would have been behind, needing a miracle on the last day. As it was, all they needed was one good afternoon.

On the morning of the final thirty-six holes, a special train carted crowds of so-called 'golf-fanatics' to the quirky little North Berwick links below Berwick

Law, a dead volcano. At its foot, crowds gathered near the first teeing-ground at the edge of a red sandstone town that had never seen anything like this.

Rain fell in sheets that morning, sluicing into the weedy old quarry beside the first fairway. The torrent peaked just as dozens of Allan and Tom's supporters were crossing the Forth on the Burntisland Ferry. By the time they reached the course they were clammy and miserable and outnumbered ten to one by the Dunns' supporters. The rain moved offshore, leaving clean sky and a breeze that blew several spectators' hats down the fairway. Allan and Tom had the honour, which meant that Allan did. Before teeing off he took a moment to look around at the huge, still-growing crowd around him, a throng that stretched along the fairway almost to the green. There were more than a thousand people watching. So many faces, all silent for one long moment before he sent the ball on its way.

Allan's drive was straight, but short. Willie Dunn's drive flew past it. Willie held his driver high at the end of his swing, waving it forward as if to chase the ball farther. The Dunns' backers cheered and shook their fists. 'I never saw a match where such vehement party spirit was displayed,' Tom Peter wrote in his memoir, *Reminiscences of Golf*. 'So great was the keenness and anxiety to see whose ball had the best lie, that no sooner were the shots played than off the whole crowd ran, helter-skelter.'

The Dunn twins' power impressed Peter: 'They went sweeping over hazards which the St Andrews men had to play short of.' With twenty-six holes played and eight to go, the Dunns were four holes ahead. Gamblers in the crowd raised their hands and shouted offers: 'Fifteen to one against Robertson and Morris.' 'Twenty to one!'

Allan had been useless all day, hitting crooked drives and funking putts. Tom Peter heard a catcall from the crowd: 'That wee body in the red jacket canno' play golf!' That yell may have been the spur the proud Robertson needed. A minute later he sank his first putt of consequence in more than a week. He and Tom took that hole and the next one, too. They halved the one after that and won two of the following three in what one report would call 'a most extraordinary run of surprises'. Suddenly the match was even with two holes to play. Two holes for £400. The Dunns wore identical frowns. The crowd pushed close enough to hear the whisk of Allan's swing as he drove his and Tom's ball into one of the worst spots in sight, a patch of shin-high grass 130 yards out. The ball hopped once and disappeared.

Tom slashed it out, but two shots later he and Allan lay four in a greenside bunker. The Dunns lay two only twenty yards away. But their ball had come to rest against a paving stone bordering a path near the green. 'They wished the stone removed, and called for someone to go for a spade,' Tom Peter recalled, 'but Sir David Baird would not sanction its removal, because it was off the course and a fixture.' The match referee was the same Baird who'd given Allan the eponymous club he was using. Musselburgh fanatics hissed at him, but the ruling was correct. The Dunns slapped at their ball three times before it popped loose, costing them their two-shot advantage and one more. Peter watched them unravel: 'Both men had by this time lost all judgement and nerve, and played most recklessly.' The most pivotal hole of the century's first half went to Robertson and Morris, who took the final hole as well. Their backers were delirious, and £400 richer. Tom and Allan got a beggar's cut of that, plus their end of several side bets, and for weeks after returning to St Andrews they enjoyed free meals and free pints. Tom was his home-town's particular hero – hadn't he downed the Dunns almost in spite of Allan? Following 'the Famous Foursome', Tom Morris' health was toasted so often that it seemed he would surely live to be 100 years old.

Almost before the cheers died down, his luck went south. The coming months would test Tom's courage and even his faith.

It began with a new ball. In the late 1840s, a few golfers in England began using balls made of rubber. The stuff was called 'gutta percha'. Made from the sap of a Malaysian rubber tree, it was easy to mould into a ball and was more durable than leather and feathers. It was cheaper, too. A gutta-percha ball resisted rain better than a feathery, which tended to split at the seams in wet weather, and the 'gutty' cost less than half as much – a mere shilling versus half a crown for a feathery ball. When Gourlay, the Musselburgh feathery-maker, got his hands on one of the first gutties, he saw the future coming.

Allan Robertson was frantic. He had always said that nothing good ever came from the south. Now here came a threat to his livelihood in the form of a grey orb bouncing from England via Musselburgh to the St Andrews links his father and grandfather had stocked with featheries. Allan could not even bring himself to pronounce 'gutta percha'. He called the new balls 'the filth'. Playing with them was 'no' golf'. He paid boys pennies to hunt down gutties and bring them to his house, where they watched Allan burn the balls in the kitchen fire. These public burnings filled the room with acrid blue-black smoke. Tom and Lang Willie, stuffing and sewing featheries in a fog that made their eyes itch, had to swear they would never play golf with the filth.

The Famous Foursome had lifted Tom's standing with the gentleman golfers of the R&A, who now insisted on getting him as a caddie or partner. One morning Tom went out for a friendly match with a prominent club member, the preeningly handsome Mr John Campbell, a man another member described as 'magnificent and pompous'. On the inward nine, Tom ran out of golf balls. Campbell gave him one of his own gutties to finish the round. Tom thought nothing of it; he couldn't leave Mr Campbell out there alone. Over a hole or two he found the rubber ball nothing special – easier to putt than a feathery, since it was seamless and a little heavier, but shorter off the tee. They were nearing the Home Hole when Allan, playing the outward nine, came storming towards them, shouting. His own Tom, playing that filth! Despite his vow! Tom tried to defend himself, but Allan was beyond reason. As Tom would recall half a century later, 'Allan in such a temper cried out to me never to show face again.'

Just like that. After more than ten years of working side by side, ten years and some 25,000 golf balls made of leather and feathers and sweat, Tom was fired. When he tried again to explain, Allan turned his back. But Tom also had his pride. He would not beg. He would take up the loom first. He would take his wife and child and leave his hometown before he begged.

Just like that a life changes forever. Heading home, Tom may have looked back towards the links, dark green in late-day sun, to see golfers gathered at the first teeing-ground. He did not want to leave home and surely did not relish the thought of giving his wife the news. He might believe, might *know* that God closes no door without opening another, but Nancy was prone to gloomy spells. She had fretted and wept over

Wee Tom's latest illness, though the doctor said it was nothing. How much would she fret over a jobless husband? Tom steeled himself as he kicked his boots clean at their door.

The child was sicker. The doctor called it baby fever, though Wee Tom was four years old, no baby. Four-year-olds were thought to be safe from the thousand things that pulled babies underground. But the boy wheezed and grew hotter. The doctor said they should keep the curtains drawn and let the child rest. A day later he said they should pray. Tom sat and prayed with Nancy, each of them holding one of Wee Tom's hands, hands that were small and too hot. The child's hair was wet with sweat, his eyes glazed.

Thomas Morris Junior died on 9 April 1850. Tom, with Nancy beside him, wrapped the little body in spotless linen. He lifted Wee Tom and placed him in a box of yellow elm, the wood so fresh that it wept sap. Later that week they put the box in the ground in the cemetery at the east end of town, beside the ruins of St Andrews cathedral.

Tom Morris, so recently St Andrews' hero, walked the town in a daze. His friends worried about him. What would Tom do? The answer came from an R&A member who found him a job as golf professional at a brand new club in Prestwick, on the far side of Scotland. Tom agreed to pack up his golf clubs, his wife and his sorrow and go west to Prestwick.

Before they left, he and Nancy bought a tall white

stone for Wee Tom's grave. They paid a stonecutter to etch the child's name and his birth and death dates on the slab, along with a verse that looked forward to Resurrection Day.

Their departure was put off until 1851. There were details to iron out. Where would they live in Prestwick? Who would join the new golf club there? The Prestwick course was another matter – Tom would have to build one. But for every trouble, he thought, the Good Lord provides a reason to rejoice. As he and Nancy prepared to leave home she was plump and happy, with a new life kicking inside her.

## TWO

# Prestwick's Pioneer

THE SUN OVER Prestwick moved backwards. It rose over inland hills, not the grey water that meant east to Tom, and set behind a mountain in an unfamiliar sea. Tom knew this water was no proper sea but the broad Firth of Clyde. He knew the mountain in the water, Goat Fell, was part of the Isle of Arran, a twenty-mile rock that rose from the firth. He knew he was on Scotland's west coast, so far west that to go much farther you would need gills. But knowing his location on a map did nothing to ease Tom's sense of dislocation. He was homesick.

Not that he complained. His wife was homesick, too, tired and fretful, and Nancy had other worries – a house to furnish, a child to clothe and feed. Their second baby, another son, had been born that spring, just before they left St Andrews. 'An extra gift from God,' she called him. They named the boy Thomas Morris Junior, after the boy they had lost. It was common when a son died young to give his name to the next son. It kept the father's name alive. But they never called this boy Wee Tom. This one was Tommy. Loud and hungry from the start, he seemed to have life enough for two.

The Morrises lived in a tidy cottage provided by the Prestwick Golf Club. Members kept their golf clubs in wooden lock-boxes in the Morris cottage and held their meetings in the parlour. The cottage sat across a rutted road from the Red Lion Inn, where on 2 July 1851 the Earl of Eglinton and forty-nine other gentlemen had founded the club over dinner and drinks. It was Lord Eglinton's friend Colonel James Ogilvie Fairlie, one of the R&A's most prominent members, who convinced Tom to bring his wife and son to the world's edge and rebuild Prestwick's golf course. There was much to rebuild. What Tom found was fifty-odd acres of dunes, brush and ragged grasses with knee-high flagsticks scattered here and there. Some Prestwick golfers played randomly, aiming for any flag they could spot from wherever they found a ball. They clambered up and down towering dunes, slipping on sandy pathways, shouting 'Fore' and 'Bloody hell!' This was the thimble of turf where Tom was supposed to build the best links in the west.

That autumn he walked the links until he knew every acre. As Keeper of the Green, Tom was charged with teaching lessons and supervising caddies, but his prime task was maintaining the links, known collectively as 'the green'. Prestwick's threadbare green was a funnel-shaped patch of straw-coloured dunes, tan and purple heather, red poppies and wind-whipped bentgrass, the last of which was at least green. To the west was the beach. On the inland side ran a muddy stream, the Pow Burn, and the railway to Ayr and Glasgow, with the vine-covered ruins of a church beyond the railway. A rough road marked the links' southern border; the northern edge, 770 yards away, was a low stone wall. Sheep roamed the dunes and dells, keeping the grass down and leaving their droppings on half-bare putting-greens. There were rabbit scrapes everywhere – oval depressions where buck rabbits shat and then rolled in their scat, marking their turf. Tom marked his territory with sticks, pacing off distances, imagining and re-imagining these dunes and hollows in hundreds of configurations. Suppose he put a putting-green here and dug a bunker beside it – where would the next hole be? Suppose he filled in a bunker, grew grass on top and made it a putting-green?

Tom had helped Allan lay out a few holes at Carnoustie, across the Firth of Tay from St Andrews, but this would be the first course he built himself. Sitting on a dune that cast a fifty-yard shadow, scratching his side-whiskers, he looked out over the Firth of Clyde to Arran, the long island on the western horizon. Sunsets made Arran appear to be on fire. The shore swept south towards hazy cliffs called the Heads of

Ayr. Between Arran and the cliffs a little bump called Ailsa Craig poked out of the water. Prestwickers had another name for Ailsa Craig: they called it Paddy's Milestone because it marked the midway point between Belfast and Glasgow, a crossing thousands of starved Irish had made and were still making in their coffin ships only to find the potatoes blighted here, too. The only work for them, the lucky ones who found work, was slaving in mines or feeding coal to the blast-furnaces that made Glasgow thrum all day and glow reddish brown at night.

Walking the wall of dunes between the beach and the links, Tom watched steamers and clipper ships going to and from Glasgow, thirty miles northeast. Closer to shore, brown seals broke the water. Still closer were knee-high waves, seaweed, driftwood, foam and sand. When golfers appeared on the links he turned to watch them, but sheep almost always outnumbered the golfers. One day the Earl of Eglinton's greyhounds came streaking across the links, training for a race.

Tom learned to enjoy Prestwick's weather, which was less raw but no less fickle than Fife's. Low clouds rolled in to pelt the coast with rain that turned to long white darts of sleet. Then the sky would relent as the land held its breath. The light changed in these lulls. It might turn yellow, purple or grey. Next might come drizzle, hard rain or diffident sun, or sometimes a mist that moved inland like a curtain, bright sunshine behind it, endless sky over water so clear that you could see fish in it.

At night, sitting up by an open window while Nancy and the baby slept, Tom made pencil sketches of the links on landscaper's paper. He drew holes and combinations of holes, with arrows showing the line of play. The arrows started out sensibly enough, then tangled like seaweed. It was a maddening exercise – there wasn't room for eighteen holes. But each night he also read his Bible: *Ask the Lord to bless your plans . . .*

Pacing, thinking, hearing the surf at the foot of the links, he might walk to the room where his wife and son slept, Nancy with her worries and Tommy with his chestnut curls and long lashes. What man hearing the sleeping breaths of his wife and child, could fail to take courage into the next day?

Tom saw what he should do. His course would be twelve holes, not eighteen. It would start with a long, unforgettable monster. The second hole would climb over towering dunes to a putting-green guarded by a huge, hungry bunker. Golfers who made it that far without surrendering would forgive him the zigzags ahead.

The club paid several labourers to help, but Tom did much of the digging and carting himself, using shovels, wheelbarrows and his bare hands. His opening hole was the longest in golf, measuring 578 yards at a time when a 200-yard drive was a long poke. The drive had to clear a swamp, the Goosedubs, staying clear of the humpbacked dunes to the left, and from there it was three solid clouts to the putting-green. The second hole, called Alps, led golfers up dunes that presented an optical illusion: they appeared to be mountains much further away. Tom planted surprises all over the links, turning the shaggy ground's limitations to his advantage with deceptions that rewarded local knowledge. Club members who knew the course's tricks would have an edge. The approach to the Alps Hole, for instance, called for a shot from a hollow called Purgatory. The shot had to clear towering dunes. Those dunes were so steep that caddies sometimes lost their footing and tumbled backwards on the way up. But clearing the dunes was not enough. A ball that summited the Alps could fall into a vast, deep, putting-green-sized bunker called Sahara. Only by clearing both the Alps and the Sahara Bunker could the golfer reach a green that sat in a grassy bowl, welcoming shots that were strong enough to find it. 'The course went dodging in and out among lofty sand-hills,' wrote the amateur champion and golf historian Horace Hutchison half a century later. 'The holes were, for the most part, out of sight when one took the iron in hand for the approach, for they lay in deep dells among those sand-hills, and you lofted over the intervening mountain of sand, and there was all the fascinating excitement, as you climbed to the top of it, of seeing how near to the hole your ball may have happened to roll.'

With so little acreage to work with, Tom had no choice but to let holes crisscross. That was a minor defect at a time when a dozen rounds might complete a day's play. Still, it could be unnerving to stroke a putt on the fifth green while someone's second shot on the first hole zipped under your chin.

While working on the course Tom played it every day but the Sabbath. He was dead-set on knowing every inch, every shot his course could ruin or create. Often he played with his patron, Colonel Fairlie, who was as near to being Tom's friend as a gentleman could be to a hireling. The gruff, clever Fairlie was forty-two, twelve years older than Tom, with a high forehead and a high, starched collar. Sporting a black, bristly moustache that curved down to meet his side-whiskers over a clean-shaven chin, he had the look of a sea-captain, scanning the horizon with squinted eyes, seeking his next challenge.

Colonel James Ogilvie Fairlie came by his title by serving the Queen as an officer of the Ayrshire Yeomanry Cavalry, a reserve unit that marched in formation on the village green on holidays, striking fear into any seals or hungry Irishmen intent on attacking the coast. But while he was no warrior the colonel was an accomplished sportsman, a cricketer who had played for the home side in Scotland–England matches and who now purchased racehorses as casually as Tom bought hiking boots. Fairlie had taken up golf late in life but had made the most of his frequent trips to St Andrews from his home near Prestwick. With Tom's help he became one of the best of the R&A's gentleman players. He had never taken to the cocksure Allan Robertson, preferring Tom's calm competence, and after bringing Tom west he was determined to see him succeed. Fairlie and Tom would sit on the grass near the twelfth green, watching golfers finish their rounds while Fairlie smoked a cigar. Soon Tom had a new gift from his benefactor: a lifelong habit. 'The colonel would often give me a cigar. Then one day, I well remember, he gave me a pipe,' Tom recalled decades later, 'and after that I was a smoker for life. I had never smoked at all when I was a boy, and I would not now advise boys to smoke, young boys at least. But if I did not smoke until I was well on in life, I think I have made up for it.'

Fairlie had a short, graceless swing, but he was strong enough to rise on his toes and hit the ball as far as Tom did. The two of them played crown-and-shilling matches, with the colonel getting strokes. Fairlie marched ahead with Tom following, carrying the clubs. After a morning round the colonel sometimes hurried to Prestwick's railway station for a trip to Ayr or Glasgow, returning in time for another round before dark. As he liked to say, the world was running faster these days, running on steam.

The rails were changing everything from golf (a fellow could play at Prestwick and Musselburgh in the same day) to food (fresh beef from Aberdeen!) to time itself. Until the 1840s every town and village had kept its own time, but railway schedules required them to synchronize their clocks. By 1855 all of England, Scotland and Wales followed Greenwich Mean Time, or 'railway time', transmitted by telegraph in periodic updates from the Royal Observatory in Greenwich. Still there were some things the machine age could not change, like a nobleman's power to stop a train with his bare hands. To Fairlie's great amusement, his friend the Earl of Eglinton, who owned half the region, had the right to flag down any train that passed through his lands. The earl would walk out from Eglinton Castle to the railway, lift his hand and create an unscheduled stop on the Ayr–Glasgow line. He rode free of charge and named his destination by saying, 'Stop here.' Sometimes he hopped off within hailing distance of a Prestwick caddie or, better yet, his man Fairlie and the new greenkeeper.

Fairlie would wave and shout hello to the man he called 'Lord E!' Tom would turn and see a man in spotless white breeches and a cape, dark hair spilling to his shoulders. Archibald Montgomerie, thirteenth Earl of Eglinton, was western Scotland's leading sportsman. His stable of racehorses featured Flying Dutchman, winner of the 1849 Derby at Epsom. Eglinton raced greyhounds and sponsored archery, curling and lawn-bowling clubs. Tall and almost pretty with his heroic hair parted in the middle, he could have played Sir Lancelot in a pageant – or tested the knight in a joust.

'Hullo, Jof,' said Eglinton, using J.O. Fairlie's nick-name, 'And Tom Morris!'

'M'lord,' said Tom, doffing his cap.

The smiling earl was always full of questions about the course. How good would it be? When could they hold a first-rate event on it? Fairlie explained Tom's latest plans to build a prodigious first hole, to trick the eye at the second, to move a green or two or three and possibly shoot several hundred sheep. Tom was happy to let Fairlie do the talking. He was not certain how to speak or even stand in the presence of this Eton-educated noble who lived in a castle. Would it be improper to turn his back on the earl? Should he keep his shadow off Eglinton's boots? Fairlie wasn't shy around Eglinton, thumping the earl's noble shoulder and speaking of horses and hounds, club dues, prospective members – Mister this and Sir that – and the upcoming season. Eglinton nodded enthusiastically. 'Jolly good! Well done, well done.'

Fairlie said Prestwick's links would give the earl more honour than 'the Mudbath of '39'. Mention of the Mudbath made them both laugh. One day Fairlie told Tom the story:

In 1839 the world went mad for medieval nostalgia. There were pageants, parades and minstrel shows in every corner of the empire, but the Camelot craze found its greatest proponent in Eglinton Castle. There the earl, who could trace his lineage twenty-four generations back to the wellsprings of chivalry, decided to stage an event that would make history live again, and on 29 August 1839, nearly 5,000 spectators came from all over Scotland and England to witness the chivalric spectacle of the century. Thirteen armoured knights on armoured steeds paraded from the castle to a newly built arena to re-enact the jousts of old. One of the knights was Napoleon III, prince of France. Another was James Ogilvie Fairlie, bedecked in a suit of armour that had cost him £400. The parade of knights and their retinues stretched for half a mile. As it neared the arena, the skies opened. A downpour turned the castle grounds to fast-flowing mud. Spectators tumbled under skidding, kicking horses; squires ran for dear life; knights dropped their lances, tumbled into the mud and lay there like turtles, weighed down by their armour. The great medieval tournament was a debacle that cost Eglinton £40,000.

'Forty thousand pounds!' said Fairlie, waving his cigar. Such a fortune would pay Tom's salary for a thousand years. At least Fairlie got some good out of it. He won the rescheduled joust as well as the favour of the tournament's Queen of Beauty, who went on to become Mrs James Ogilvie Fairlie.

Tom, ever the agreeable partner, would nod and smile while the earl and colonel laughed. Then it was back to business. 'Carry on, Tom,' said Eglinton.

Tom Morris was born to carry on. Determined to spend the club's money wisely, he would pioneer a handful of greenkeeping techniques, including several that were widely imitated and one that became universal.

Many of Prestwick's bunkers had walls that were crumbling, falling inward. Tom could have shored them up with sod, but that would have been expensive. Railway ties, however, cost nothing. The Glasgow and South Western Railway that ran past the course left old railway ties in a heap beside the railway station; they were rubbish to everyone but Tom. He carted them away and used them to bulwark his bunkers, creating a shot that was new to the game, the near-miss that caromed crazily to parts unknown.

He shored up bunkers and dug new ones. He scythed heather, trimmed greens and cut neat-edged holes in the greens. By the end of his first year in Prestwick the course was a fair challenge for Tom's own game, but equally fair to Mr Sampson McInnes, a Prestwick member who was odds-on to leave any shot in his own shadow, and to the earl, who seldom finished twelve holes in fewer than eighty strokes. Tom gave the links' landmarks colourful names: the dunes were called Alps and Himalayas; a patch of trouble was known as Purgatory; a sand pit was called Pandemonium. Some of the names were traditional, others he coined himself. He promoted them all with a wink, a smile and endless repetition. And, at the tenth hole, he made a discovery that changed greenkeeping forever. The putting-green there had been in worse shape than the Hole o' Shell green at St Andrews. Tom moved the green to a new spot a few yards away – back-breaking work that took weeks. One day he spilled a wheelbarrow full of sand on the putting-green. When spring came he found hundreds of yellow-green shoots of grass sprouting on the sandy part of the green, while other spots lay bare. He filled his handkerchief with sand from a bunker, sprinkled the bare spots and kept returning to the bunker until the whole green was dusted with sand. Club members complained: did the tenth hole have a putting-green or a bunker with a hole in it? But the greenkeeper carried the day: by summer that putting-green was as smooth as a billiard table. Tom Morris had introduced top-dressing, a way to cultivate greens that golf-course workers still employ. From then on his refrain was 'More sand!' When golfers grumbled, Tom said, 'Tut-tut, sand's the life of a green, like meat to a man.'

As the course shaped up he settled into his other duties as golf professional. Tom caddied for Fairlie, Eglinton and other gentlemen. He taught lessons. He played rounds with club members, a chore that earned him three shillings per round. Tom also had the delicate task of handicapping the club members. Over several months he took each of them out on the links and observed each man's swing, making notes in a cloth-bound book. Then he posted the members' handicaps. Even Fairlie was handicapped fairly, which was all the colonel expected, knowing that Tom wouldn't fudge a stroke to save his soul. But other club men were miffed. 'Who is this caddie,' they asked, 'to rank a gentleman?' Tom's cause was aided by Eglinton, whose stabby putter was as deadly as Lancelot's lance – deadly to his score. After the earl accepted an unflattering double-figure handicap with his usual what-a-fine-day-to-be-me smile, the others accepted theirs as well.

Soon the keenness of Tom's eye was apparent to all. Matches stayed tight to the end; he knew the golfers' skills better than they did. By the end of his first year, club men were congratulating Fairlie for recruiting this greenkeeper. Some went so far as to shake Tom's hand.

The first autumn meeting of the Prestwick Golf Club was a feast for the palate and the eye. There were platters of meat, fish and duck; gallons of claret, gin and champagne; garlands of flowers; hours of singing and dancing. Fairlie wore a tartan cravat that cascaded down his chin, posing a hazard to his soup. He and the other club members sported brass-buttoned suits. Their jewelled ladies wore gowns festooned with silk ribbons and bows. Tom, dressed in his best Sunday tweed, stood at the festivities' edge where a hired man belonged. After midnight the last of the food gave way to drink and more merry drink, with toasts and speeches lulling the moon into its cradle behind the Isle of Arran. At last the Earl of Eglinton stood up. Silverware tap-tapped on wine glasses; the ballroom went quiet. The earl's gaze swept the room and found Tom.

Nodding towards the links outside, Eglinton announced that the course, their course, was 'a wonder of our new golfing age'. To applause and calls of 'Hear hear', he raised his glass. His hand was smooth and pink, his teeth as white as perfect health.

'To Tom Morris,' he said. 'Our perfect pioneer!'

As a player Tom was famous but not perfect. In 1851 he lost a match to Willie Dunn on the final hole. After his last putt missed, 'Tom gave his ball a kick in disgust,' wrote Hutchison, 'while Dunn took a snuff with great gusto and smiled satisfactorily.' Tom turned the tables the following year when the golf world descended on St Andrews for the R&A's autumn meeting. In one foursomes duel he and Colonel Fairlie pipped Dunn and another Musselburgh golfer, the expert amateur Sir Robert Hay, who had 'challenged the world' with Dunn as his partner. Then Tom delighted his hometown by teaming with none other than Allan Robertson, who had 'forgiven' Tom – Allan's word – and now made gutta-percha balls in his kitchen by the old links. The reunited Invincibles gave Hay and Dunn odds of two to one. Tom made side bets giving as much as five to one. 'The betting was extreme in this important piece of golfing warfare,' reported the *Fifeshire Journal*, 'this all-absorbing trial of dexterity betwixt St Andrews and Musselburgh ... The match was witnessed by doctors, lawyers and divines (young ones at least of the latter profession), professors, bankers, railway directors, merchants' clerks, tradesmen, workmen ... as well as a goodly sprinkling of general idlers.'

As at North Berwick three years before, Allan and Tom were out-driven by taller, stronger foes. Worse yet was Tom's putting. He kept missing short putts, a fault that would dog him for most of his life. According to the *Journal*, 'Tom, it was insinuated, was at his old trade of "funking".' But, in another late reversal, the Invincibles stormed back. On one eventful hole Allan wound up and slugged a drive that 'shot far ahead of Mr Hay's corresponding one; indeed, one could hardly conceive how Allan's little body could propel a ball so far.' Tom sank a crucial putt; he and Allan won in a walk. 'In the progress inward, some boys removed the flags ... and held them aloft in the procession, giving it the appearance of a triumphal entry,' the *Journal* story concluded, calling Robertson and Morris 'the cocks o' the green. Long may they hold that honourable elevation. St Andrews for ever!'

That account was too negative for one St Andrean, who fired off a letter to the editor. '[Y]our correspondent says that at one stage of it he was afraid Tom was at his "*old trade of funking*" – that is, showing a want of nerve,' wrote A GOLFER, who claimed that the match's outcome 'ought to dissipate every doubt – should any really exist – as to Tom's *pluck*'.

Another dispatch lent weight to the charge that Tom Morris was a short-range funker. When an R&A member mailed a postcard addressed to THE MISSER OF SHORT PUTTS, PRESTWICK, the postman took it straight to Tom, who might have torn it apart or hidden it in his pocket. Instead he laughed and showed the card to half the town.

In the 1850s the Invincibles swept aside challengers in St Andrews, Prestwick, Perth, Musselburgh and half a dozen other Scottish towns.

Allan claimed never to have lost in single combat – despite his 'wee coatie' match with Tom and other losses he considered unofficial. As the '50s progressed he defended his 'perfect' record with Jesuitical zeal. Singles mattered more after Willie Dunn moved south to be greenkeeper at Blackheath, near London, where he earned ten shillings a week – about twenty-five pounds per year – for serving Englishmen like the peevish Lord Starmont, who broke two sets of clubs over his knee during his first round of golf and pronounced himself satisfied with the day's exercise. Dunn's departure left Scotland to Allan Robertson and Tom Morris, only one of whom could be the country's King of Clubs, a title the east-coast newspapers gave to Allan. The king's crown would be hard to dislodge. On one visit to St Andrews, Tom played his old boss and beat him. Allan called it a casual, unofficial match, though bets had been laid and paid. The west-coast *Ayr Observer*, loyal to Tom, crowed, 'The palm of victory, which has so long reposed in quiescence in the sombre shade of St Rule, is gracefully waving in the westering breezes.' But the *Fifeshire Journal* defended the rule of St Rule's, the tallest cathedral tower in St Andrews, by sniffing, 'Who would have conceived aught so preposterous as that insignificant match should be seized and a claim to the championship constructed upon it by anyone conversant with the usages of golf?' Or, more simply put: frontiersman, go hang.

The newspaper war escalated, with the *Observer* denouncing the *Journal*'s 'treasonable discourses' and claiming, 'Tom is "the King of Scotland", and reflects the highest credit on Prestwick.' To which the *Journal* shot back: 'The Prestwick colony is in open revolt against the lord liege of golfers – the "bona fide" King of Clubs – Allan.'

The problem was that no one had found a way to identify the best golfer. Most clubs held annual and semi-annual tournaments, but the cracks were not allowed to play; instead they caddied for the gentlemen. The cracks had their challenge matches, which may have made for much amusing betting among the gentlemen, but which could not crown a true King of Clubs for two reasons. First, there was no way to say which of many matches was *the* match, the big one.

Second, a ranking based on challenge matches could be stymied by a king who would not risk his crown.

'I prefer having Tom as a partner,' said Allan, royally coy.

Fairlie and Eglinton urged Tom to issue a loud, once-and-for-all challenge, but Tom would not shame Allan into playing him. Still, he let his patrons know that if they arranged a £100 match, he would show up. But Allan declined repeated offers and Tom let the matter drop, leaving the nascent sport of professional golf in uneasy equilibrium, tippingly balanced between east and west, Robertson and Morris, a balance that would hold until a new player barged onstage to send everything ass-over-teapot.

His name was Willie Park. The son of a farmer who scraped up a living by pushing a plough for a Musselburgh landowner, Willie grew up with seven brothers and sisters in a cottage on the high road that passed the links just east of Edinburgh. As a gaunt, hungry lad Willie caddied for members of the Musselburgh Golf Club. He learned to play the game on summer evenings after the gentlemen went into the clubhouse for dinner and drinks. He started out with one club, a hooked stick he'd whittled down from a tree root. Thanks in part to a handy source of calories – a baker who played the local boys for pies – the caddie with the whittled stick grew strong and bullish.

After winning enough bets to buy a set of real golf clubs, he beat every caddie in sight. He went into business making the new gutta-percha balls, which he carried in the deep pockets of a long coat he wore around the links. But Willie Park made his name as a player and, in 1854, he did what strong young men are born to do. He went looking for older men to fight.

Whether you played Park for crowns and shillings, for twenty pounds or for a pie, he left no doubt that he wanted to kill you on the links. He claimed he had never played a round of golf for pleasure. For the better part of a year he issued challenges to Allan Robertson, the living legend he planned to debunk, daring the King of Clubs to play him in messages sent through other golfers and finally in a newspaper advertisement. The response from St Andrews was silence. But if Robertson thought Willie Park would take no answer for an answer, he was wrong. In 1854 Park bought a rail ticket to Robertson's town. The young tough was twenty years old on the day he stepped off the train in enemy territory. As a Musselburgh man he was allergic to the staid old snoot-in-the-air town. He began playing practice rounds alone, smacking booming, parabolic drives that sent caddies hurrying to Allan's door with news of the stranger's arrival. Park, with his slightly open stance and fierce downswing, made contact so clean that his drives sounded like pistol shots. His drives carried to places where R&A members often found their second shots.

After one such exhibition Park strutted to Allan's cottage on the corner of Golf Place and Links Road. He introduced himself and demanded a match.

Allan was amused. He admired pluck. But he was not about to risk his crown playing a potentially dangerous upstart, so he accepted the challenge with a proviso: young Willie would have to earn his shot at Allan by beating another St Andrews professional.

With Tom Morris far away in Prestwick, they agreed that Park would play Tom's older brother George. George Morris was smaller and darker than Tom. A passable golfer who could make his way around the links in 100 strokes or fewer, George played in a white cap that from a distance made him look like a button mushroom. Park proceeded to pound him into paste. After losing the first eight holes in a row poor George cried, 'For the love of God, man, give us a half!' Allan, an interested spectator, allowed that, 'Willie frightens us with his long driving.' Park would not get his shot at Allan anytime soon, but by demolishing George Morris he earned the next best thing, a big-money match against Tom, who stepped up to defend the Morris family's honour.

Their scrap would be Willie Park's debut on the national stage. The betting favoured Tom, who was thirty-three years old and at the height of his powers. But he too fell to Park in a one-sided match that ended with the boyish victor mobbed by Musselburgh fans chanting a clamorous call and response:

*'Where's the man who beat Tom Morris?'*

*'He's not a man, only a laddie without whiskers!'*

A week later, at North Berwick, Tom and Park played again. Colonel Fairlie went along to provide moral and financial backing. He bet heavily on Tom. But Tom's precise drives and iffy putting proved no match for the strength and pinpoint short game of Park, who won by nine holes. 'Park,' wrote Hutchison, 'was now the rising, or rather the risen, sun.'

On 4 November 1854, readers of the *Edinburgh News* saw a notice that revealed itself in the second paragraph to be a dare:

A GREAT MATCH at GOLF was Played at St Andrews Links on the 19th October by THOMAS MORRIS, servant of the Prestwick Golf Club (late of St Andrews) and William Park, Golf-Ball Maker, Musselburgh. This was played at St Andrews, North Berwick, and Musselburgh – Three Rounds on each Green – WILLIAM PARK leading Morris Nine Holes at the conclusion of the game.

WILLIAM PARK Challenges Allan Robertson of St Andrews, or William Dunn, servant of the Blackheath Golf Club, London or Thomas Morris, for Fifty Pounds, on the same Greens as formerly. Money Ready.

WILLIAM PARK, Golf-Ball Maker

A St Andrews newspaper deplored the cheek of 'this braggart'. A less biased source called Park 'a golfing crack of the first water, young and wiry, with immense driving powers; cool as a cucumber'. According to Hutchison, 'So strong a player had he become that money in abundance was forthcoming to back him against Allan Robertson, but the latter could not be induced to play.' Like the heavyweight boxing champions of later eras, Allan was more than happy to let the contenders beat each other up.

Tom Morris and Willie Park would swing away at each other for the better part of a decade. Tom won a match to restore his good name, lost another when his putter betrayed him, then regained the upper hand when Park's hell-bent playing style got him into trouble. After his stellar debut in '54, Park endured a partial eclipse (an 'obnubilation', Hutchison called it), not because his talent waned but because Tom got better. In the next five years the two of them squared off more than twenty times, usually for £100 or more, only to prove that they were as evenly matched as two boots. Those battles spurred the growth of professional golf. Newspapers dispatched reporters to the latest 'great match' between the two. Bettors shouted odds while vendors hawked lemonade and ginger beer to spectators. Before long there were dozens of challenge matches pitting local heroes against the best golfers from other towns, with civic honour at stake. Park was Musselburgh's warrior; Bob Andrew was Perth's; and Tom played for Prestwick, though St Andrews claimed him too. Meanwhile Allan Robertson stayed above the fray while occasionally trumping them all. After Tom set a scoring record by shooting 82 in a match at St Andrews, Allan made that look like small beer with a 79 of his own. He was forty-three years old, past his prime, and his magical score came in a casual round, a quick eighteen with an R&A member. Still, he and his supporters had no doubt that it was the finest performance ever.

Tom rode the train east to play matches at St Andrews and dreamed of going home to stay, but as long as Allan reigned there, the town had no need for another professional. So Tom made the best of life in Prestwick. He carved and trimmed the links, taught lessons, recalibrated the members' handicaps and refereed their disputes. He supervised the caddies and slipped the poorest ones a shilling when they went hungry. He set up a small shop where he made gutta-percha balls, cooking the rubber and moulding it into a ball while the rubber was still hot – a simpler task than stuffing featheries. He kept up his old habit of sleeping by a window and leaving it open several inches, even in winter, a habit that drove Nancy to take little Tommy to another bed near the fire.

He watched his family grow. Each birth was a terror to Nancy, borne down as she was by thoughts of fever and death. Her birth pains grew worse. She was sure she would die, but out came Elizabeth in 1852, as strong and healthy as Tommy. By the time Nancy entered her next confinement four years later, a numbing substance called chloroform had spared Queen Victoria the pain of her most recent labour. Yet many doctors were reluctant to tell women about the chloroform, country doctors most of all. Their reservations were religious, not medical. Had not the Lord cursed Eve, saying, 'In sorrow shalt thou bring forth children'? Should medicine nullify Genesis? The doctors thought not, so women went on suffering the old way and most had a glad result, as Nancy did in 1856 with the birth of her fourth child and second surviving son, James Ogilvie Fairlie Morris, named after the colonel.

With three healthy children and a husband to fret about, Nancy was as content as she would ever be. She greeted neighbours, sang out in church. She smiled most of all on Tommy, her first answered prayer, a bold, happy boy who chased dogs and birds on the links and played soldier by parading behind the Ayrshire Yeomanry Cavalry. Townspeople noticed the Morrises' eldest child. Tommy seemed to have some spark that was not like Tom or Nancy or some mix of the two of them but something of his own, some force that made the boy think he could outrun a greyhound or leap and pull a gull out of the sky.

Tommy was waist-high to his father when he took

his first swings at Prestwick, whacking old gutties with a cut-down club. Tom taught the boy how to grip the club in the palms of his hands and pull it back, keeping his right elbow high, until the shaft was almost flat against the back of his neck – the old St Andrews swing. Tommy showed no great talent at first, but he had heart. Teeing up an old gutty on the beach, he would aim seaward, knock his ball into the surf, wait for it to wash back up and smack it again, trying to drive it across twenty miles of water to the Isle of Arran.

Tommy turned eight years old in the spring of 1859. Nancy often dressed him in a sailor's togs and cap, the boys' fashion of the time. That autumn he noticed that his mother moved more heavily as she dressed him. She was pregnant again, plump, flush and happy. But soon there was unsettling news from St Andrews.

'Allan Robertson is dead,' Tom said. 'Dead of jaundice.' Allan had been forty-four, only six years older than Tom.

Golfers mourned the great Robertson. He was remembered as 'a giant, a titan ... pleasant, fearless, just, gentle and invincible'. Tom could have disputed 'invincible' and Willie Park 'fearless'. Both could have quibbled with 'just'. But, of course, they held their tongues. Tom never uttered a word against the man who had hired and fired him, though he may have allowed himself a smile when one eulogist invoked

Allan's 'great grit' by telling how 'the little giant would roll up his shirt-sleeves before playing an important drive'. Tom knew the shirt-sleeves tactic wasn't grit. It was a trick. Before a crucial shot, Allan would pause and hand his jacket to his caddie. He would pace the teeing-ground, roll up his sleeves and spit in his hands – not to bolster himself but to unnerve his opponent, to slow the crucial moment, giving the other fellow time to lose his nerve.

Allan Robertson was buried in the cathedral cemetery at St Andrews, a hundred paces from Wee Tom's grave, in the warm September of 1859. Three weeks later Nancy Morris gave birth to another son, John, in the cottage at Prestwick. They would call the baby Jack, and would soon find there was something wrong with his legs.

Tom began 1860 the way he began every day. On New Year's Day he woke, pulled on his bathing long-johns and took a dip in the bone-chilling Firth of Clyde. Afterwards, shivering as he climbed the beach to the links and his cottage beyond, he felt strong, washed clean.

His wife hoped the new year would take them home to St Andrews. With Allan gone, the way was clear for Tom. Nancy and Tom both had family there. Family mattered most in troubled times. Nancy was worried about baby Jack, who grew but who did not kick or crawl. Tom, though, was in no hurry to flit back to Fife. He wanted no one saying he had rushed to fill Allan's place. He said it was better to bide in Prestwick for now, and if baby Jack would not walk just yet, Tom was glad to carry him around the house.

Tom and Colonel Fairlie saw the new decade as a time for Prestwick to rise in the golf world. Fairlie and Lord Eglinton had already run a Grand National Interclub tournament for amateurs in 1857. Eglinton provided the trophy for that event, just as he had given a silver Eglinton Jug to Ayrshire's curling champions, another jug to its lawn bowlers and a golden belt for Irvine's archers to shoot for. Now he proposed to outdo himself with a Championship Belt for the world's best professional golfer. Fairlie tried to persuade other clubs to share sponsorship duties and expenses, and got a collective yawn for his trouble, so now he and Eglinton agreed to go it alone. They reasoned that a tournament for the cracks could promote Prestwick as a golf hub and establish Tom Morris as the new King of Clubs. The earl would preside over the event, smiling and waving, weakening the knees of women of all classes, while Fairlie handled the details.

Fairlie and Lord Colville, another officer of the Prestwick Club, dashed off letters to eleven of the thirty-five golf clubs then in existence – those that were large and important enough to have likely contenders for a professional championship. Knowing that many of the cracks were uncouth, Prestwick's officers took precautions. 'I have just been talking to Lord Eglinton in regard to the entry of players,' Fairlie noted, writing to club secretaries from Eglinton Castle, 'and to avoid having any objectionable characters we think that the plan is to write to the secretaries of all golfing societies requesting them to name and send their *two best professional players* – depending on them for their characters.' Having the clubs vouch for their entrants, he believed, would make the contest 'quite safe'.

The Prestwick officers made up invitations, written in blue ink on pale blue paper, and posted them to St Andrews, Musselburgh, Perth, Aberdeen and six other Scottish towns, plus Blackheath in England. But not all the blue notes were well received. Didn't Eglinton and Fairlie know what sort of crowd they were inviting? Prestwick's own professional might be an upstanding fellow, but the common crack was, in Hutchison's words, 'a feckless, reckless creature ... His sole loves are golf and whisky.' These glorified caddies might embarrass everyone with their drinking and cursing. They might cheat. What right-minded gentleman would vouch for them?

In the end only eight professionals turned up for what would become the first Open Championship, the world's oldest and greatest golf tournament. Even so the one-day event threatened to overshadow the autumn meeting of the Prestwick Club that followed a day later. One newspaper writer came up with a more dignified name for the cracks: they were 'golfing celebrities'. Still they kept their hosts improvising to the last minute. During practice rounds in the days before the tournament the professionals offended club members and their wives with ragged dress and worse manners. One was said to have spent a night in the town's drunk tank. Fairlie found a way to improve the players' dress if not their morals: he gave each golfer a lumberman's jacket to play in. The jackets were heavy black-and-green tartans, the kind worn by labourers on Eglinton's estates. Seen from a distance, the players in their chequered jackets resembled a lost team of woodsmen, searching in vain for a tree to cut down.

The Championship Belt they would vie for was made by Edinburgh silversmiths James & Walter Marshall for the news-making sum of twenty-five pounds. Fashioned of Morocco leather festooned with silver plates showing golf scenes and the Burgh of Prestwick's coat of arms, it featured a wide gleaming buckle, minutely filigreed, that showed a golfer teeing off. Bizarrely, the little golfer on the buckle swung a shaft without a clubhead – an oversight that escaped notice at first. The Belt was lauded as 'the finest thing ever competed for'. It was so valuable that the winner, who would gain possession of it for a year in lieu of prize money, would have to leave a security deposit before taking it home. Eglinton and Fairlie added spice to the fight by announcing that the tournament would be an annual event, and any player who won it three times in a row would own the Belt forever.

On the clear, windy morning of 17 October 1860, the players gathered in front of the Red Lion Inn, the hotel where Eglinton and Fairlie had founded the Prestwick Golf Club nine years before. Milling about in their lumber jackets, rubbing their hands to keep them warm, Tom Morris, Willie Park, Bob Andrew and five others were told the event's particulars: they would go around Prestwick's twelve-hole course three times for a total of thirty-six holes; the rules of the Prestwick Golf Club would apply; the winner by the fewest strokes would keep the Belt for a year; each pair of competitors would be accompanied by a club member who would ensure that there was no cheating. The professionals were required to sign a form affirming that they accepted these conditions. Some were illiterate, so they signed with Xs.

At half-past eleven the golfers walked to the first teeing-ground beside the twelfth hole's putting-green. About a hundred spectators followed them – gentlemen golfers leading their wives and children, Prestwickers of all classes and occupations. Fairlie scanned the horizon, seeking omens in the weather. Tall, smiling Eglinton stood nearby, his hair flowing in the wind. Nine-year-old Tommy Morris slipped between gentlemen's jackets and ladies' frills to get a clear view of his father. As the home-club professional, Tom had the honour of teeing off first. He was favoured to win. After all, he had built the course. He stood a few club-lengths from the twelfth hole's knee-high flag and waited while his caddie teed up a ball on a lump of wet sand. Tom took a last look at the fairway ahead – his Herculean first hole, well over a quarter of a mile of turf – and began his ticktock swing, the first swing in the history of major-championship golf. At that moment, according to one account, a gust sent his tie up over his chin and momentarily blinded him. He managed to strike the ball soundly, but missed his target. He would struggle with his aim for most of the day.

Bob Andrew played next. The lanky, glum-faced crack Andrew was called the Rook for his beady-eyed resemblance to a crow. He was second choice in the day's betting. The Rook's backers were delighted to take him at three-to-one odds. Andrew hit a low, skimming drive, then followed Tom past Goosedubs Swamp along with their caddies and most of the spectators, including the gentleman marker who would keep their scores. Spectators in those days tracked their favourites from hole to hole rather than staying put and letting the golfers pass by. They tromped across putting-greens and often stood in bunkers if that helped them see the putting. No one raked bunkers during play; that would have seemed like cheating.

According to Prestwick's club history, 'generally there was a feeling that the championship lay between Morris and Andrew.' Willie Park, the second pairing's featured player, disagreed with the general feeling.

Park made a slew of side bets, backing himself. He was the bettors' third choice at Prestwick; the smart money figured that the twenty-seven-year-old's reckless style would hurt him in a medal-play event in which one wild spell or one unlucky hole could cost him the Belt. But Park got off to a strong start, launching a drive that one writer described as sounding 'as if it had been shot from some rocket apparatus'.

On Tom's epic first hole and the long uphill second, Park's power tipped the balance in his favour. 'At the commencement of the game the interest was concentrated in Tom Morris and the Rook, who were paired together,' the *Ayr Advertiser* reported, 'but it very soon had become apparent that the struggle for supremacy would be betwixt Park and Tom Morris. Park made the best start, four ahead of Tom in the first two holes. At the end of the first round Park had scored 55, and Tom 58.' Both men shot 59 in the second round, leaving Park three strokes ahead. By then it was a two-man tournament.

As the final round unfolded, Park made a tidy four at Prestwick's 400-yard fourth hole, where a stone wall crowded the back of the green. Tom, playing a minute ahead of his rival, kept finding his ball in the bunkers he had shored up with railway ties. 'At this crisis the excitement waxed most intense,' one observer noted, adding that, 'frequenters of the links will also admit that in all their experience of Morris they never saw him come to grief so often.' But Tom kept grinding out fours and fives, whittling a stroke off Park's lead, then another.

The sun fell towards the Isle of Arran, painting the sky purple and orange. At the last putting-green, Park had his chance to win or lose. His ball lay ten bumpy yards from the hole. Get it down in two and he would claim the Belt. But if he took three putts – a likely result from that distance – he and Tom would play another round to break the tie. Now Tom, Fairlie, Eglinton, Lord Colville, the Rook, Tommy Morris and scores of others went silent as Park drew back his putter and sent his gutty on its way.

There were shouts, and then cheers as the ball rolled, bounced and dived into the cup. The Belt went to Willie Park.

Tommy couldn't believe it. The bad man had won.

The entire three-round event had taken five hours. In a brief ceremony afterwards, the Earl of Eglinton presented the Belt to the champion. Tom Morris, standing a few paces away, applauded. He had lost fair and square. Later that autumn Park posed for his official photograph as Champion Golfer of Scotland, wearing a satin bow tie and a hound's-tooth suit, one jaunty thumb under his lapel: Willie the Conqueror.

# THREE

# The Belt, the Ball and the Juvenile Celebrity

TOMMY LOVED TO RUN. Down the beach he ran and up to the links, over and around the dunes, moving in and out of shadow and sun until he fell in a heap in the grass. He was the nemesis of the fat partridges and squawking, long-elbowed blue herons he flushed from the reeds that lined Pow Burn. Lying still where he fell, catching his breath, he smelled heather and salt air. He listened to bees. He heard birds carry on their girlish conversations, clicking and whistling in the weeds. He watched gulls ride air currents, peering down with their black pellet eyes. He watched clouds whose edges turned silver when the sun was behind them, mile-high clouds shaped like sea monsters and ships' sails, sheep and puffs of smoke from his father's briar pipe. Springing to his feet, he chased rabbits that scooted to safety, their white tails zipping into high grass like bad golf shots.

Prestwick was his kingdom. The dunes were mountains and the bunkers were dungeons, black as night when the sun was low. When a train from Glasgow appeared behind the Tunnel Hole green, trailing a plume of white smoke, it looked like a toy. Now and then he knocked a scuffed golf ball around with the half-club his father had made for him. Golf was hatefully hard for a ten-year-old whose best shot went a hundred yards, but as he grew he got better and his father made him a set of cut-down clubs. At the age of eleven Tommy could chip and putt better than most of the club members who employed his father. Golf was hard, but it was far more fun than playing with his sister. In any case, Lizzie had household chores to do. As a girl of ten, she spent most of her day helping Mum cook and clean, picking up after Tommy and their little brother Jimmy, washing and folding the boys' clothes and blacking their Sunday shoes. The boys' only chore was reading Bible stories. Tommy did his Bible reading, then escaped.

On his links jaunts he ran up the lofty, grass-covered dunes called the Alps. Reaching the top he kicked sand out behind him like a buck rabbit. Better yet was the downhill part. Every boy in town liked to lie sideways and roll down grassy hills, but running was more daring. From the top of the Alps he would lope down the path towards the first putting-green, gaining speed with every step. At the point where he reached top speed there was a spot where he could turn to the left, down a still-steeper hill. The pitch of this slope was almost forty degrees. He often lost control of his legs and fell on the way down, but in the brief stretch of time between running and falling, he felt he was flying.

His way home from the links led from rough turf to cobbled streets. Tommy saw horses pulling coaches and wagons while dogs, goats, chickens and ducks skipped out of the way. Labourers moved stones in wheelbarrows. Late in the day the air carried warm smells of biscuits, meat pies and fish soup as well as those of mud and horse-dung. The greenkeeper's son passed the town's round-headed Mercat Cross, a stone monolith etched with a weathered misspelling of the town's name: PRESTICK. He rounded a corner and faced the Red Lion Inn, a stone box with four chimney pots on top and a scarlet lion painted on one corner. The dragon-tailed beast stood upright, scratching air – the Lion Rampant that symbolized Scotland. Tommy remembered his father's saying that the lion symbolized both Scotland and England, but that the English lion was a carrion-eater.

The Red Lion's double doors dwarfed a boy Tommy's age. Poking his head inside he could see gentlemen handing their hats, coats and canes to a valet. The smoke of their cigars drifted to the door along with the scents of buttered beefsteak, meat puddings and pies.

The Morris house was a minute's run away. The Prestwick Golf Club paid five pounds a month to rent the cottage for its greenkeeper and his family. There were no beefsteaks cooking inside, but Nancy's table was respectably stocked with fish and mutton, boiled turkey, carrots and turnips. If Tommy was lucky there were stovies, too – potatoes and onions mixed with fat – or apple fritters. He would arrive to find his mother instructing Lizzie, whose job it was to help with plates and table settings while her younger brothers Jimmy and little Jack, the crippled one, watched. Five-year-old Jimmy might shout a greeting to Tommy and draw a stern look from their father, who sat beside an oil lamp reading his Bible. Tom Morris owned many books but read only two, his Bible and his Burns, and Robert Burns' poems ran a distant second to the black book with its frayed ribbon and crackling, threadbare spine. Each evening Tom read Bible verses aloud to the rest of the family.

The Morris house and its contents were valued at eighty pounds by the Scottish Union Insurance Company. Each spring the treasurer of the Prestwick Golf Club paid fifteen shillings to insure the cottage and its 'furniture, bed and table linen, wearing apparel ... golf clubs, brass tools and such like things'. The insurance agent didn't measure the looking-glass over the mantelpiece, which was surely taller than it was wide, a sign of the good taste Nancy had acquired working in Captain Broughton's house. The mantelpiece held flowers and a clock covered by a bell jar to protect it from the soot in the air. Tommy thought the mantelpiece would be a fine place to put the

Championship Belt once his father won it away from Willie Park.

Tom's next chance to win the Belt came in 1861. That year's tournament was the first true Open: it was 'open to all the world', cracks and gentlemen alike. Eight amateur golfers, unimpressed with Park's winning score the previous year, reckoned they could give the cracks a run for the Belt. The amateurs included Colonel J.O. Fairlie, a fact that brought Tommy close to a sort of blasphemy: speaking ill of the colonel. 'He thinks he can beat you, Da!' But Tom only smiled. If he couldn't beat the colonel over three rounds on a course he had built himself, he said, then the world was surely upside-down.

The event's growing fame led the Dunn twins, Willie and Jamie, to make the two-day trip from Blackheath, near London, where Jamie had gone to work with his brother. On arrival they encountered the Earl of Eglinton, fresh off his second term of running Ireland for Queen Victoria as her Lord Lieutenant in Dublin.

Autumn rains drenched the links on the day of the Open, leaving the players to splash through puddles in Tom's fairways. Markers again followed Tom, Willie Park, Bob 'the Rook' Andrew, the Dunns and the other cracks to make sure they didn't cheat, while the eight amateurs were trusted to keep score on their own.

In less than an hour it was clear that the gentlemen

were no match for the cracks. Fairlie would post the lowest score by an amateur – twenty-one shots behind the Belt-winner. The Dunns, too, fell back in a hurry. For all his brilliance in match play, Willie Dunn could not last thirty-six holes of stroke play without stumbling, not at his age. Dunn, a decade older than Tom, finished seventeen strokes off the lead. As for the Rook, he hung close for two rounds but could not hit the ball high enough to make up strokes on Prestwick's uphill holes. He came in fourth, shaking his head.

By mid-afternoon several hundred spectators had abandoned other groups to follow the leaders, Park and Morris. The previous day Park had gone to the treasurer of the Prestwick Golf Club and handed over the clanking silver-and-red leather Championship Belt, as he was bound to do or else pay a twenty-five-pound penalty. The treasurer placed the Belt on the long table in Prestwick's clubhouse, where it dared the professionals to claim it. Park boasted that he would take it back to Musselburgh, and for most of the day he looked to be as good as his word. With twelve holes to play, Park led by three shots while Tom stayed close in second place, tacking his way from one safe spot to the next. Then Park reached the second hole of the final round, the treacherous Alps Hole, where Tommy liked to run and tumble downhill. With his usual brio, Park tried to clear the hole's mountainous dunes in two. To succeed he had to go 385 yards in two clouts of a gutta-percha ball that might fly 200 yards if Hercules hit it. It was a brave, horrible choice. According to the *Fifeshire Journal*, 'A daring attempt to "cross the Alps" in two brought Park's ball into one of the worst hazards on the green, and cost him three strokes – by no means the first occasion on which he has been severely punished for similar avarice and temerity.'

While Park's hopes sank in the huge Sahara Bunker, Morris tick-tocked his way home and reached the last hole with a cozy lead. Or so it seemed. The *Journal* reporter saw him 'driving a magnificent ball from the teeing-ground towards home'. But the shot was unlucky, landing 'in a bed of fog at the edge of a pool of water . . . spectators thought that Tom would pick out the ball and forfeit a stroke'. Instead he courted disaster. The most careful of golfers found his ball, gave it a wallop and 'with a self-reliance rising to the emergency, he dexterously sent it bounding into the air'.

Tom won by four strokes. His score of 163 was eleven shots better than Park's winning total the year before. That score put paid to the notion that amateur golfers might be as skilful as the cracks. At its highest level, golf was already a game for professionals.

Willie Park went home empty-handed, while Tom took the Belt uphill to his cottage, a journey of a few hundred yards, and put it on his mantelpiece under the looking-glass. The Earl of Eglinton took the train from Prestwick to St Andrews, where he was joined on the links by R&A members including James Balfour. As Balfour wrote in his *Reminiscences of Golf on St Andrews Links*, 'Lord Eglinton ... expressed his delight with the scenery at the High Hole – and indeed he frequently admired the whole landscape, as the descending sun lengthened our shadows on that October afternoon.' After dinner the earl felt ill, but soon found his usual good humour and said he was right as rain, but 'while the butler was helping him on with his great-coat, he fell down in a fit of apoplexy, was carried to a bedroom, never spoke again, and died two days after'. The thirteenth Earl of Eglinton, dead at forty-nine, was honoured with a statue that still stands in the west-coast town of Ayr, just south of Prestwick. Friends including Napoleon III of France and the heartbroken Colonel Fairlie chipped in to pay for the statue, which shows Eglinton holding a scroll, looking stone-faced out to sea. It is a more reverent monument than the Eglinton statue the Irish built in Dublin. The one in Dublin, blown up by the IRA in the 1950s, showed the sporty earl with a deck of cards in his hand.

Not far from Scotland's Eglinton statue was a school called Ayr Academy. Founded in 1794 as a warren of schoolrooms under a thatched roof, the academy could trace its roots to a school founded in 1233. It secured a royal charter and, in 1810, moved to a building that cost a princely £300. Half a century later its students included Colonel Fairlie's sons, the children of other gentlemen and a contingent of lower- and middle-class youngsters. One of the latter was Tommy Morris, who on school days – Monday through Saturday – traded his little-boy sailor suit for the jacket and tie of an academy scholar.

Tommy knew he was fortunate to be going to school with the Fairlie boys. If he forgot, his father could remind him that lads his age worked hand looms from sun-up till dark and thanked the Lord for the work. Other boys sweated through twelve-hour shifts in smoky factories.

In the 1860s only one in 140 Scots attended secondary school. A tradesman's son who succeeded at one of the country's handful of 'famous academies' would be thought of as a 'lad o' pairts' whose virtues offset his lack of social standing. The rise of the clever, industrious lad o' pairts was as mythical as that of plucky American boys in Horatio Alger's tales of the same time – for every bright lad who rose from rags to riches, tens of thousands lived and died in rags. Yet here was young Tommy Morris, bypassing the Prestwick Burgh School by the links, a lesser school, to make the three-mile trip to Ayr, a port town bisected by a muddy river dotted with swans. Here a boy could study navigation, astronomy and bookkeeping as well as Latin, mathematics and science, which was then called natural philosophy. Classes began at seven in the morning. Discipline was strict, with schoolmasters beating and flogging students who got out of line.

Tom Morris scrimped and scraped to pay the school fees of twelve to fifteen pounds a year, and six mornings a week Tommy made his way three miles down the coast to the academy. At the age of twelve, Tommy was better educated than either of his parents. They joked about how he could chatter about Ajax and Alexander, Hector and Achilles as if they were golfers from the next town. Their son would not have to be a caddie and greenkeeper. He wouldn't need to be a crack, living on wagers. Tommy Morris could be what he chose to be.

Still the boy had to eat. He needed food, shoes, jacket and tie, pencils and schoolbooks in addition to his academy fees, and he was but one of six Morrises in the cottage across from the Red Lion. The task of feeding and outfitting them all fell to Tom, who was now in his early forties and showing flecks of grey in his hair. A Scotsman of his era had a life expectancy of forty-one, but Tom showed no sign of slowing down. Every dawn he rose from his bed beside the cracked-open window and dressed for his morning ablutions. He padded down the links to the shore, where he removed his coat and hat and placed them on high ground. Under the coat he wore a long-sleeved bathing costume of dark blue linen with nine buttons up the front. It weighed twenty pounds when wet, which it soon was. Without hesitation, Tom plunged into the Firth of Clyde, which was cold even in July. In January and February the shallows froze over and he had to walk across ice to reach the frosty water. A Prestwick memoirist wrote, 'We recollect a gentleman staying in a cottage shouting out one cold, frosty morning that there was "a man on the beach trying hard to drown himself". It was only Tom Morris breaking the ice to enjoy his usual morning dip in the sea.' Tom emerged shivering, hungry and eager to do a long day's work.

He had half a dozen duties: cutting holes and sweeping rabbit droppings off putting-greens; trimming back heather and other weeds; overseeing caddies; teaching lessons; keeping club members' handicaps and arranging their matches; and playing rounds with some of them, a task that called for infinite patience, but paid four shillings a round. He also settled disputes. One match turned when a Prestwick golfer swung too far under his ball and sent it straight up into his own beard, where it perched and would not budge. Tom's ruling: loss of hole.

The greenkeeper also spent long hours in his workshop, surrounded by the props and paints that preceded each day's dramatics on the links: blocks of wood; wood shavings; sheets of leather and sheepskin; glue; rubber; rags; strips of wool; chunks of black iron; jars of paint; hammers, chisels and saws; the odd, disembodied horn of a ram. When a Prestwick golfer brought him a driver with a grip that was worn or unravelled, Tom would strip off the old grip. He would wrap the hickory shaft with a wool rind, then wrap a strip of leather over the wool, then glue and tack the leather to the shaft. In those days golf-club grips could be as thick as those on modern tennis rackets. A fat grip helped absorb the shock of striking a rock-hard gutta-percha ball; it also suited the then-universal practice of holding the club in the palms of the hands rather than gripping it with the fingers, as later generations would. In addition to repairing grips, Tom mended cracked shafts and clubheads and also made clubs, but above all he was a ball-maker.

After his feud with Allan Robertson, Tom had become the leading producer of gutta-percha balls. There must have been some satisfaction in that – the ball that had cost him his seat in Allan's kitchen now put food on Tom's table. Making gutties was far simpler than making featheries. A skilled worker could turn a lump of rubber into a finished ball in two and a half minutes. Gutties sold for only a shilling apiece, the price of a jar of jam or two pints of ale. That spurred the sort of arithmetic Tom understood: instead of making four featheries in a day and selling them at four shillings each for a total of sixteen shillings – not even a pound – he could make six dozen gutties, sell them at a shilling apiece and rake in three pounds twelve. The difference would make him a prosperous man. In time he would sell gutties by mail to sportsmen all over the United Kingdom.

Gutta-percha came to Tom in dirty pink bricks that in warm weather were soft enough to hold a thumbprint. Tom cut strips from the bricks and softened them in hot water. When the rubber was warm he rolled it between his callused hands, until it was as soft as dough, rolling it into a ball, so close to perfectly round that it looked flawless. Then he dropped it into cold water to harden. He nudged and turned the ball as it bobbed to make sure it hardened evenly, for if one part stayed above the surface too long it would swell and ruin the ball. When the ball was hard he dried it and tapped it all over with a sharp-nosed hammer, leaving scores of dents that resembled the dimples on a modern ball, dents that would help the ball slip through the air.

Hammering the balls was a recent innovation. The first gutties had been smooth, and they flew like shot birds: crazily and not far. Before long golfers noticed that gutties performed better after they had been nicked and scuffed. This was golf's first lesson in aerodynamics. A smooth sphere fights its way through the air, but a scuffed one scratches the air just enough to tunnel its way through. Feathery balls, which whizzed audibly in flight, had been aerodynamic by accident: their seams worked like the raised seams of a baseball, helping them cut through the air. Gutties had no seams, but wear and tear served the same purpose. In later years Tom would make gutties in an iron mould that stamped dimples into them, but in his early days as a ball-maker he was still using a hammer, tapping every new ball like a woodpecker.

While Tommy was off at school, second son Jimmy often joined Tom in the workshop. So did Jack, who was talking now but not walking. The youngest Morris would never walk. He got around by pulling and pushing himself along on a wheeled trolley Tom had made for him. He would sit on his trolley in a corner of the workshop watching Tom hammer a ball or rub up a clubhead. 'Da,' he might say, calling Tom by the name all the children used, 'What're you makin', Da?'

Tom would smile at such a question. 'Money.'

In 1862 the defending Open champion lapped the field by thirteen strokes, a margin of victory that has never been equalled. But Tom Morris earned not a penny for his second Open win. While Willie Park, now described in the *Fifeshire Journal* as 'the ex-champion golfer', got five pounds for finishing second, another year's possession of the Belt was thought to be reward enough for the champion. Less than a week later a hopping-mad Park challenged Tom to a marathon match for £100, and Tom took the dare. The duel of the year would open with two rounds at Musselburgh, Park's backyard, followed by two rounds at Prestwick, two more at North Berwick and finally two at St Andrews. In the weeks leading up to the match, Tom prepared like a modern athlete: he went into training, playing round after round and giving up 'the divine weed', his pipe tobacco. Over four Saturdays in November and December of 1862 he beat Willie by two holes at Musselburgh; by five holes at Prestwick; and sealed his triumph with a four-hole victory at North Berwick. That made the last two rounds at St Andrews a formality. A reporter for the *Fifeshire Journal* wired an account that saddled Park 'with the heavy incubus of being eleven holes behind'. Surrounded by a final-day crowd of more than 300 including the Rook, looking as usual as if he knew some gloomy secret, Tom built his lead to fourteen holes, knocking his drives ten yards past those of Park, who trudged with his head down. Willie's supporters said he had to be ill.

For now, the debate over who was the King of Clubs was settled. The national newspaper the *Scotsman* called Tom's seventeen-hole margin 'unparalleled in the annals of golfing'. At a banquet celebrating Tom's victory, Prestwick's golfers applauded and called his name until at last he stood up. 'I would prefer playing Park to making a speech,' said Tom, whose blushing proved his point. 'There is no disguising the fact that William Park is as good a golfer as ever lifted a club, and it was my great good fortune to defeat such a formidable opponent on all the four greens.' He announced that he was swearing off eight-round marathon matches because training for this one had cost him valuable time in his workshop. It had also cost him 'one of the great pleasures the Good Lord allows us' he said, and with a flourish he fired up his pipe.

Tom could have made the Belt his property by winning a third straight Open in 1863. He played well enough through rain and hat-grabbing winds, but a familiar figure stood in his way. Park was in top form again, clouting long parabolas, his chin leading the way as he marched to a two-stroke victory. That left Morris and Park with two Opens each, while the rest of the golfing population had none. Park carried the Belt back to his workshop beside the Musselburgh links, leaving Nancy Morris with an empty space on the mantelpiece at 40 High Street in Prestwick, where the Morrises now lived.

This second cottage was farther from the links than their first, closer to the centre of town. It sat on a paved street that little Jack could get about on his home-made trolley. And though the Morrises had moved to a better home on a better street, there was talk in town that the club wanted Tom to move his brood back to the links. What good was a greenkeeper who lived so far from the green? A gentleman golfer should be able to knock on the keeper's door at any hour. The club's officers were planning to build a new clubhouse on the links; perhaps Tom could be persuaded to move his family there. The officers were not pressing the issue, at least not yet, because another strain of gossip was coursing through town. People said that the R&A wanted to hire Tom away.

In the mid-1850s the Royal & Ancient had hired a pair of greenkeepers named Watty Alexander and Alexander Herd. Under the two Alexanders, who were paid a combined six pounds a year, the putting-greens at St Andrews grew ragged. Fairways sprouted gouges dug by golfers' swinging cleeks. The minutes of an R&A meeting reported that the faces of bunkers were crumbling, 'much breached by frequent visitations'. After the *Fifeshire Journal* described a course that was 'sorely cut up . . . execrable', the club's powerful green committee fired Watty Alexander, leaving Herd to wage a lonely war against the elements. Poor Herd. If he seeded a green, the seed died. If he pushed a wheelbarrow to the beach, filled it with sand and brought it back to fill rabbit holes in a bunker, the clouds chose that moment to burst and flood the bunker, undoing his work, leaving him bailing rainwater with a bucket while seagulls and club members cackled. Such a job can change a man, if only from drunken bastard to poor miserable drunken bastard. Herd quit in 1863.

Inside the R&A clubhouse, one question became

imperative: what would it take to bring back Tom Morris? When the clubhouse was built in 1854 it was pale brown, but a decade of wind and rain had bleached its colour. Tom wasn't the first to observe that sandstone and golfers both started tan and weathered to grey. To the greying men inside, the need for a greenkeeper multiplied when Edward, Prince of Wales, eldest son of Queen Victoria and future king, agreed to become the club's patron and first royal captain. With the prince's year-long captaincy to begin in the autumn of 1863, the more-royal-than-ever Royal & Ancient could not afford to make its home on a second-rate green. And so the question of Morris' return became more urgent as the months slipped by. The Prestwick Golf Club paid him quarterly – nine pounds and fifteen shillings every three months for a total of thirty-nine pounds per year. No other greenkeeper made nearly as much, and many R&A members believed Tom would gladly race back to St Andrews for the same amount.

In Prestwick, a west wind was blowing all the flags towards St Andrews. Tommy, now twelve, was nearing the end of his studies at Ayr Academy. Nancy longed for her hometown and Tom did, too, though he said no such thing to the R&A men who visited Prestwick with growing frequency. Instead he hinted that he might look favourably on an offer of fifty pounds per year. When that record-setting number was met with splutters of disbelief, Tom took a south-bound train to Devon to lay out a course called Westward Ho!, England's first seaside links. Tom Morris was seen as a hero there. He was the King of Clubs and builder of the twelve holes at Prestwick, the best new links in a century. When he joked that there was a dire need for new courses in England, 'for nearly as many men play golf there on Sunday as go to church,' they loved him all the more. Tom would make many trips to Westward Ho!; on one visit he met a boy named Johnny Taylor – the future five-time Open champion J.H. Taylor, who would remember the encounter all his life. Young Taylor saw Tom come through a door with the sun behind him, and perhaps because of the reverence with which grown men approached the bearded visitor, or perhaps because someone mentioned the town Tom was born in, the boy believed he was looking at St Andrew himself.

Tom enjoyed his days at Westward Ho! He was in no rush to return. He knew what the R&A officers knew – that there was nothing to keep him from following Willie Dunn's example and taking a green-keeper's job in England. Nothing but the absolute impossibility in his own mind of Tom Morris becoming even temporarily, even momentarily, English. But then the R&A officers didn't know that.

Tommy was growing like a spring weed. He

excelled at the academy, but to his mother's dismay he would drop his books at home and race out to play golf. Six days a week he played – every day but Sunday. He swung in the same way for any shot – hard – and always took the straight way to the target. If the Cardinal Bunker yawned ahead of him, he challenged it. If his ball failed to clear the bunker, he would jump down into the sand, swing hard one or two or six or seven times and then emerge with a wave. His father kept pointing out better, safer routes around the links he had built when Tommy was a baby. 'It's point A to B to C, son,' Tom said. 'Do they not teach Euclid at your academy?' Tommy's answer, in a word, was 'Fore'. Alone among Prestwick golfers, he ignored Tom Morris.

By his last year at the academy Tommy was bigger than most boys his age. Now he ran up and down dunes not for fun, but to strengthen his legs. He practised even more scientifically than Tom had done while training for his marathon with Willie Park. Tommy would hit the same shot different ways with different clubs. Nancy clucked and worried – was this how an academy scholar behaves? But Tom could see that his son possessed a sort of genius. He saw it the first time Tommy checked his aggression, thought twice and played around a bunker, floating a pitch shot to the only flat part of a slanting green. The boy was starting to think two or three shots ahead. He was learning to see a round of golf as an interlocking set of options, like shards of glass in his favourite toy, his kaleidoscope. Most golfers saw only one way to play a hole, but Tommy could picture a dozen, and as he grew he gained the strength to hit the shots he imagined. But it was his academy-trained mind that helped Tommy see new ways to go from A to C, to scan a hole and find a better route than the straight-to-target line, a route that the next century's golfers would call 'the line of charm'.

On 12 April 1864, Scotland's leading professionals convened at the Rook's home course in Perth for one of the richest tournaments yet. The purse was eighteen pounds, with ten pounds for the winner – enough for a man to live like a prince for a month. The Rook led early but funked late, taking four swings to escape a vile lie in a bunker. Tom Morris and Willie Park tied for top honours, and they tied again in a playoff round. The sun was sinking fast during a second playoff when Park tried for a killing shot, a long spoon over a hazard that Tom lacked the power to clear. But Park's ball fell just short – avarice punished again. After several long, ugly minutes he recorded a ten on the hole, and Tom was ten pounds richer. Oddly enough, the winner of an amateur tournament on the same course the next day received the same prize money. Major Robert Boothby of St Andrews won his ten pounds with a score that would have embarrassed the cracks. He did it

without losing his amateur status because he was a gentleman. As a gentleman, Boothby was presumptively exempt from greed – never mind that many members of the gentry were chronically strapped for cash. The chasm in class between swells like Boothby and commoners like Tom Morris allowed both to win ten pounds without making Boothby less respectable or Tom more so.

Tommy had begged his father to let him play in the professional tournament at Perth. The cracks might all be taller than he was, but Tommy could out-drive some of them and he was brilliantly deft around the putting-greens. He begged until Tom relented, and the two Tom Morrises went to Perth together. Once there, however, they got bad news. The Perthers would not let Tommy play. They said he was too young – who had ever heard of a schoolboy crack? Yet his trip was not in vain. As a consolation, the gentlemen of Royal Perth arranged a match between Tommy and another lad without whiskers, a prodigy the newspapers called 'Master William Grieg of Perth, juvenile golfing celebrity'.

Men passed a hat and came up with a five-pound prize for the boys' match, the same sum Park earned for second place in the twenty-eight-man main event.

At the first teeing-ground, Tommy shook hands with Grieg, the young hero of Perth Academy, a rival of Tommy's elite school. A curious crowd followed the boys. Many had bets down on Grieg, who was known for pinpoint accuracy and was as meticulous as ever that day, striking his gutty with what a witness called 'astonishing neatness and precision'. Imagine the boy's puzzlement, then, as he lost hole after hole after hole. Tommy's man-sized drives and canny short game overwhelmed young Grieg, who looked more childlike as his defeat dragged on. 'It was very funny to see the boys followed by hundreds of deeply interested and anxious spectators,' read a news account. 'Master Morris seems to have been both born and bred to golf. He has been cast in the very mould of a golfer, and plays with all the steadiness and certainty in embryo of his father.'

A photograph from that week in Perth survives. It shows eleven of the cracks posing in front of a stone wall. To the right stands the Rook, with half a smirk on his face. To the left is second-place professional Willie Park, looking irked, and beside him a stoic Tom Morris. And standing on a step behind Tom, one hand resting on his father's shoulder, is Tommy. A week shy of his thirteenth birthday, dressed in his little-boy sailor suit and cap, he could pass for ten or eleven years old. Looking straight at the camera, he seems to know that he belongs among these men two and three times his age, the best golfers of the 1860s. He certainly knows one thing that the newspapers failed to notice.

His score in the boys' match would have won the professional tournament.

# FOUR

## *Return to St Andrews*

THE FOURTH OF May 1864, was a shining, windy Wednesday. The whins hid their thorns under yellow blossoms that wreathed the links like garlands. In a long, wood-panelled room in the Royal & Ancient clubhouse, ruddy men smoked, laughed and argued while servants moved among them carrying food and drink on silver platters. After lunch Major Robert Boothby called for the attention of his fellow members, some of whom knew what was coming.

'I move that Tom Morris of Prestwick, formerly of St Andrews, be brought here as a professional golfer at a salary of fifty pounds a year,' he said.

'Second the motion,' called Captain William Maitland-Dougall, lifeboat-rescue hero of the Storm of '60.

The patrician John Whyte-Melville, his moustache and side-whiskers as silver as money, rose to object. Whyte-Melville would not hear of paying a green-keeper fifty pounds. Did no one else recall what they had paid Allan Robertson for the same work? Nothing! Were they now to be held hostage by Allan's apprentice, the son of John Morris the weaver? Whyte-Melville and several other members called for a vote. But Major Boothby, whose prestige may have risen a notch with his amateur victory at Perth three weeks before, had picked the right man as well as the right moment, and his motion was passed. The club's official offer to Tom was an annual fifty pounds plus twenty pounds for expenses. According to an R&A historian 'the invitation ... will have doubtless filled him with pride and awe'.

In fact the gentlemen of St Andrews needed Tom more than he needed them. A greedy man would have held out for more money, reckoning that the gentle-man golfers could easily double that fifty pounds out of their pockets on any given afternoon. Tom also knew that accepting their offer carried risk as well as reward. If a blight struck his putting-greens next year he could be fired like Watty Alexander. And he would not be his own boss. The new greenkeeper's job would be 'to keep the putting-greens in good order, to repair when necessary', wrote Tulloch, Tom's biographer. 'For heavy work, carting, etc., he was to be allowed assistance at the rate of one man's labour for two days in the week, and it was understood that he was to work under the Green Committee.' The last clause emphasized that Tom needed to please the club's officers, who would be looking over his shoulder.

Prestwick golfers took their loss in their stride. They gave Tom a rousing send-off in the town's Burgh Council Room, where fiddlers and pipers moved through a festive crowd that ate, drank and sang until long past midnight. The *Ayrshire Express* described the scene: the event's chairman opened by praising the 'professional pioneer' who had built a golf course famous for its 'compactness and variety of hazards'. The golfers cheered. Tom's departure, the chairman announced, was no shame to Prestwick, for 'the ties of an earlier and stronger affection drew him Fife-wards to re-settle in his native county at St Andrews, known over the world as the headquarters of the grand old national pastime.' After several more minutes of chairmanly harrumphing, the host offered a toast: 'To Tom Morris, with all the honours!'

The room went white as shouting men waved their handkerchiefs over their heads. Tom waited for the noise to die down, but the din rose until he had no choice but to stand and speak. 'I am no orator,' he began. An awkward silence proved his point. 'When I first arrived in Prestwick thirteen years ago I thought I had made a mistake,' he said. Seeing the barren links hemmed in by a wall to the north, a road to the south, railway and beach on the other sides, he had wished he'd never left Fife for this strange frontier. But Prestwick surprised him, proving to be fertile ground for golf. 'I leave with regret,' he said. 'My feelings will not allow me to say more. But if you will take the will for the deed, I will offer my best thanks for the honour you have paid me, an honour which I will never forget.'

The golfers stood and cheered.

On the Monday before Christmas 1864, Tom and Nancy brought their well-bundled children to Prestwick station to await the day's first train to Glasgow. The train rolled into Prestwick just after seven. It would leave at 7.18 a.m., so there wasn't much time to load children and luggage into the second-class compartment and cast last looks over the links, the firth and the rocky peaks of the Isle of Arran, snow-capped in winter. Five-year-old Jack, sitting on the platform amid a jumble of hurrying legs, could not climb onto the train without help. Tom hoisted him up and they were on their way.

It was only a hundred miles from Prestwick to St Andrews, but the trip took all day as they switched from train to train on crisscrossing rail routes. In the forenoon they passed the short, gloomy shoulders of the Kilsyth Hills, with the higher Campsie Fells behind. They changed trains at Greenhill, where the hills were green even in December, but if you were to hike to their summits you would see smudged skies hanging over lower land, where coal and ironstone mines had turned farmland into ant-hills. The Morrises' train rolled due north through Bannockburn and Stirling, passing within longbow range of the battlegrounds where William Wallace beat the English in 1297 and Robert the Bruce beat them again in 1314. Tom and his family changed trains at Stirling station, where Tom paid a porter to trundle their luggage onto an eastbound car while the children peered up at Stirling Castle, on its flat rock pedestal a hundred feet above the trees, where Mary Queen of Scots had been crowned in 1542 at the age of nine months – Lord Livingstone had placed the baby-queen on her throne and stayed nearby to make sure that she didn't roll off onto the floor.

The train out of Stirling took the Morrises east into Fife. After a change to the Edinburgh & Northern Railway at Dunfermline their route curved northeast through Ladybank station, following the River Eden through fallow fields to Cupar and Leuchars, where the river spilled into the North Sea. Here at last was a final transfer of luggage and weary children to the snub-nosed little train that ran to St Andrews.

The rail link from Leuchars was only four miles. They would just beat December's late-afternoon sunset. Tom and Nancy's hearts must have risen as they approached their hometown. For the children, St Andrews was a foreign place, a wintry town north of Moscow or Copenhagen, huddled on a promontory whipped by sea winds. From a mile away they saw rooftops, chimney pots and crow-stepped gables, the tall clock tower of St Salvator's in the middle ground, the spires of the crumbling cathedral behind. Near dusk, the town's west-facing windows mirrored the setting sun and St Andrews seemed to glow. 'I never saw anywhere such winter sunsets as at St Andrews,' wrote the local pastor. 'Regularly each afternoon, through all November and December, the sky all round the horizon blazed with crimson and gold ... The men came out of the club daily, and gazed their fill.'

The train moved past the wide Cottage Bunker on the fifteenth hole, following the golf course to the west edge of town. Here the tracks ran right beside the course. The knee-high flagstick that marked the fifteenth hole, topped with a square of red flannel, was twenty paces from the rails. The train came in at fifteen miles per hour, slowing to a walking pace on its way to St Andrews station, where it huffed to a stop, exhausted. Tom helped his wife and children down to the wood-plank platform at the station. He picked up little Jack and led the way to town.

They took rented rooms on Golf Place. Tom also rented a shop nearby, an old candy shop where he set up a workbench and began turning out gutties and working on clubs. During the winter months when few golfers played, he paced the links, chewing his pipe, strategizing. Like his contemporary James Balfour, Tom relished what Balfour called 'the grand history of St Andrews and its sacred memories – its delightful air – the song of its numberless larks –

which nestle among the whins – the scream of the sea-birds flying overhead – the blue sea dotted with a few fishing boats – the noise of its waves – the bay of the Eden as seen from the High Hole when the tide is full – the venerable towers and the broken outline of the ancient city.'

But as the Custodier of the Links, as Tom was officially called, he was in hard fact the keeper of a dilapidated green. The links had deteriorated since Allan Robertson's death five years before, a slide that continued through the unhappy tenure of Watty Alexander and Alexander Herd. After Herd quit there was no greenkeeper at all for more than a year. By the time Tom arrived, cows grazed fairways gouged by studs. The putting-greens, too small for the traffic they endured now that golf was ever more popular, were bumpy and brown; many were as rough as the fairways and teeing-grounds. Women dried and bleached their wash by draping it on whin bushes near Swilcan Burn. Horsemen, shepherds and seaweed-pickers crossed the line of play, stamping the links with hoof-prints and barrow tracks. At the Heathery Hole, bits of shell deflected putts on a bare brown putting-green.

One of Tom's first moves was getting the cattle off his turf. With aid from influential R&A members, he established a new local law: cows could graze on public land, *except* on the golf links. Tom doctored the Heathery Hole putting-green with hardy grass seed he ordered from Holland. He started work on new putting-greens for the first and Home holes, and introduced a practice that would last for most of his life: each morning Tom Morris inspected the St Andrews caddies, a ragged lot that included grimy barefoot boys of ten and eleven years old as well as grizzled men of sixty. Some of the older caddies reeked of cheap whisky, as did one or two of the boys. Tom told the caddies that he was not their father or pastor, but that they were now in his charge, and he would sack any caddie who disgraced himself or these links with drink or coarse language. Furthermore, there would be no golf on the Sabbath, with no exceptions.

Some of the caddies pitched in during Tom's early labours, but few could keep up with him. He rose early for a dip in St Andrews Bay even when there was ice on the shallows. His sun- and wind-burnt skin stayed red all winter as he took up the work of mending and modernizing the old course, work that Allan Robertson had started eight winters before. Back in the cold months of 1857–58 the R&A had paid Robertson a one-time fee of twenty-five pounds to enlarge most of the putting-greens so that two holes could be cut into the greens. Before then, golfers had gone outward to the Eden for nine holes and then played the homeward nine on the same narrow path, using the same putting-greens. In his *Reminiscences of Golf on St Andrews Links*, Balfour recalled fairways 'no wider than a good, broad street', with thick whin bushes on both sides. A large bunker could fill most of the space between. It was no wonder that players of Tom's generation learned to sacrifice distance for accuracy. As J. Gordon McPherson marvelled in his 1891 book *Golf and Golfers*, 'What skill was needed – especially with a side-wind – to avoid the Scylla of the whins without being caught by the Charybdis of the bunker!'

In those days holes like the third, Cartgate Out, and the fifteenth, Cartgate In, shared a small putting-green and the very same hole in the ground, which meant that golfers playing the third hole had to wait while others putted on the fifteenth or vice versa. (The group reaching the green first had priority.) And since the next hole's teeing-ground had to be within eight club-lengths of the hole, golfers who had waited to putt out often did so while drives and curses whizzed past their ears. As more players took up golf, the links grew so crowded that gutties sometimes struck each other in mid-flight. A dozen or more golfers might be approaching, chipping, putting and teeing off in a space the size of a dining room. More than one player had the shock of swinging down at his ball just as another ball came flying in to strike his club and cannon back the way it came. By the 1850s, the links were so congested that a few R&A members avoided the crowds by playing at night. They placed lanterns beside the holes, creating an eerie, firefly effect.

Allan Robertson relieved the congestion by en-larging the putting-greens. Each of his new double greens featured two holes and two flags. Now, rather than tussling for space like miners going opposite ways in a yard-wide tunnel, golfers moved smoothly out and back. To show them which hole was which on each double green, Robertson used flags of different colours – white for the outward nine, red for the inward. The first red flags were cut from worn-out golfing jackets donated by R&A members.

It was soon clear that St Andrews' new, wider putting-greens called for wider fairways. Otherwise players left Robertson's spacious greens only to duel for space in the same narrow pathways Balfour had compared to a city street. Robertson had done some clearing of whins, heather and long grass, but Tom inherited the bulk of that task, which would occupy him for years. He would widen the fairways, giving golfers more room for error, opening the way to a more freewheeling style of play.

After cutting back swathes of heather and high grass, Tom attacked the whins. There were no whins at Prestwick, but the thick, sharp-bristled bushes choked the links at St Andrews. Tom was a terrier with them. The club paid local men to help – Hutchison called them Tom's 'horny-handed sons of toil' – but Tom's hands were anything but soft. He could strike a match on them. Still, no bare hand could win a round with the whins' skin-tearing thorns. Tom wore thick gloves on the days he battled whins, chopping off their branches, undermining them with picks and spades, yanking, grunting and wrestling until the gnarled brown bushes came out by the roots. Only then did he have the satisfaction of tossing a whin carcass into a barrow and lighting his pipe. And that was one bush out of thousands. All through the late 1860s Tom would come home with whin thorns sticking out of his jacket, his hat and even his beard. Nancy and Lizzie would pick out the thorns and throw them in the fire. Tommy wondered which foe his father would rather be rid of, Willie Park or the whins.

Tommy wondered, too, whether his father's back-breaking work was hurting his golf. After winning his third Open in 1864, Tom had failed to finish first or even second in the next two.

Both Morrises went to Prestwick for the 1865 Open. Fourteen-year-old Tommy, by far the youngest in the field, was making his first try for the Belt. His father was the betting favourite, but after two rounds Tom stood nine shots behind Andrew Strath, the gaunt St Andrean who had succeeded him as Prestwick's greenkeeper. Strath came from a large, colourful family. His younger brother, Davie, was a gifted golfer who would become Tommy's foe and great friend. Another Strath brother called Mad Willie was a thug who specialized in home invasions. He would burst through your door at the dinner hour, beat you up and steal your valuables – banknotes, teapots, silverware, even your hat if he liked it. Golfers joked that if Andrew Strath won the Belt he'd have to hide it from

Mad Willie. But the joke was whispered, for everyone knew the Straths were an ill-starred family prone to consumption. Twenty-nine-year-old Andrew already showed signs of the tuberculosis that would kill him.

He was apparently better at golf than greenkeeping. As the *Ayrshire Express* reported, 'Never since the Belt was competed for has the weather been so good, the only drawback being that some of the putting-greens were not as smooth as hitherto.' Tom Morris, weary and scarred after months of whin-wrestling, fell apart in the second round. According to the *Express*, 'No little consternation prevailed among the backers of the favourite when it was known that he had been beaten by his own son.' Not that Tommy was anywhere near the lead. Eight shots behind with twelve holes to go, Tommy picked up his ball and quit. At the last hole, scrawny Strath edged Willie Park for the Belt.

By 1866, Tom's second full year on the job, the cost of maintaining the St Andrews links was eight times what it had been in 1860. He had stayed under his twenty-pound expense limit in his first year, billing the R&A for seventeen pounds, two shillings and sixpence for 'labour assistance, cartage and grass seed . . . and a new wheel for the links barrow', but the next year Tom nearly doubled his budget, spending a bit over thirty-six pounds for labour and equipment, including an innovation that shored up the hole in the High

Hole's crumbly putting-green, an iron collar that may have been the first cup on a golf green. No one complained about the money he was spending. Even R&A members who had opposed Tom's hiring praised him now. The fairways were wider, bunker walls re-sodded, divots filled with sand and grass seed to help them grow over. Best of all were the putting-greens. Tom made some of the course's double greens still larger as well as smoother and greener. He top-dressed the greens with sand as he had at Prestwick, and helped his workmen whisk them with long, rough brooms made of dried evergreen branches strapped to old broomsticks. His conifer brooms resembled the kind that witches rode in fairy tales, and they worked a similar sort of magic, scraping the top layer of soil just enough to stimulate young grass. He said brooming a putting-green was like scratching an itch – the green *liked* it.

For greens other than the one at the wet High Hole he used clay pipes as hole-liners. The pipes, made in nearby Kincaple, happened to be four and a quarter inches in diameter. Due to that quirk of the Kincaple brickworks, four and a quarter inches became the standard diameter of the cup on every green. (Or at least that was the story in St Andrews. Musselburgh golfers claimed they'd been cutting holes that size since 1829.)

While Tom mended the course, his son hit balls. Tommy's swing would be imitated by a generation of golfers who saw themselves as his apostles. Gripping the club with his hands about a finger-width apart, Tommy kept the 'V' between his right thumb and forefinger aimed at his right shoulder at address, as golfers do today. Twisting so far on the backswing that he nearly lost sight of the ball, he swung down with a fast move that one witness compared to 'the shutting of a jackknife'. He hit the ball low, drilling it into the wind. In golf, as in all things, Tommy was a sceptic: nobody could tell him how to hit a shot; he would find out for himself. He improved by making mistakes and then trying again a different way, or just trying harder. In the words of Bernard Darwin, grand-son of the evolutionist and golf correspondent for the *Times* early in the next century, Tommy Morris was 'palpably filled with golfing genius'. Tommy would have agreed with Darwin that 'golf at its best is a perpetual adventure, that it consists in investing not in gilt-edged securities but in comparatively speculative stock, that it ought to be a risky business'. The boy played more like the daring Willie Park than like his own father, who was by nature a feather-ball player. Tom's style was needlepoint – knitting a round together with straight lines from one safe spot to the next on ragged, narrow links. Tommy's more imaginative, attacking game evolved along with the gutta-percha balls and the wider fairways and iron-headed clubs that came with it.

Far from mistrusting irons, as older players did,

Tommy found new uses for them. One favourite was his rut iron. A forerunner of the sand wedge, the rut iron was made for digging a ball out of cart-wheel ruts. Most links were crisscrossed with ruts – cart tracks barely wider than a golf ball. The rut iron was a lofted specialty club, designed to flip the ball out of a rut to safe ground. But Tommy used his rut iron from the fairway. As a Prestwick Golf Club historian wrote, he 'developed the art of playing approach shots with a rut-iron, a shot so difficult as never to have been attempted before'. By swinging sharply down with the lofted little cleek, Tommy launched high approaches that stopped or even backed up when they hit the green. Backspin! As a tournament tactic, he invented it.

He perfected a different shot while practising at his father's workshop. Tom and his workers would be moulding, cooling and hammering gutties, while Tommy, who did all he could to avoid such tedious labour, worked on his chipping. Fashioning a clay ring the size of the hole, he dropped the ring on the saw-dusted cement floor and chipped balls at it. He was already a brilliant putter. His stance on the green was unique – right foot almost touching the ball, so close that it appeared he'd bump that foot with his wooden putter on the backswing. He gave putts a firm rap, coming upward through the stroke to add overspin that kept the ball rolling over bumps and bits of shell. 'Young Tom was of an entirely different temperament from his father. He played with great dash and vigour,' reads Prestwick's club history. 'He was a notably good putter, always giving the hole a chance ... the hero of the golfing world and the pride of Scotland.' It seemed he never missed inside five feet. 'Of the short ones,' the golf chronicler H.S.C. Everard recalled, 'he missed fewer than any player the writer has ever seen.'

Nobody ever said that about Tom. The elder Morris was a generally solid putter bedevilled by what later generations would call 'the yips'. His putting woes earned him frequent ribbings from his son. 'The hole'll not come to you, Da,' Tommy said. 'Be up!' Still Tom left crucial putts short. Tommy teased him, telling other golfers, 'My father'd be a brave putter if the hole were always a yard nearer to 'im.' Tom shook his fist, citing the Fifth Commandment: *Honour thy father!* But he liked the boy's spirit. Tom may have feigned indifference when his son hit brilliant shots; may have offered only a handshake when the boy beat him for the first time, on a windy morning when Tommy sank a putt and threw his putter into the air; may have scolded Tommy later for making a show of himself. But Tom was quietly pleased. The boy wasn't afraid to win.

As the 1860s progressed, father and son began playing as a team. Small-stakes contests at first, but the wagers Tom made with cracks and club members grew to ten, twenty, even fifty pounds – Tom's annual salary as greenkeeper. He said little about these matches to

Nancy, who wanted more for their bright, academy-taught son than the life of a crack. Indeed, Tommy lacked a prime credential for that low trade. Unlike all the other cracks, he was not a caddie. This privilege was unique to him – from the start Tommy Morris was a player, never stooping to tee up someone else's ball.

There was no golf on the Sabbath. Golfer Andra Kirkaldy recalled the town's 'broad clean streets in the quiet of Sunday, when every tavern door is closed'. Six fresh-scrubbed Morrises made their way up North Street, passing the little house where Tom was born, nodding to other churchgoers. They wore their 'Sunday best', a recent Sabbath custom that signalled respectability. Tom had on a well-brushed tweed suit he wore only to church. Nancy wore a long dress and a bonnet with a ribbon that tied under her chin; if the sun was out she carried a parasol. Tommy walked stiffly in his short black jacket, frilled cotton shirt and black tie, striped breeches, peaked cap and gleaming shoes freshly blacked by his sister, Lizzie, who was dressed in starchy frills and a little bonnet of her own. Jimmy, to his deep satisfaction, was decked out just like Tommy. Little Jack wore plain black. Unable to walk, he rode on his wheeled trolley, sometimes pushed by one of his brothers, sometimes pulling himself along. He wore leather half-gloves that protected his knuckles.

Holy Trinity church covered half a block in the middle of town. A stone castle dating to 1412, it was rebuilt in the 1700s with crouching gargoyles and a bell tower that climbed twenty-five yards high. Tom had been christened here. He led his family through the church's iron gate to arched oaken doors that moved with the weight of centuries. Inside was grey Calvinism: cutty stools for sinners to sit on while the pastor scolded them from his stone pulpit; a Seat of Repentance for golfers caught playing on the Sabbath. The Seat of Repentance had fewer occupants after Tom came back from Prestwick and helped the pastor enforce the church's ban on Sunday golf. 'If the golfers don't need a day of rest,' Tom always said, 'the greens surely do.' His ban has remained in force from then until now for more than 7,000 weeks; it still bars Sunday golf except for one week every five years when the Open Championship returns to St Andrews.

Morning services began at eleven and ended at half past twelve. Like many other families the Morrises then walked from the kirk down to the cathedral cemetery. Little Jack enjoyed this jaunt; the street was downhill here.

When they reached the graveyard, some of the stones were so old that weather had erased them. Others held seven or eight sets of names and numbers. A twelve-foot deep plot could accommodate eight coffins with newer generations stacked tight on top of the ones that came before.

One gravestone was an obelisk with an elfin mutton-chopped face bulging out of it, as if the elf inside were trying to force his way out. Here lay Allan Robertson, under crossed golf clubs and the words *Far and Sure*.

South of there stood a thick white stone. It marked the Morris family plot, purchased by Tom after his and Nancy's first son died. Tommy stood by his father, mother, sister and brothers, reading the side of the stone that faced each day's sunrise. This was the grave of Wee Tom, the first Thomas Morris, Jr.

Erected

by

Thomas Morris and Agnes Bayne

in Memory of their Beloved Son

THOMAS

who died 9 April 1850, Aged 4 years

In the silent Tomb we leave him

Till the Resurrection Morn

When his Saviour will Receive him

And Restore his lovely Form.

Under this marker was the elm box into which Tom had lifted his firstborn. His consolation stood beside him, a strong son with a jackknife swing and the same name. Names mattered. Nancy was *Agnes* on the stone because that was her given name. Lizzie was named in honour of Nancy's mother, Elizabeth;

Jimmy for Colonel Fairlie; Jack for Tom's father. Tommy's name honoured his father but also Wee Tom, the eldest son who never lived to outgrow his nickname.

The Morrises then walked back up South Street to Holy Trinity, passing through the same iron gate and oaken doors to attend afternoon services, filing into a pew under a vaulted ceiling that climbed into shadows. They listened and prayed. They sang the '*Magnificat*' and '*Nunc Dimittis*'. By the time they got home it was almost time to eat. After a quiet dinner, tea, Bible reading and bedtime prayers, everlasting Sunday gave way to Monday morning. Tom would be out the door early, headed for the beach and his morning swim. Tommy would wake early as well, and reach for his golf clubs.

By Tommy's sixteenth year, professional golf was growing fast. The cracks were no longer mere sideshows to the club members' medal competitions. They were coming to be seen as showcases for the game's leading talents – the national game most expertly played. Until 1864, the Open was the only significant event for professionals, but from 1864 to 1870 there would be fourteen more: five open to all-comers and nine for professionals only. Such contests were still primarily excuses for gentlemen to lay down a bet – in the absence of a good cockfight, the gentlemen would bet on a duel among the cracks. And the professionals didn't object to being so used as long as they were not bought too cheaply. Willie Park for one scowled at the sight of fistfuls of twenty-pound notes he saw changing hands at events in which the winning player got two pounds or five. As usual, he went public with his gripe. 'If better inducements are not held out,' the *Fifeshire Journal* warned, 'William Park at least will hesitate before he comes.' Park's mood was understandable; his luck was running sour. He had narrowly lost the '65 Open to Strath, and also lost a pocket-watch to the Grim Reaper. According to Musselburgh golf historian George Colville, a gentleman promised Park an expensive watch if he could drive a ball off the watch for nine holes without scratching the face. Park did just that, but the man died two days later and Willie never collected his prize.

'We are underpaid,' Park told his fellow professionals. They seldom received a tenth of what was bet on them. One percent was closer. They paid their own way to tournaments and bought their own food and drink – plenty of drink – but were treated as if their very souls were as soiled as their boots. The cracks were never allowed in the gentleman golfers' clubhouses. Any professional golfer who spoke out of turn or failed to tip his cap when a gentleman passed was asking for a poke in the ribs with a walking stick: 'Mind your manners, laddie.' The cracks all knew the club members could easily turn their two-pound and five-pound prizes into twenty-five pounds, but the gentlemen hesitated and the cracks knew why: the gentlemen golfers were worried. Might not these golf-playing caddies with their booming drives and trick shots eclipse the amateur game? The men of the R&A and other golf societies saw the typical professional as a drunken, foul-mouthed lout. They saw amateur golf as the true game, more skilful and pure than the shabby sport of the cracks. By supporting professional events, would they sabotage their own? No one expected such a thing, not yet, but spectators and newspapers were paying more attention to the cracks and less to amateur medalists. It was an ominous sign.

The youngest of the cracks was not yet a fully fledged professional and wasn't sure he wanted to be one. But with wrists as thick as a blacksmith's, Tommy Morris was already doing things no professional could do. His pre-swing waggle of the club, a forceful half swing, was so vigourous that he sometimes snapped a club's hickory shaft while waggling. Not even muscly Willie Park broke shafts without hitting the ball. Tommy loved doing that, for it proved his own strength and put worry in other golfers' eyes. His father only rolled his eyes – there's one more shaft to repair. But while Nancy hoped their son would find clean work in an office, Tom was dogged by a growing feeling that no golfer Tommy's age had ever played half as well. It was a strange idea, sobering, intoxicating. If the boy kept improving, Tom might not be the King of Clubs for long. But there might soon be a new, even more profitable edition of the Invincibles.

In 1867 the two Morrises went to Carnoustie on the north side of the wide Firth of Tay. Twenty years before, Tom had cut his teeth as a course designer here, helping Allan Robertson lay out ten holes over tilting land threaded by the yard-wide Barry Burn. Now a purse of twenty pounds drew golfers to those same ten holes for the biggest professional tournament yet.

Stepping off the train behind his father, Tommy was practically Sunday-dressed in his clean black jacket, vest, high collar and tie, topped off by a Balmoral bonnet he wore cocked to one side. He was one of the few male travellers with no beard or moustache; he had barely started shaving. He and Tom were approaching the links when they encountered Willie Park. The reigning Open champion looked Tommy up and down. 'Tom,' he asked. 'What have you brought this boy here for?' Park was needling them – he knew who 'this boy' was, having regained the Belt at the '66 Open while Tom finished fourth and Tommy struggled home in ninth place, eighteen shots behind.

'You'll see what for,' said Tom. 'You'll see.'

There were few level stances on Carnoustie's wind-lashed links. Thirty-two professionals, the largest field ever, slashed, spat and cursed ill winds, bad lies and worse bounces. Tom fell apart in the second round, but Tommy stayed close to the pace set by Park and Bob Andrew, the Rook. After learning to slap balls out of waist-high whins at St Andrews, Tommy wasn't flummoxed by hanging lies at Carnoustie. He slashed low, medium-length drives, sent chip shots rolling up to peek at the hole, and on the last green of the third and last round, he stood over a putt to tie for the lead. He spent so much time looking the putt over, settling into his stance, that some spectators thought he was afraid to make the stroke. At last he gave the ball a sharp rap. In it went.

Tommy had outlasted twenty-nine professionals including his father. Now he would go to a playoff round with Park and the Rook. While the three of them headed for the first teeing-ground, bettors shouted odds for the playoff, making Tommy a distant third choice. Just before the extra round began, a gambling man found Tom Morris in the crowd and offered generous odds if he'd bet on his son. Tom turned the man down, saying the boy was 'over-young'. He thought Tommy would lose.

The boy held nothing back in the playoff. If anything he swung harder than before, his bonnet flying off as he followed through. Spectators rose on tiptoe to watch his low, wind-cheating drives. Schoolboys ran to see where they bounced. Safe again! Tommy gained a quick stroke on Andrew, who soon gained it back, and on Park, who fell far behind and would settle for third-place money. Tommy traded shots and glances with the Rook, whose squinty smile seemed to suggest that he saw some dark humour in the game. As the playoff wore on, Tommy's focus narrowed until he didn't see the Rook or the crowd, only the ball and the target. Drive, approach, chip, putt. Nothing could be simpler. When Andrew faltered, Tommy added to his lead. The Rook, who had often lost to the first Tom Morris, was left gritting his teeth while this hard-swinging boy outplayed him. For him, Tommy was surely one Morris too many.

On the last green, spectators shouted and pounded his back. Tommy, knowing better than to make a show of himself, nodded thanks. The Carnoustie gentleman who held the purse stepped up to hand him eight pounds, the winner's share.

Walking the St Andrews links, Tommy looked north towards Carnoustie. On clear nights the northern sky was not black but the deepest blue, as if lamp-lit from the other side of the horizon. He was schooled enough to know why: that faint light was the reflection of polar ice. A glow that had mystified the ancients could be explained by science.

More than most St Andreans – more than his father – Tommy was a modern, even at sixteen. Unlike the phrenologist who taught classes in town, he did not believe that the bumps on people's heads told their futures. Unlike the fishwives at the bottom of North Street, he did not believe that the souls of drowned sailors lived in seagulls. Tommy smiled when his mother spoke of a sea monster that had frightened St Andrews' children since the moon was new, a creature made of kelp, rope and dead men's hair: 'Beware the shallows, or the Water Skelpie'll git you!' If there were such a creature, he thought, it would run in terror from the sight of Tom Morris in his longjohns, rising from his early morning dip in the bay.

Looking north over miles of black water, Tommy saw a pinpoint of light sweeping an arc around Inchcape Rock. Its source was Scotland's newest, finest lighthouse, a man-made marvel. Even from fourteen miles' distance the beam was bright, sharp white, and yet here was a mystery: sometimes the lighthouse beam and the polar glow were blotted out by brighter lights – shimmering streaks of unearthly green, yellow and red that filled the night sky. Science could not explain them but had given them a name, *aurora borealis*. The Northern Lights. Scots called them the Merry Dancers.

Tommy stood watching the Northern Lights climb over the water. He did not believe in magic, but the sky seemed to disagree.

# FIVE

## *Collision Course*

WITH HIS GREYING beard and forward-leaning gait, walking with one hand in his pocket and the other under the bowl of his pipe, Tom was one of St Andrews' best-known figures. Good old Tom Morris was never too busy to stop and chat, to doff his cap to a lady or (with a wink) to a little girl, or to ruff a lad's hair and ask to hear a favourite Bible verse. But he wouldn't tarry long. Tom always had work to do. On Sundays it was God's work: Bible reading before and after church, handing round the bag for collections during services, walking his family to the cemetery, Bible reading in the evening. On other days he did his own work: inspecting caddies, uprooting whins, top-dressing greens, hammering and painting gutties, winning bets.

By 1867, three years after returning from Prestwick, Tom had won praise from all quarters for refurbishing the links. He had also matched Allan Robertson's most famous feat by shooting 79 there. Only he and

Robertson had visited the low side of 80. Yet, for all his titles, the Custodier of the Links and King of Clubs was still a caddie when his social superiors crooked their fingers his way. He often carried for Colonel Fairlie, and occasionally for R&A officers and visiting dignitaries. When the English novelist Anthony Trollope came to town and tried his hand at the Scottish game, Tom teed up his swings and misses.

Watching his father kneel to tee up another man's ball set Tommy's teeth on edge. Tom, unbothered, said there was an art in making a sand tee just the right height for a golfer's swing, and applying a drop of spit to the ball so that a few grains of sand stuck to it, adding backspin when it landed. There was no shame in kneeling, he said. Had not our Saviour told his followers to render unto Caesar? After all, Tom said, it was not his immortal soul that bent, only his knee.

On the days he caddied for Fairlie, Tom would start by fetching the colonel's sticks from the R&A clubhouse, where they were kept in a wooden locker the size and shape of a small coffin. He readied them for play in the time-honoured fashion, by rubbing them up. He rubbed cleeks with emery paper, applying a good shine to the edges of the blade while leaving the middle of the clubface a darker grey. A darker sweet spot, he said, 'helps the eye be easily caught when aiming.' After finishing the cleeks he rubbed his man's wooden clubs with a rabbit's foot, dipping it first into a pot of linseed oil, then buffing the shafts and clubheads with the oily rabbit's foot, giving the wood a waterproof coating as slick as an otter's back.

After the clubs were rubbed up he stuck them under his arm and went to meet his man at the teeing-ground. It would be twenty years before anyone thought to put golf clubs in a bag the caddie could swing over his shoulder. If Tom was partnering Fairlie in a foursomes match that day, he left his own clubs behind. When a caddie and his man played as a team, both of them used the gentleman's clubs – a custom that played a part in the 1867 Open.

Taking his dip in the Firth of Clyde on the morning of the Open, Tom watched fast-moving clouds and felt a freshening wind that blew gulls sideways down the shore. He remembered a black, flat-faced wood that Colonel Fairlie employed to hit low drives under the wind. A driving putter, it was called. Tom thought the colonel's club might help him get the Belt back.

Willie Park had the same thought on the same morning, but for once Park was not bold enough. By the time he found Fairlie and asked to borrow the black driving putter, Tom already had the club tucked under his arm.

Through the first two rounds on Prestwick's up-and-down links, Tom led Park and Bob 'the Rook' Andrew by two shots. Willie Dunn, who would finish last in a field of ten, must have wished he had spared himself the long trip north from Blackheath. For all his brilliance in match play, he was undone by stroke play and would never come close to winning an Open. Perhaps Dunn bought a pint that night for another of fate's victims, the Rook, who fell apart yet again in the late going.

Afternoon winds hummed and then paused as if holding their breath, daring the golfers to swing. Tom, wielding the black driving putter, led most of the day but could not shake Park, who kept hammering drives and knocking in putts, pressing the issue as he had throughout their ten-year duel.

'No competition excites more interest among the lovers of the grand national pastime', intoned the *Fifeshire Journal*, than one between 'the two most distinguished professionals' Morris and Park. The gruff Fairlie followed along, clenching his fist each time Tom smacked another low-hanging drive. After the first two rounds, which was all the Prestwick scorecards could accommodate, the scorekeepers turned their cards over, as they did in all the early Opens, and recorded the third and final round on the cards' blank backs. In the end it was Park who missed a crucial putt and forty-six-year-old Tom was the champion again – the oldest Open champion yet. That was no great distinction after only eight Opens, but even today, after 135 Open Championships, no other winner has been as old as Old Tom was in 1867. He earned a year's possession of the Belt and seven pounds while Park, who now trailed his rival four Opens to three, won five pounds for finishing second. Andrew Strath got three pounds for third place. That left the last pound of the sixteen-pound purse for the fourth-place golfer, sixteen-year-old Tom Morris Jr, who came in five shots behind his father.

After the Belt ceremony there was still enough light for one more round. Tommy found Park and dared him to play a money match. The Musselburgh man smiled. Willie Park, who had yet to duck a challenge in his thirty-four years, nodded and headed for the first teeing-ground. The match prompted spirited betting and drew a curious crowd to what often appeared to be a duel to see which golfer could swing harder. Tommy may have led by that measure, but despite fighting Willie down to the final tee, he was humbled two-and-one.

Once again the Belt sat on the mantelpiece in the Morris house. This was a new mantelpiece in a new house beside the St Andrews links, a tall stone house at number 6 Pilmour Links Road. Tom had bought it the year before. The doorsill sported a big black 6, a poor omen for golfers. Occasional snows between Martinmas and May Day piled up like white icing on the flat roof until the town's sooty air turned the snow as grey as the house.

It was a gossiped-about house. One cause for talk was the fact that Tom had *bought* it. Victorian Scotland was a rental society; not one in ten Scotsmen owned his home. It was curious, too, that the previous owner, a club-maker and part-time crack named G.D.

Brown, had agreed to sell his house so soon after Tom came home from Prestwick. Brown was a dapper, coarse-talking cockney who had married money; his wife was the daughter of a rich London ale-seller. Brown never quite managed to fit in St Andrews – too loud, too English – but he hadn't talked about leaving. Then, just when Tom Morris needs a house by the links, Brown ups sticks, packs up his ale heiress and disappears, leaving behind an eight-room house in a prime spot and a shop full of golf clubs waiting to be sold. Why?

There was a hidden hand in the sale. As part of the deal that brought the Morrises home from Prestwick, town officials agreed to help Tom find just such a place. They pressured G.D. Brown to sell and seven months after taking up his shovel and barrow as St Andrews' greenkeeper, Tom received a loan from town provost Thomas Milton for £500 – the precise amount it took to pry Brown out of his house. The town was betting that Tom Morris would help make St Andrews the undisputed capital of golf. But that £500 and the house it bought were both a boon and a burden to Tom, who took on a debt that was ten times his annual salary.

The Morris children peeked out from the windows at 6 Pilmour Links Road while their mother filled the house with respectable things, herself included. It was a sign of respectability that Nancy did not work outside the home, performing instead the still-new role of stay-at-home wife, the so-called 'angel of the household'. Such a woman personified the values of a nascent middle class. Rather than milk cows, gut herring, or clean another woman's house, she stocked her own with table linen from Dunfermline, carpets from Kilmarnock, upholstered chairs and a grand-father clock. She put a potted fern on either side of the fireplace. She bought a blue-and-white china teapot that never held tea but only sat, dry and haughty, on a shelf with Nancy's cups, saucers, stoneware mugs and her favourite nutcracker.

The man of the house, whose paternal authority came straight down from heaven, gladly ceded rule over pots, pans and linens to Nancy while spending every day but Sunday on the links or in the shop. Every morning after his dip in the bay he returned, still wet, and changed into dry tweeds. Walking past the sitting room, kitchen and scullery he went out the back door to a small garden between the house and the shop. Nancy grew roses, turnips and onions in the garden. The light was poor, with direct sun only for the hours around noon, and her vegetables grew small and sickly. Her roses were hardier, particularly those near the family's dry-hole privy, a shed that spiders haunted in the summer. Nancy's rose bushes climbed halfway up the privy's paint-chipped walls.

A gravel path led through the garden. Tom would clomp down the path on his way from the house to the shop, with little Jack not far behind. Eight years old, Jack had strong hands and wrists, thickened by years of dragging himself around on his wheeled trolley. Children in his condition did not go to school, so Jack stayed at home and helped his father in the shop. He got around the house, garden and workshop by pulling himself along on railings Tom had built into the walls at knee level, giving Jack a hand-hold wherever he was. The boy would grab a rail at the back door and yank himself into the garden, where the gravel path ran downhill; he would zoom through the garden, pebbles flying behind him, and barrel into the shop.

Jack did finishing work on new clubs. He polished the heads of spoons, as fairway woods were called, and drivers. He tightened the whipping that bound clubheads to shafts. He worked beside James Foulis, a young carpenter Tom had hired to help in the shop. They made quite a trio – greying Tom and the bony, hollow-cheeked Foulis on the workbench with fleshy Jack sitting below them, gripping the head of a driver in his fists, rubbing it up until its surface gleamed like glass.

The heart of any golf shop was a sturdy workbench. According to J.H. Taylor, the English golfer and club-maker, a proper workbench 'must be strongly built, and should not be more than 33 inches high' This was the same Taylor who as a boy caught a glimpse of Tom Morris at Westward Ho! and thought Tom was St Andrew. Taylor, whose clubmaking was as precise as his golf, listed the items on his workbench: a vice with a 3½-inch jaw; a 14-inch bow saw; a 12-inch tenon saw; a 14-inch half-round wood rasp; a 14-inch half-round cabinet rasp; a 14-inch half-round cabinet file; a ³/₈-inch gouge; a 1-inch chisel; a medium hammer; a brace; a lead ladle; a ³/₁₆-inch twist drill; a small bit; a 12-inch screwdriver; a scraper; a screw for leads; a steel-bottom plane; a glue-pot; an oil-stone; an oil-can; a pair of scales; and weights up to 8 ounces. Tom's shop held all that as well as a spherical iron mould for making gutties, Tom's primary business. Each gutty went into the mould as warm putty and came out as a near-perfect sphere that was hammered all over to make it fly better; given two coats of white paint and then set aside for three months to cure before it was sold. Each ball was stamped with the same letters emblazoned on the sign over the workshop door: T. MORRIS. A name that meant probity and good golf, if not good putting.

Outside the shop lay the broad green links. Four years of axe- and spadework had turned narrow trails through bramble into outward and inward nines, side by side. The putting-greens Allan Robertson had doubled grew bigger under Tom, who seeded, sanded and broomed them until their piebald turf was soft and true. R&A men joked that Tom was making the greens so smooth that even Tom could make four-foot putts. Balfour and other old-timers complained that the course was now six shots simpler. Tom said no, it was fairer, and he had the numbers on his side. In his first five years as greenkeeper the winning score in the R&A's annual medal competition ranged from 92 to 98. Lesser medals went to gentlemen shooting no worse than 99 and no better than 96. If the course was getting easier, the difference was hard to detect. Of more than 500 R&A members, only a handful ever broke 100.

Tom knew better than the members that the 'Old Lady', as he sometimes called the course, had many ways to defend her virtue. Tom had not stilled the wind. He had not warned golfers about the invisible breaks on several greens. If St Andrews' links lacked the blind shots found at Prestwick, optical illusions were at work here, too. At St Andrews the grass itself was deceptive: more than forty varieties of bent and fescue grasses ranged in colour from near yellow to the deepest forest green making it hard to judge where the ground undulated and where it only appeared to.

Somehow the old course changed but did not change. That was a trait it shared with golf, a game that owes much of its character to its fields of play, no two alike. A case in point was the new first hole at St Andrews.

When Tom became Custodier of the Links, the ground in front of the clubhouse was often under water, swamped by high tides. Storms sent saltwater sloshing up the clubhouse steps. It took a visionary politician and a pair of poetry lovers to beat back the tides.

The politician was Hugh Lyon Playfair, the most famous St Andrean since the mythical jumble of bones that was St Andrew. Born in 1786, Playfair served Her Majesty's Army in India, where he marched in formation and played golf. Playfair was a founder of the Dum Dum Club, the first golf club outside the British Isles, laid out on a stretch of scorched grass that is now the site of Calcutta's international airport. Like other gentleman soldiers with room in their luggage for Indian gold, rubies and emeralds, Playfair came home a wealthy man. Sporting the whiskers and jowls of a white walrus, he paraded around town in a top hat, silk tie and black greatcoat. As provost of St Andrews he launched a modernization campaign. 'The new broom,' Playfair called himself, and his twenty-year rule swept dunghills and horse carcasses from the muddy streets, which were soon paved for the first time. Provost Playfair brought the rail link from Leuchars. He brought the telegraph that clicked news at lightning speed from Edinburgh, London and the world. It was he who saw the town's future as a tourist centre, with golf its prime attraction. An avid golfer, he was elected captain of the R&A in 1856, the same year he turned seventy and went to London to be knighted by Queen Victoria. After that he had his clubs engraved with a line to foil pilferers: *This was stolen from Sir Hugh Lyon Playfair.*

Affronted by the tides that swamped parts of his home links, Playfair envisioned a breakwater between the course and the beach. He dispatched workmen to bury old boat hulls at the top of the beach. When the sea crept over and around the buried hulls, Playfair ordered more wrecks to be buried, and in time the land in front of the clubhouse was reclaimed from the sea. Playfair's project would be re-launched decades later by Tom Morris and George Bruce, a builder who followed Playfair in the chain of town provosts and who followed Tom into meetings of the town's Burns Society.

On the course, the job was to contain what Burns called the 'roar o'sea'. What Playfair began, George Bruce would continue by using construction debris as a breakwater. Hundreds of cartloads of rocky soil, rubbish and cement were dumped into wrecked fishing boats. Bruce directed the horse-drawn carts of rubbish and the sweating labourers who unloaded the carts and buried hulls. He got his hands dirty, too. He and Tom looked on while the workmen over-turned a cement-laden sloop, pressing their shoulders to the hull until the splintering husk gave up and rolled into place. Victory!

The breakwater, called the Bruce Embankment, would create a dry mile north and east of the first teeing-ground. Along with Playfair's work, it remade the seaward side of town. Tom used a quarter of a mile of reclaimed land to build a new first hole in front of the clubhouse. He re-turfed the widest fairway in Scotland and built a green on the far brink of Swilcan Burn, so near the stream that a golfer's power was neutralized. Tom's new first hole was a finesse player's hole. A gimmick hole, some would say. Still, it has a thought behind it: the first hole at St Andrews is a good Presbyterian hole, one that rewards those with the good sense to play it humbly. Hit your second shot to the back of the green, two-putt and move on.

Not that the greenkeeper's son played it that way. Tommy wanted to make three. While his father made four after four after four on the hole, Tommy would loft a daring approach inches over the burn in the hope of getting his ball close to the flag. As a result, he made threes, fours, fives and sixes. But that is what makes it a good hole: you can disagree on how to play it, and no answer is right every time.

The adjacent eighteenth was a forgettable thing, its fairway crossed by Granny Clark's Wynd, a dirt path that led to the beach. Golfers stood waiting while men on horseback clopped across the path. They also waited for mule-carts, dogs, wrack-gatherers and courting couples. They waited for the town's volunteer lifeboat crew to drag a thirty-foot lifeboat to the beach for lifesaving drills. The boat and the carts left deep ruts that golf balls dived into. And the patchy little putting-green beyond Granny Clark's Wynd was not much better. It lay in a dark hollow where grass refused to grow. So Tom set to work digging another hollow, the Valley of Sin. He and his men used all the earth they dug from the Valley of Sin to build a new putting-green for the Home Hole at the southeast corner of the links, a broad green that sloped from right to left and back to front. Tom said that greens on plateaus kept the golfer looking towards heaven. But this one had an unholy beginning. 'In the course of the work,' wrote Andra Kirkaldy, whose father helped Tom build the Home green, 'human bones were exhumed.' The workers struck a shallow burial pit that had been dug during the cholera outbreak of 1832. Tom, who had turned eleven that year, remembered the fear that gripped the town. Now his workmen were affrighted by the sight of human bones. He could have left this green-site to the ghosts but he forged ahead, telling the men that they would dig if they wanted to be paid. After all, a man with a shovel could strike bone all over town.

The burial ground at the east end of the links was re-buried as Tom's new Home green took shape. Even Balfour, grumbling that the eighteenth was 'quite changed by the formation of an artificial table-land', called it 'a beautiful green'. Few modern players or spectators would guess that every champion who has won at St Andrews, from Bobby Jones to Jack Nicklaus and Tiger Woods, has walked over the Valley of Sin to stand on an old boneyard as he finished his round.

The course was improving but Tom's own game

was going stale. He knew that if he didn't play better he would lose the Belt – perhaps to his namesake, who made no secret of his hunger to win the clanking old thing for himself.

The Championship Belt was part of the furniture of Tommy's youth. It was no mere symbol, but a thing with heft and texture, its red leather darkening with age, smooth to the touch but shot through with hairline cracks. Its silver buckle, showing tarnish, was slightly ridiculous with its engraver's error, the little silver golfer swinging a headless club. Still, the Belt meant more than any other trophy a golf professional could win. Its winner was the Champion Golfer of Scotland.

After losing to Park in their singles match after the 1867 Open, Tommy got even in a rematch. Park was longer off the tee, though the gap was shrinking, but Tommy could hit shots no one else had imagined. He didn't need a driving putter to keep the ball under the wind. He naturally hit a low ball, and could smack chin-high screamers by closing the clubface at impact. Such a shot took exquisite timing – just as club met ball he turned his right wrist as if he were turning a door key from right to left.

He had ambitions beyond golf, but they would wait. His mother might have dreamed of seeing him in a business office, but Tommy had no yearning to push a steel-nibbed pen down columns of numbers day after humdrum day. He relished the slight stickiness of a tacky suede grip; the powerful shifting of forces at the top of the backswing; the crack of impact and the sight of the ball in the air, hanging for an instant before it falls to a thudding bounce on the putting-green, a fine flat thud that sounds nothing like a ball landing on longer grass. And then there was the crinkle of a ten-pound note between his fingers, the texture of victory.

By the spring of 1868, seventeen-year-old Tommy and forty-seven-year-old Tom were making real money in foursomes matches. Ten, twenty, *fifty* pounds in a day. No office job paid that much.

One money match pitted them against another talented pair, former Open winner Andrew Strath and pug-nosed Bob Kirk, the son of Tom's longtime caddie, now grown and winning bets left, right and centre. According to the *Fifeshire Journal*, 'either party considered themselves lucky if they got a single hole ahead, and when they did so, it was generally to be brought down the next one to "all-square".' They were all-square at the Home Hole in the first of two rounds. Tom could have won the hole with a long putt – still called a 'put' in the *Journal* – but left it so far short that the Morrises' backers moaned. After Strath missed, it was Tommy's turn to hit his side's ball. He paced between the ball and the hole, studying the mess his father had left him. A three-yard putt, sidehill. Settling over it, he pictured the ball curving to the hole and rapped it hard enough to diminish the curve. By the time the ball felt gravity's pull it was nearly to the hole. When it fell in, Tom breathed again.

'On coming back the second round, father and son gained the match by three holes and two to play,' the *Journal* reported. 'Young Tom played a splendid game, and was admired by the large concourse of spectators as a youth of great promise. A good deal of betting was on this match.'

Sometimes the Morrises teamed against a pair of R&A golfers, giving them a handful of strokes or generous odds. Sometimes Tom and Tommy split up, each taking a club member as his partner, with the members betting each other. Tommy came to know dozens of the gentlemen his father worked for. A few were soldiers who had fought in the Crimean War of 1854–56 or the Indian Mutiny of 1857–59. Captain Maitland-Dougall had joined the Royal Navy at the age of thirteen as plain old William Maitland. He served in Persia and China, where the Chinese fractured his skull but couldn't kill him, and came home in time to rescue those shipwrecked sailors in the Storm of '60. As progressive as he was brave, he added the name of his wife, the former Miss Dougall, to his own name when they married. Oddly enough, the heroic Maitland-Dougall was a nervous, twitchy golfer, but Tommy liked him.

Other R&A golfers were men of leisure who had no careers beyond spending their family fortunes. They hunted fox and grouse, played golf and whist, drank, smoked and filled their bellies with more good meat in a fortnight than a factory worker's family got in a year. One was Mister Cathcart, a fop whose motif was citrus. He traipsed the links in his lime-green jacket and yellow neckerchief. Two other gentlemen anticipated the age of golf carts by riding ponies between shots. One of the pony riders, Sir John Low, employed three caddies at a time: Lang Willie to lug his clubs, a second caddie to lead the cream-coloured pony, which left loose impediments on the greens, and a third who carried a stool that he planted on the green so that Sir John could rest his knightly bottom while he waited to putt.

Tommy was polite to the gentlemen, lowering his eyes and tipping his cap, for they were his father's employers. But he didn't have to like them. Some called themselves golfers, but were only playing dress-up in their leather breeches and red golfing jackets. Butchers who worked the way these golfers played would have no fingers. And they looked down their noses at Tom Morris!

'See here, Tom,' Mister This or Major That would say. 'Fetch me my putter, Tom.' At the end of a round the nabob dropped a coin into Tom's upturned hat. Still, the gentlemen said they loved Tom Morris as one of their own. Tommy heard that very phrase from one of them. 'Good old Tom,' the man said, 'I think of him almost as one of my own ...' Then came the next word: '... servants.'

Tommy preferred the caddies. The renowned caddies of St Andrews were 'no' saints', as they gleefully admitted. They were poor, unshaven, often drunk, occasionally insolent. One R&A man called them 'gentlemen of leisure, who for a consideration will consent to sneer at you for a whole round'.

Caddies were 'bronzed like Arabs' from their days in the sun, wrote Andra Kirkaldy, who joined their ranks as a boy. Each morning they gathered at the corner of the links by the Golf Hotel, waiting for loops that paid a shilling apiece. They saw that corner as their own property, 'consecrated by the expectoration of tobacco-juice,' Kirkaldy wrote, 'and the fumes of threepenny cut.' They chewed the same tobacco that they smoked. They lit matches on their stubbled chins. Some drank on the job, sneaking sips from flasks called 'pocket-pistols' and swore they weren't breaking Tom's rule against caddying drunk, because they could hold their liquour. Their thirst was such that when the gentlemen put on a tournament for caddies, with a turkey for first place and a bottle of whisky for second, the finalists kept missing putts on purpose, trying to finish second.

They loved Tom, their supervisor, who always had a few pennies for the poorest. In the winter, when there was hardly any work, he'd give a needy man five shillings. 'Take this and buy meat,' he said. 'Don't drink the little that I'm able to give you.' Tommy saw the money go from his father's hand to the paw of some poor wretch, money that could have put meat on the Morrises' own table, and he loved his father even more.

Tommy never cared who carried his clubs – he sought no advice on the links – but he liked to gab with the caddies and hear their stories. There was one about a fishwife who bit off a piece of her husband's nose: when the magistrate ordered her to 'keep the peace', the crone said, 'I canna – I fed it to the cat.' Another tall tale concerned a golfer whose playing partner dropped dead on the High Hole. Unwilling to leave his friend behind, he carried the poor bugger to the clubhouse, where a gentleman said, 'What a fine Christian thing you've done!'

'Aye,' the golfer said. 'The worst bit was layin' him down and pickin' him up between shots.'

Some of the caddies' tales were even true. One concerned Auld Daw Anderson, the white-haired fellow who lived in an upstairs apartment next door to the Morris house. Every morning Auld Daw pushed his wicker cart across Granny Clark's Wynd and then west to his post beside the End Hole, the ninth, where he sold ginger beer and lemonade. He also kept a flask of sterner stuff for those who knew how to ask for it. Handing over the flask, he always said the same thing: 'A wee nip for the inner man.'

The caddie called Hole-in-'is-Pocket made sure his man never lost a ball. If the ball was in the whins he dropped another down his trouser leg and cried,

'Here 'tis, and no' such a bad lie!' His opposite was Trap Door Johnson, who wore a boot with a hinged, hollow sole. When Trap Door stepped on a ball the sole opened and the ball vanished – until the next day, when he sold it.

One caddie towered over the rest. By 1868 Lang Willie, Tom's colleague at the workbench in Allan Robertson's kitchen, had trod the links for sixty years. He still wore his trademark blue swallow-tailed jacket, white moleskin trousers and wrinkled black top hat. While other caddies taunted the R&A men or angled for tips by praising them – 'Well struck, sir; a bonny lick!' – Lang Willie did neither. Asked how his man was doing, he always gave the same reply.

'Just surprisin',' he said.

Caddies who reached forty often looked sixty and lost some of their skills if not their wits. But Lang Willie, due perhaps to some miracle of alcohol's preservative power, reached the Biblical age of three-score and ten. Then he sat down to porridge with his sister one morning. She said his face looked crooked. 'Nonsense,' he said, but the word came out blurred.

The town doctor said it was a stroke. Lang Willie said it was 'just surprisin''. Later strokes clouded his eyes and put a quaver in his step and by 1868 his mouth moved only on one side. By then Lang Willie walked with such a stoop that his top hat some-times fell off. There were days when no golfer hired him. At the end of such a day Tom would clasp his hand and there would be a coin in the handshake.

That July, Lang Willie was lugging a gentleman's clubs at the Corner of the Dyke hole when he fell like a chopped tree. The undertaker had to make an extra-long coffin. After the funeral, Tom, Tommy and the other caddies drank toasts and told Lang Willie stories in a haze of threepenny smoke. The men must have wondered who would be next to climb the ladder to heaven. None expected to see threescore and ten. Tom, who was forty-seven, had read a story in the newspaper saying that the average Scot had a life expectancy of forty-one. 'Lads,' he said. 'It seems I've been dead for six years.'

That autumn he and Tommy rode the train past Stirling Castle and the shoulders of the Campsie Fells and the smudged air of Glasgow and weedy Paisley to Prestwick. Father and son made their way to the club-house through a scrum of players, caddies, spectators and gentleman golfers. Many of the gentlemen were there to play in the Prestwick Golf Club's medal competition, which they considered the main attraction of the week. The professionals playing in the eighth Open Championship would serve as their caddies in the medal event – except for Tommy, who was nobody's caddie.

A new stone clubhouse stood beside the links. It had cost the club £758, an imposing sum offset in part by the £170 the old Morris cottage fetched when the club sold it. Tom admired the long windows and black tile roof of the new clubhouse, but noted that the ground around it was uneven. Little Jack would have faced an uphill climb from the clubhouse to the village. This would be no place for a child who got around on a home-made trolley.

Tom took the Championship Belt to the clubhouse, surrendered it to the treasurer and reclaimed the money he had left the year before. Not even he was trusted to keep the Belt without paying a security deposit.

At eleven in the morning on Wednesday, 23 September 1868, the first group teed off under fast-moving clouds. Bettors in the crowd called out their offers.

'Two five-pound notes to one on Tom Morris.' Tom and Willie Park were the gamblers' choices, with Bob 'The Rook' Andrew available at longer odds.

'The Rook at five to one!'

A pound on Tommy would fetch seven or eight. Bettors knew the teenager had talent, but what had he won? A tournament in the wind at Carnoustie. The Open favoured seasoned professionals who could endure three circuits of the course under ever-mounting pressure. Open pressure had undone the Rook and turned the once-feared Willie Dunn into a last-place finisher. And now that the 1865 winner Andrew Strath had succumbed to tuberculosis, only two proven champions remained. Tom Morris and Willie Park had won the Belt seven times; no other living golfer had won even once.

Park looked north from the first teeing-ground towards the green almost 600 yards away. His open stance gave his muscled arms room for a forceful swipe at the ball. Picking his driver almost straight up, he shifted forward and brought the club down hard, sending his ball on a high line over the waving reeds of Goosedubs Swamp. Tom poked a shorter drive. The hunt was on.

There was no 'par' on Prestwick's prodigious opening hole, or on any hole. Along with 'birdie' and 'bogey' the term had not yet been coined. Still there was a number the professionals expected to make on each hole. In that sense the idea of par existed, and in that sense the 578-yard first at Prestwick was a par six. In a quickening breeze off the firth, Park nearly reached the green in three. Chipping on and two-putting for six, he tipped his cap to his backers. Tom and the Rook matched Park's work on that hole and the Alps Hole that followed.

Back at the first teeing-ground, Tommy walloped his drive past the swamp. Next he swung his long spoon, a graceful, goose-necked fairway wood, and it got him within sight of the green. He tracked it down and stood over it again, waggling the club almost hard enough to snap its neck. Setting up with the ball forward in his stance, almost level with his left foot, he swung, opening the clubface a fraction at impact, and watched as the wind carried his third shot high over the rise in front of the green, over the edge of the Cardinal Bunker. The ball bounced on the green with a fine thud. He nearly made four, but settled for five.

The second hole, Alps, was where he used to race the wind downhill. His drive cleared the huge dune ahead, his approach skirted the immense Sahara Bunker and his putt cut the hole in half. He was the early leader, listening to hear the other golfers' fates in the cheers and groans of their supporters.

At the seventh, Green Hollow, Tommy peered 140 yards to a green perched sideways in the Alps' grassy foothills. With the sun straight overhead he hit a niblick shot that kicked hard to the right, towards the knee-high flag. The ball spun and stopped. His three at Green Hollow began a stretch of near-perfect golf as he closed the first round 3–4–4–4–3–4. With the first of three rounds complete, he was alone in first place.

'Young Morris has shot 51!' a man said. It was the lowest score yet in an Open.

Tommy played more like a boy in the second round, losing the lead to his father, whose course-record 50 said *Take that*. Two rounds, two new scoring records on Tom's obstacle course. Around they came for a third and final tilt, with the sun leaning towards the Isle of Arran. Tom had a stroke on his son while Park lurked four behind. Willie Dunn, twenty strokes behind, would finish last again.

Park took chances in the last round and bunkered too many balls on his way to a fourth-place finish. The Rook, however, was in full flight, hitting the ball higher than he had in the first seven Opens, sailing through the Alps Hole where his low sweepers had always struck the dunes and fallen back. His doomy countenance lightened, and when a last putt fell and his backers sang 'Hoorah for the Rook, the Belt to the Rook!' he gave them a smile full of whisky-coloured teeth. He finished at 159, three strokes better than Strath's record total of 1865.

News moved fitfully around the links. With no scoreboards, players' positions were a matter of rumour. No one was sure who had won until all the scorecards were turned in and tallied up. Even so it was soon clear that the Rook's only Open victory would be a moral one. He hadn't funked, but he had waited too long to play the best golf of his life. Both Morrises were coming in with lower scores.

Tom defended his title with guile. He was not about to make an error that would cost him two or three strokes, as Park had done, as Tommy was likely to do. So Tom gentled his ball up, over and around the dunes, protecting his narrow lead. He did nothing very wrong, but left several putts short and yielded the advantage midway through the round, when his son made his third consecutive three at Green Hollow. From there Tommy went 3–5–3–3 on the next four holes, a stretch where amateur champions like Colonel

Fairlie made sixes and cracks hoped for fours. Still Tom would not give in. When Tommy fired a three at him, Tom matched it. Each time the famous Misser of Short Putts faced one that might sink him, he steeled his nerves and knocked it in. He stayed close, giving the boy a chance to stop and think, to let doubt enter his mind, to look around at all the people looking at him: the haughty Earl of Stair and several other noblemen, gentleman golfers with their ladies, bettors with scored of pounds riding on the outcome, professionals including Park and the Rook, newspaper reporters and curious Prestwickers – all watching to see if a seventeen-year-old boy could outplay the King of Clubs, his father.

Ten years before, lying on this turf after a pell-mell run down the Alps, Tommy had looked up and seen white dragons and sailing ships crossing the sky. Today they were only clouds. They were the vapour of water, as he knew from his natural philosophy classes at Ayr Academy. Clouds were the seas' breath drawn into the sky to fall as rain that flowed through rivers and burns, mills, distilleries and our own bodies until it found its way back to the seas. The more he knew of the world, the more he believed that a world without magic could still be full of wonders.

He turned to his father. 'Far and sure, Da,' he said.

Tom nodded. 'Far and sure.'

They both knew the last hole by heart: 417 paces, wind right to left, dunes to the right and Goosedubs

Swamp to the left. One hole for the Belt. Tommy had the honour.

He waggled. He pulled his driver back behind his head, twisting until his left shoulder touched his chin and the driver's shaft brushed the hairs on the back of his neck. At the top of his swing he was coiled so far to the right that he nearly lost sight of the ball. Then he uncoiled, his right elbow digging into his side, his hips and shoulders turning, pulling the clubhead through an arc that blurred into a sound. *Crack!* The ball went long and straight. Spectators ran after it. Someone shouted that Tommy had won.

Not yet. A misfire could still cost him two or three strokes, enough to give his father a last putt to force a playoff. Tommy would win if he played the last hole the safe way, knocking a niblick to a broad part of the fairway a hundred yards short of the putting-green, then another niblick to the green where he could take two putts, make his five and claim the Belt. But five was not a number that Tommy cared to shoot for. He had a long spoon in his hands and a flag a little more than 200 yards away. He would try to make three.

It was all Tom could have hoped for. Not even Willie Park tried for threes when fives would win. It was a foolish choice, the only choice that could still cost Tommy the Open.

Tommy's second shot took off on a low line, cutting through the wind. For a second it looked bound for the Goosedubs, but the ball held its line against the wind, safely to the right. It was still in the air when Tom nodded as if to say *Good for you*. Tommy's ball was headed for the green and the tournament was clinched. His backers shouted. *Young Morris has done it!*

*Young Tommy . . .*

*Tom Junior . . .*

*The boy has won!*

He chipped close and made four. His third-round score was 49, another course record, the third of the day. Spectators, bettors and golfers gathered round to see the Earl of Stair present the Belt to the new champion. Tommy held the Belt up for all to see, spurring the loudest cheers of the day.

Seventeen-year-old Tommy had smashed the Open record by eight strokes. The *Ayrshire Express* noted, 'the winner of the Belt was the youngest competitor on the links,' a distinction he won even more handily than he won the Belt, for he was the youngest by ten years. His victory made golf-watchers think that Tommy might win two or three Opens in a row. Who would stop him?

# SIX

# *Tommy to the Fore*

The champion stood with his fist on his hip. While taking his pose he rustled the arras behind him, a velvet curtain meant to add a touch of theatre to the photograph. Tommy Morris wore his Sunday best, all black except for a high white collar, his watch fob and the broad silver buckle of the Championship Belt. His eyes challenged the camera. He wanted the photographer to hurry up and let him go. Tommy could barely stand still for ten seconds, much less the minute it took to expose a calotype image. He was itching to *move*. Even worse than standing stock-still was holding this pose, fist on hip, as if he were some pretentious nabob. The pose was forced on him by the size of the Championship Belt – there were no clamps or notches on the Belt, which was far too big for Tommy's thirty-inch waist. His fist pressing the Belt to his hip was all that kept it from sliding down to the floor.

He stood in a little glass house, the outdoor studio

of 'calotype artist' Thomas Rodger, who had built this greenhouse in the sunniest part of his garden. It was hot inside Rodger's glass studio. The light was strong enough to show the weave of Tommy's necktie and the texture of his thin moustache. Rodger captured the image on thick white paper coated with silver nitrate. Tommy appeared first as a pale grey ghost. Rodger washed the paper with gallic acid; the grey parts darkened and there stood the seventeen-year-old Champion Golfer of Scotland. Long before his image was fixed on paper, however, Tommy was crossing North Street on his way to the links. It was late in the forenoon and he had his own things to make: wagers, putts, money.

His era was the true dawn of professional golf. Club members still saw their medal competitions as the game's most important events and lauded their medal-lists with banquets, long speeches and innumerable toasts, but golf-watchers were increasingly drawn to the professionals, who played the game better. A new idea was afoot – the belief that there was something special about seeing the national sport played at its highest level, even if the player was not well-born or well-to-do.

The men of the Royal & Ancient Golf Club of St Andrews were not above encouraging the profes-sionals. Prestwick had stolen some of the old town's thunder with its Open Championship, but the Open was, by definition, open to all golfers, amateur and professional, and by 1868 it was clear that the amateurs were overmatched. William Doleman, a Glasgow baker who was the best amateur in Scotland, led the amateurs in that year's Open with a score of 181, a far cry from Tommy's 154. The R&A members reasoned that if all the best golfers were professionals, a professionals-only event might help drive home St Andrews' claim to be golf's capital.

It wouldn't take much money. The cracks would pay their own way from one end of Scotland to the other to play for ten pounds. They groused when Prestwick cut the Open's prize money in 1868 – Tommy got only six pounds for his victory, a pound less than his father had won the year before – but most of them made the trip anyway. So it was not surprising that they hustled to St Andrews when R&A members topped the Open's prize money at an event of their own, offering a purse of twenty pounds with eight pounds for the victor. The St Andrews Professional Tournament, conceived in 1865 and all but forgotten today, instantly became a legitimate rival to the Open.

The crack golfers of Scotland were, with few exceptions, a rough-hewn, money-hungry bunch, smelling of tobacco and whisky. Two weeks after Tommy's Open victory, they gathered in the shadow of the R&A clubhouse, where they chaffed and made final side bets. Tommy stood at the first teeing-ground, waggling his driver almost to snapping point. The others, his father included, had no intention of letting this stripling pocket prize money they needed for eating, drinking, betting and, in Tom's case, tithing. They could not be bothered to watch Tommy slash a drive that nearly reached Swilcan Burn.

There was another young golfer on hand that morning, a tall, thin fellow of twenty-seven with a smoothly elegant swing. Davie Strath, a friend of Tommy's who worked as a clerk in a law office, had learned the game by tagging along with his brother Andrew, the 1865 Open champion. After Andrew succeeded Tom Morris and Charlie Hunter as greenkeeper at Prestwick, Davie followed him there. In the summer of 1868 he spent long days sitting in a stiff-backed chair by Andrew's bed, watching his tubercular brother sputter for breath, praying out loud with Andrew and praying for him when he had no breath to pray, until the merciful day when Andrew sank into his cow's-hair mattress and lay still. He was the latest in a long line of Straths to die of consumption, and when Davie returned to St Andrews, half the town expected his own handkerchief would soon be spotted red. Thinly handsome with dark, lustrous hair that he combed straight back from the widow's peak above his high forehead, black-clad Davie often looked preoccupied, like a nervous undertaker. Even his slow backswing had a melancholy air. Like Tommy, Davie had never done much caddying. Instead he studied mathematics and bookkeeping. He was a reader, equally keen on Homer, Plato and Archimedes. Like Tommy he believed that a professional golfer could also be a respectable young man – a radical thought that triggered golf's first dispute over amateur status.

By entering the St Andrews Professional Tournament in 1868, Davie Strath challenged the R&A members' conception of the game. 'It was objected to him that he was not a professional,' the *Fifeshire Journal* reported, 'because he is a clerk in a lawyer's office, and not at the call of gentleman players.' In short, he wasn't a caddie. The men running the event still equated professionals and caddies: a professional golfer was a caddie who also played for money. Tommy had slipped through the cracks by playing for money before anyone objected, but Strath was no greenkeeper's son. He was a law clerk with designs on middle-class respectability. Club members urged him to drop out of the tournament. They said he was risking his future if he played.

On the eve of the event, Strath was called to a meeting chaired by Major Robert Boothby and General George Moncrieff of the R&A. Boothby and Moncrieff were in a bit of a hurry, for it was the night of the club's annual ball, a highlight of the town's social calendar, a night of feasting, music and dancing until dawn. They had decided 'to give young David a choice', noted the *Journal*, 'either that he decline to play as a professional, or by playing on the morrow as one, elect to be regarded as a professional for ever.' The fact that Major Boothby had won ten pounds at an 'amateur' event at Perth didn't matter because he was already a gentleman.

Strath did not back down. 'He foolishly, we think, elected to cast in his lot with the professionals,' the *Journal* sniffed. The next morning, Davie Strath sealed his fate with one of his slow, mournful backswings and a drive towards Swilcan Burn.

The eighteen-hole St Andrews Professional Tournament of 1868 was finished before many R&A members got out of bed – 'before the gentlemen awoke from the recuperative slumber of the Ball morning to the fact of the existence of a new day,' in one report. Tommy won; Strath came in fifth. Tommy's eight pounds first prize, along with the six pounds he won at the Open and five pounds from another tournament the next week gave him nineteen pounds in prize money in less than a month – a fraction of what others had won by betting on him and perhaps less than he'd won in side bets, but a tidy sum in an era when farmhands earned ten pounds a year and some houses in St Andrews still sold for twenty pounds. No one had imagined that a golfer would ever earn so much simply by swinging his sticks. Tommy was starting to think that it might be possible to do nothing else – to play a tournament or money match in one place and then move on to the next.

Could a man be a touring professional golfer? That far-fetched notion was much discussed at the Cross Keys Inn on Market Street, where Tommy sat by the fire nursing a pint of blackstrap, a golden mix of porter and soda water that was his father's favourite drink. He and friends, including Davie Strath, James Conacher, a fellow member of the local Young Men's Improvement Society, gathered at the Cross Keys to celebrate Strath's professional debut. Strath, so often nervous or morose, brightened in Tommy's presence. They joked about certain snuff-sniffing majors and generals, ancient men who believed that no money golfer could be more than a low-living crack. Who needed the Royal & Ancient? The ambitious young men of St Andrews could form their own club.

As tradesmen's sons, Tommy and his friends had no hope of ever joining the R&A. Not being tradesmen themselves, they didn't fit into the St Andrews Golf Club, a band of plumbers, tailors, cabinet-makers and other so-called 'mechanics' who played when the R&A men were not using the links. And so, in 1868, Tommy and his friends banded together and gave themselves a cheeky name: the Rose Golf Club.

There was already a Thistle Club in town, named after Scotland's national flower and dedicated to upright Scottish values. The thistle's opposite was the rose, the national symbol of England, the sign of modernity and empire. In making the rose their symbol Tommy, Strath, Conacher and their circle were claiming to be citizens of a modern world whose capital was London, 400 miles away. They believed that Scotland should be less Scottish and more British, and might better be called North Britain. They aligned themselves with Dr Samuel Johnson, who had written that 'the best prospect a Scotsman ever sees is the high road to London'. (On a 1773 visit to St Andrews with his Boswell, the Scotsman James Boswell, Dr Johnson remarked on the town's 'silence and solitude of active indigence and gloomy depopulation'.) The members of the Rose Club thumbed their noses at Burns, haggis, kilts and other things Scottish, except, of course, for golf, and while officially a golf club they seldom played the links as a group. More often they met to dine, drink and debate world events into the wee hours.

The Rose Club's emblem was as provocative as the name. Its petals suggested an aspect of female anatomy. The club members' sexual lives were furtive at best, at least until they married, and even then the realities of sex could be a rude surprise to their brides, who were expected to be virginal until marriage. Some Scottish lassies were kept in such ignorance that they did not know where babies came from until they gave birth. Scottish lads of the time, however, were as randy as those of any country or century. The adventurous visited prostitutes in the dark corners of Edinburgh or in the fisher-folk's quarters in St Andrews, where a fellow could sin with a toothless woman while the salty blood-scent of herring-guts filled the room and a piglet rooted under the bed – or was it a child?

Lacking a clubhouse, they met in pubs. They were regulars at the Criterion and the Cross Keys, where they ate lamb stew and drank small beer – a low-alcohol brew – or blackstrap or claret, while arguing about books, politics, money, sometimes even golf. Young men born in fast-changing times, they wished they could ride the new underground railcars that crawled under London like iron moles, open carts pulled by steam engines through tunnels lit by oil lamps. The Rose Club discussed the Crown's recent ban on public hangings in London, a law enacted not because hangings were barbaric but because they were getting too popular. The Rose Club debated the schemes of Glasgow surgeon Joseph Lister, who cleaned wounds and scalpels with carbolic acid on the theory that the acid killed 'germs'. Even after Lister's trick cut the death rate for major surgery from fifty percent to ten, surgeons scoffed when he suggested that they wash their hands between operations.

After midnight the innkeeper would shoo the debaters through the door and the merry men of the Rose Club would spill into a darkened town, for the lamplighter had already made his last rounds, extinguishing streetlamps to save gas between midnight and dawn. They found their ways home by moonlight.

While Tommy and friends founded the Rose Club, another young golfer was making his name in Musselburgh. Bob Fergusson was no debater and no drinker, but a teetotaller who rarely spoke above a whisper. Long-legged, spare and goateed like the martyred American president Lincoln, twenty-four-year-old Fergusson was the best Musselburgh golfer to come along since Willie Park and, like Park, he first attracted wide notice by challenging a famous St Andrean.

'There was doubtless jealousy between St Andrews and Musselburgh,' Bernard Darwin wrote, 'but it seems fair to say that St Andrews was unquestionably the metropolis of the game, where on the whole the best golf was played by the best players.' That sort of talk could get a man punched in Musselburgh, where partisan crowds hissed St Andrews golfers and cheered their mistakes. Fergusson, though, was a gentle soul who shied from inflaming the old civic rivalry. One St Andrean called him 'uncommonly civil for a Musselburgh man'. When Fergusson issued a challenge he did it not with a newspaper ad but with a whispered suggestion followed by a handshake.

Before trying his luck against Tommy, Fergusson challenged the senior Morris. In a series of six matches he made short, cruel work of Tom, sweeping all six. The chronicler Everard called it 'the most exemplary castigation, for he won the whole series and each of them by a pretty substantial majority'. The worst drubbing of his father's career spurred a quick response from Tommy, who announced that he would play a series of matches against Fergusson.

Tommy's duels with Bob Fergusson were the most hotly anticipated money matches since the Famous Foursome contests of 1849 pitted Allan Robertson and Tom Morris against Musselburgh's Dunn brothers. The players were polar opposites – bold, slashing Tommy swinging and even walking faster than his treelike opponent, who moved grudgingly except to unwind a long, powerful motion that slammed drives well over 200 yards. Fergusson hit cleek shots with such force that he dug gouges in the firmest turf. More than once he had hit a gutty so hard that it broke into pieces. He was so deft at running the ball onto the green with his putter that his supporters dubbed that stroke a 'Musselburgh iron' long before anyone called the same shot a Texas wedge.

Fergusson's showdown with Tommy Morris began at St Andrews. Musselburgh loyalists came by rail and ferry to the town where they were as welcome as cholera, but went home dejected after Tommy swept the day. The series then moved to the Musselburgh links, where hundreds of locals stalked the golfers from the first tee to a stirring finish that saw Tommy and Fergusson finish dead even. So they went around again, and on the last hole of their playoff round Fergusson fired a cleek shot that brushed the flag, setting off a frenzy of cheers and dancing in the hometown crowd. 'Bob,' wrote Everard, 'after most determined play … managed to win by one.' The series swept on to the links of Luffness, just west of Edinburgh, where bettors made Tommy a six-to-four favourite. The short money proved to be the smart money as 'the science and calculation of young Tom told most decidedly in his favour. His putting was deadly, and before the match was half over, the result had almost become a foregone conclusion.'

He enlivened the Luffness match with a gesture that almost everyone present remembered. After striking a putt he would start for the next teeing-ground. Musselburgh writer George Colville recalled the scene: 'Time and again when Morris had putted he would say to his caddie, "Pick it out the hole, laddie," and it went in every time.' Fergusson played his best golf at Luffness only to see his teenaged opponent sink putt after putt to overrun him, eight holes up with seven to play. For the rest of his life Fergusson called Tommy's performance that day the best golf he ever saw.

A return to Musselburgh 'caused great excitement in the town', Colville wrote, 'and there were many wagers.' Fergusson was in command late in the match, three holes up with nine to go. At that point he lifted his game another notch – clouting long dart-like drives, using his putter to slap forty- and fifty-yard chips that rolled up and over greenside mounds and died beside flagsticks. He carded an errorless 40 over the final nine. On most days he would have won in a rout, but Tommy reeled off one of his trademark runs of threes and fours to pull even, then won the last hole and the match, leaving Musselburgh's crowds as still as if he had knocked the air out of them.

Tommy had now avenged his father's castigation at Fergusson's hands, but he wasn't through with Bob Fergusson. They met again at the St Andrews Professional Tournament of 1869, in which the two of them outplayed the rest of the field to tie for top honours, shooting 87s in heavy wind and sideways rain. After an eighteen-hole playoff they were still tied again, so they returned to the first teeing-ground for yet another playoff. As the news spread, townspeople hurried down North Street and Golf Place to watch. Soon it seemed the whole town had left work, school and home to follow the marathon match. When Tommy pulled his driver back and peeked over his shoulder, he saw that a scatter of spectators had become a throng. Fergusson, unfazed, sent outward-nine drives booming towards Lucklaw Hill beyond the River Eden. Between shots he stood in silence, scratching his goateed chin. Tommy was louder. He told his ball to *go* or *run* or *duck in*. He cursed himself for making six on the long Hole o' Cross going out, but clean fours on the next two holes kept the pressure on Fergusson, and on the quartet of holes that formed the shepherd's crook at the far end of the links, Tommy flirted with perfection: 3-3-3-3. His 37 going out was the best nine-hole score ever shot at

St Andrews. His 40 coming in won the long playoff and completed a course-record round that would stand for twenty years. Seventy-seven! Tommy's townspeople crowded around him, reaching out to shake his hand, pound him on the back, pat the top of his cap, *touch him*.

The runner-up stood a dozen yards away, casting a long shadow that climbed the brown picket fence between the Home green and the R&A clubhouse. After several minutes of waiting, Fergusson caught Tommy's eye. Bowing his head, the civil Musselburgh man touched the bill of his cap. It was a quiet man's way of saying, *Well played*.

Tommy's victories over Fergusson restored the Morrises' honour but did nothing for Tom's reputation. There were whispers on both sides of the Forth that 'Old Tom' was no longer a golfer of the first rank. Wasn't it sad that only two years after winning the Open he needed his son to fight his fights? Or if you lived in Musselburgh, wasn't it amusing?

Tom heard the questions. He joked about them. It wasn't idle gossip that said Tom Morris was twenty yards shorter off the tee than his son and worse than ever with his putter. It was plain fact. Putting practice was no cure – he could hole twenty consecutive three-footers in practice and then miss half of them in a match. The caddies joked that Tom should make the hole bigger. He was the greenkeeper; he could find a brickworks that made hole liners six inches across; or he could make the hole a bucket. But Tom laughed and said no. He knew he could sink putts if he kept his head still and his wrists calm. But it was easier vowed than done, and it didn't help that his current plight echoed an earlier embarrassment.

As everyone knew, Tom had made his name as a golfer by avenging his brother George's loss to Willie Park. George Morris, routed by Park in 1854, was renowned for asking for mercy: 'For the love of God, man, give us a half!' Tom had no desire to be remembered as a charity case, not after four Open titles. Yet he could feel the game moving past him like a quickening breeze. After yielding the Belt to Tommy at Prestwick he had lost the course record at St Andrews – the famous 79 he'd shared with Allan Robertson – to Tommy's now-famous 77. When people saw Tom on the street these days, they asked about Tommy.

Tom was proud of his son, but he also felt stirrings of regret. A sharper pang than Burns' nostalgia, this was the regret of an athlete who feels his body faltering. The reflexes slow, the muscles ache. A physical forgetting erases part of what the athlete is, the main part, leaving him as clumsy as other men, but unlike other men he remembers a time when he never stumbled.

Tom sensed he had set all the records he would ever set. Still there were reasons to rejoice: Scotland and

England were full of golfers who thought they were better than they were; even an aging athlete could part them from their money. Tom's family was increasingly respectable, the children healthy. Tommy was the best golfer the game had ever seen; seventeen-year-old Lizzie was a pattern girl, well schooled in manners, Bible stories and piano playing; Jimmy was a golfer of promise and still Tommy's acolyte; even lame Jack, a diligent club-finisher, had a trade. And the golf course Tom tended was in such fine fettle that golfers considered it perfect. After Tom filled in a little bunker on the fifteenth hole in 1869, A.G. Sutherland, a lawyer who summered in St Andrews, demanded that he restore it. When Tom refused, Sutherland sued him and the R&A, claiming that the greenkeeper and his bosses were despoiling the links. Three nights later, two golfers sneaked onto the course. They re-dug the bunker by moonlight and left a note with Sutherland's name on it.

Tom thought that was funny. He could have undone their sabotage with thirty barrows of dirt, but he waved his workers away from the pockmark on the left side of the fifteenth fairway, a hazard that has been known ever since as the Sutherland Bunker.

A morning storm assailed the 1869 Open. Thick fog hid the Prestwick links until thirty-mile-an-hour winds tore the fog apart forcing players and spectators to pull their caps down tight. Fourteen men teed off that Thursday morning, but only nine finished. The others, including a golfer from Perth who soon found himself forty-four strokes off the lead, spent the last round in the clubhouse, warming their hands by the fire. They warmed their insides with drams of whisky and peered out through the building's slot-shaped windows, waiting for the survivors to appear on the last hole.

Tom stayed close to the lead in the early going. He had trained with an eye towards this day. The weather suited him – cold and wet were no bother to a man who had begun his day by wading in the Firth of Clyde, and gusts that blew longer hitters' drives off course had less effect on his lower, shorter ball.

Davie Strath stayed closer to the lead, his swing as syrupy as ever despite the wind. A tobacco chewer, he worked his jaw nervously between shots. Strath matched Tommy shot for shot in the morning and often looked poised to overtake him, but the leader kept wriggling out of trouble. Once after his ball bounced into a whin bush and stuck there, waist-high in a cluster of thorns, Tommy swung and hit it like a cricketer, slapping the ball over a bunker to the putting-green.

In the first round of the 1869 Open he made his usual three at Green Hollow, the seventh of Prestwick's twelve holes. Next came the Station Hole, 166 yards over the Alps to a green guarded by the Sahara

After winning the Open Championship, Tommy posed proudly with the Belt in Thomas Rodger's studio.

Tom's mentor Allan Robertson, who claimed he'd never lost a match, was hailed as Scotland's 'King of Clubs'.

In Tom's later years these images held pride of place on his mantelpiece: the old man flanked by sons Tommy (left) and Jimmy.

*Above* Willie Park of Musselburgh, Tom's nemesis, prevailed in 1860 and went on to win three more Opens.

*Above* At the first Open in 1860, Tom (right) and other golfers wore lumbermen's jackets donated by the Earl of Eglinton.

*Right* Tommy's star-crossed friend, the gifted Davie Strath, was nearly the champion's equal.

As golf's Grand Old Man, Tom was the game's leading figure at the turn of the century and beyond.

The first and last holes at St Andrews occupied sandy turf between the town and the beach.

A long stone pier, built with rocks from ruined St Andrews Cathedral, protected the harbour from North Sea storms.

Tom (left) and Allan (centre, in dark trousers) watched Major Boothby play a shot beside the ancient Swilcan Bridge.

Caddies carried clubs in loose bunches under their arms until a late-century invention, the golf bag, eased their burden.

At the northeast end of town, the gasworks fouled the air and fishermen took refuge in a pub called the Auld Hoose.

*Above* Golfers including Allan Robertson (crouching, third from right) and Tom Morris (fourth from right) watch Willie Dunn putt.

*Left* By winning the Open three years in a row, Tommy made the Championship Belt his personal property.

Courting couples would stroll through the ruins of St Andrews Cathedral, once the seat of religion in Scotland.

Playing his last Open at age seventy-four, Tom putted well but was too weak to muscle the ball from the bunkers.

When the blizzard of 1875 froze the links, Tommy and challenger Arthur Molesworth played through the snow.

Tommy's memorial, dedicated in 1878, still stands beside the Morris family plot in the Cathedral churchyard.

Bunker's half acre of sand. Fall short and you could make five or six on the Station Hole. The professionals hoped for three, settled for four.

The line was just right of the clubhouse. Tommy's tee shot started low, then rose. He liked the shot; spectators saw him take a step forward, shielding his eyes. The ball landed on the front edge of the putting-green, five yards short of the knee-high flag. It hopped and began rolling, not directly towards the red flannel flag, but off to one side – a superior shot that looked ever better as the ball lost speed, curling towards the flagstick. The more speed the ball lost the more it curled until, on the last turn, it fell into the hole.

There was a silence, a sonic blink. Tommy stood at the teeing-ground, unable to see the ball, listening for cheers or groans, but hearing nothing.

Then a roar went up. He'd holed it in one! Men and boys ran onto the putting-green to gape at the ball in the hole. The gallery cheered every step of Tommy's march along the fairway, the noise ebbing when he reached the green, cresting again when he picked his ball out of the hole and held it up for all to see. With one swing he had added two shots to his lead and a boost to his legend. This was the first recorded ace in the history of professional golf.

Tommy finished the round in 50 strokes, one shy of his record. A second-round 55 put him four ahead of Strath and six up on Bob Kirk. Tom had fallen back by now – first by ten strokes, then fifteen, feeling no music in his hickory shafts and little strength in his legs. In the third round, climbing the dunes of the course he had built, Tom used a golf club as a walking stick.

Strath was next to lose hope. His syrupy tempo never varied, but gusts off the firth buffeted his scarecrow figure, bumping him off balance. Strath foozled an approach along the ground into the Cardinal Bunker, took three swings to get out and was finished. He tramped in with an ugly 60 in the final round, letting the snub-nosed Kirk slip past him into second place, good for four pounds. But it was a distant second: when the scores were tallied and the scorecards signed, including the card showing Tommy's ace on the Station Hole, the defending champion had won by eleven strokes.

In Everard's words, 'He absolutely spread-eagled the field.' The *Fifeshire Journal* noted, 'It is worthy of notice that "Young Tom" has won the Belt both last year and this with the lowest scores ever recorded.'

Tommy worked his way to the clubhouse through thickets of well-wishers, accepting the usual handshakes and backslaps. After a brief ceremony he left twenty-five pounds with the Prestwick Golf Club treasurer – security for the Championship Belt's safekeeping – and threw the Belt over his shoulder. He and his father walked uphill to the railway station.

When the news from Prestwick reached the sandstone clubhouse at the head of the St Andrews links,

R&A golfers drank to the health of their greenkeeper's son. Toasts to 'Young Tom' echoed along with the old refrain 'St Andrews forever!' The gentlemen's spirits were high but not undiluted, not on an evening when they could look out over their empty links while the rest of the golf world was focused on Prestwick. As they pictured the middling crowds the Open lured to Tom Morris' up-and-down links on the western frontier (next year, with the lad gunning for his third Belt in a row, there might be a few hundred more) they couldn't help wondering how many thousands might come if the Open were to move to St Andrews.

Tommy's ball hung between clouds, carried forward by the lightest breeze, falling towards the Cardinal Bunker. A year had passed.

The date was 15 September 1870. In the year since Tommy's second Open victory his father and Willie Park had played a raucous series of matches; Tommy and Bob Fergusson had clashed again, with Tommy winning once more; and golf had kept growing. There were now fifty-four active golfing societies in Britain, up from ten in 1800. As the summer of 1870 dwindled, all eyes had turned to the autumn meeting of the Prestwick Golf Club and its annual sideshow, the Open Championship. If Tommy Morris could win a third consecutive Open, the Belt would be his forever. Losing would leave him as only one of three living former champions, along with his father and Park and, with fewer Open titles than either of them, he would be the junior member of that threesome.

One thing was sure: the wind would not drive anyone off the course this year. The 1870 Open enjoyed the sort of weather that Scottish golfers say isn't weather at all, but its absence. The London sporting journal *The Field*, which billed itself as 'The Country Gentleman's Newspaper', told of 'a genial warmth . . . only a zephyr coming from the golden island of Arran to the west'.

'There was scarcely any wind, and the heat was tempered by light, fleecy clouds, which hid the sun's face,' the *Fifeshire Journal* reported. 'Considerably more than the usual interest was manifested this year, as it was known that Young Tom was in excellent form, while other players were in equally good play, and all determined to do their best in order to prevent the young champion from permanently retiring the Belt.' The day began with hundreds of spectators waiting for the champion at the first teeing-ground. They applauded as Tommy smacked his drive and set off after it. The lion's share of the crowd followed him down the fairway of the monster of an opening hole his father had laid out. Prestwick Golf Club members were so proud of the hole that they had measured it down to the inch: the longest hole in tournament golf was 578 yards one foot and seven inches long. Spectators heard Tommy grunt as he struck a long-spoon second shot that left him with an uphill third of about 200 yards. Within seconds of reaching his gutty he swung again, his long spoon nipping the turf under the ball, and now the ball was a dot between clouds, starting its descent, headed for trouble.

A low ridge between him and the green blocked his view. He saw his ball arrowing towards the railway ties that shored up the long, deep Cardinal Bunker yawning to the right of the green. If his ball ricocheted off a railway tie or buried in the sand, he might have trouble making six. Watching the ball dive towards the Cardinal, he talked to it: '*Go.*'

It cleared by inches. Spectators yelled as the ball kicked left onto the green. It was running too quickly; someone shouted, 'Stop!' Next came whoops and even laughter as the ball clacked the flagstick and disappeared.

Tommy couldn't see it, but he knew what had happened from the crowd's reaction. His arms went up, holding the club over his head with both hands as if it were a broadsword. A three!

An old sport who had bet against him turned away in disgust, saying, 'It's no' golf at all, it's just miracles.'

The first three ever made on Prestwick's first hole was more singular than his ace had been the year before; three perfect shots are better than one. Tommy's third shot of the 1870 Open was also the best-timed blow in golf's early history. All over the course, players awaiting news of his round heard a burst of cheering so loud that only Tommy Morris could have triggered it. Whatever he had done, it was bad news for them.

With threes at the first, third, sixth, seventh, eighth and tenth holes, he blazed through the first round in 47, breaking his own record by two. Forty-seven broke another barrier: four was a good score on any hole; his 47 on Prestwick's twelve-hole links made Tommy the first golfer to average less than four over a full round. Already he stood nine shots ahead of his father and thirteen ahead of Willie Park. Only Davie Strath and Bob Kirk had stayed close to Tommy's pace. When Strath shot 49 in the second round to Tommy's 51, he drew within five shots of the lead.

One round to go. Twelve holes stood between Tommy and permanent possession of the Belt – the same twelve stretches of grass, dunes and scrub he grew up on.

He stood at the first teeing-ground between the Home Hole and the beach. This spot was no more than ten paces from where his father had sat with old Colonel Fairlie almost twenty years before, when Tom picked up the tobacco habit that gave him the dusty sweet scent that Tommy loved. Tom was now too far behind to sniff the lead, but Strath and Kirk still hoped to catch Tommy. As the last round began, spectators squeezed in around the first teeing-ground, standing four and five deep on the cobbled Station Road, jostling and standing on tiptoe to see the golfers. Tommy waggled. He coiled his driver behind him until it brushed the back of his neck, paused for an instant and let fly. Applause and glad shouts pursued him up the first long fairway to the green, where there was no miracle this time, no three, only a five that fortified his lead. Solid play on the Alps and Tunnel holes left him with a start of 5–5–3. But at the fourth, where the reedy Pow Burn ran beside the fairway and a stone wall stood behind the green, Tommy faltered. He bunkered his second shot and left his recovery short. He took two more swings to reach the green, where he missed a putt and tapped in for a seven. It was his worst score in the Open since his Belt-winning run began, a span of a hundred holes. For once Tommy Morris had given strokes away.

The fifth teeing-ground was in the northwest corner of the course, within spitting distance of the tall grass at the top of the beach. The surf was loud here. The breeze was gently inland, the crowd fretful, quiet. Tommy stood with his back to the weathered stone wall that marked the north border of the course. He shook his head at his stumbles on the Wall Hole. *Seven!* He had given himself a chance to lose. Still angry, he stepped to his ball and swung hard, eager to leave the Wall Hole behind. After a long, low spoon shot he lay two about seventy yards short of the fifth green. He aimed for the red flag, swung his rut-iron and sent the ball so high that men in the crowd, looking up to follow its flight, held on to their hats to keep them from falling off. The ball dropped almost straight down. It thudded and fell silent a yard from the flag. Tommy stepped to the green and banged it in. *Three*.

Over the next ten minutes he made threes at Green Hollow and Station. His three at the Station Hole was two strokes worse than his now-famous ace there, but was still good enough to stretch his lead. His gallery had swollen; it was ten deep in places. Everyone wanted to follow the leader whose every swing brought him closer to permanent possession of the Belt. His last full swing was a long, bouncing approach to the green at the 417-yard Home Hole. His putt for a closing four brought cheers that Prestwickers remembered a generation later. Tommy yanked off his Balmoral bonnet and flung it straight up into the air.

His three-round total of 149 set a record that would never be broken. His finishing kick gave him a twelve-shot triumph over Strath and Kirk, who tied for second place. Tom Morris finished another stroke back, thirteen behind his son. William Doleman set an amateur record by shooting 169, but was still twenty strokes behind, while Willie Park trailed by a humbling twenty-four.

Gentleman golfers crowded into the clubhouse for the last presentation of the Championship Belt. Spectators outside pressed their noses to windows, angling for a peek at Tommy as he approached the white-whiskered Earl of Stair, who stood holding the Belt.

'His play was excellent – in fact we never saw golf clubs handled so beautifully,' *The Field* reported. 'And he was at the end of the third round hailed as the champion for the third time in succession and consequently the permanent custodier of the Belt ... The Earl of Stair formally presented the Belt to young Morris in the clubhouse.'

That evening, with the Belt under his arm, Tommy celebrated with his father, friends and golf-fanatics until Prestwick's pubs had all barred their doors. Doleman, the amateur who would later help define the concept of par, told anyone who would listen that Tommy's score that day had set a new standard. By Doleman's calculations, Tommy's 149 was 'two strokes more than perfect play'.

'A man generally wins a championship by the narrowest possible margin,' Bernard Darwin wrote. 'Tommy for the three years he won the Belt was on an average nine strokes better than the runner-up.' Tommy's total of 460 strokes in his three Open victories was thirty-five shots better than the next-best total – 495 by Tom Morris – while only five shots separated Tom's 495 from Bob Kirk's third-best 500. No other player would so outshine his peers until 130 years later, when Tiger Woods began winning major championships by double-figure margins.

The *Fifeshire Journal* of 22 September 1870 had the

view from St Andrews: '"Young Tom has won the belt for the third time," were the words in everybody's mouths when the news arrived of his success, and they seemed to convey the *acme* of satisfaction. A flag was displayed from Mr Morris' workshop, and when it became known that the champion would arrive on Saturday night with the ten o'clock train, a number of his friends awaited his arrival, and he had scarcely set foot on the railway terminus 'ere he was hoisted shoulder high and borne in triumph to Mr Leslie's Golf Inn, where his health was drank with every honour.'

He was seven months shy of his twentieth birthday.

# SEVEN

## *Interregnum*

HE WALKED THE links with a crowd behind him – schoolboys and red-coated gentlemen, gamblers waving money, curious townspeople, travellers on holiday, lace- and ribbon-decked ladies and their blushing daughters, all craning for a look at the Belt-winner. Some handed him slips of paper and asked for what they called his autograph. That puzzled him. What use was his signature? Tommy shrugged and signed with the loops and flourishes he had learned from Laurence Anderson, the hard-eyed old writing master at Ayr Academy who would cuff you if your pen hand slipped. Tommy chatted with the autograph-seekers. He was handsome and polite, this bonny braw lad who played the old game better than his elders. He had grown a fuller moustache – more manly he thought – that drooped around the corners of his smile.

When Tommy came home to St Andrews with the

Belt, his return was greeted with church bells. Allan Robertson and Tom Morris had been local celebrities after winning the Famous Foursome contests of 1849, but the hubbub around Tommy's three-Open sweep was something new. The *Fifeshire Journal* described a gathering at the Golf Inn, near the links: 'Mr Denham, London, who proposed the champion's health, said the feat he had performed had never been done before, and in all probability would never be repeated. By it he had brought the highest honour which any golfer could confer upon the ancient city and on all interested in the national game of golf.' Then the champion stood to acknowledge his supporters' applause, nodding to his Rose Club friends as well to his father and his brothers Jimmy and Jack, the latter sitting on his wooden trolley on the floor. The *Journal* scribe took down his words: 'Thank you for this highly complimentary demonstration,' Tommy said. 'Three years ago, I determined to become proprietor of the Belt. As you all know, I had the satisfaction of realizing that goal last Thursday at Prestwick.' Amid loud cheers, he lifted his glass to toast to another golfer. 'To Tom Morris Senior,' he said.

The applause went on, led by Tommy, until his father stood up. After apologizing as usual for being a poor speaker, Tom cleared his throat. 'Seven years ago, I almost succeeded in making that Belt my own,' he said, 'having held it for two years and lost it in the third by a very little. I feel proud, however, that my successful rival, the ultimate winner of the Belt, is my son.'

Each year's Open-winner earned a year's reign as the 'Champion Golfer of Scotland'. By carrying the Belt off for all time Tommy made that title forever his as well, at least in the popular mind. According to one of the first published histories of the game, 'a new star rose in the golfing firmament, one before which all others had to pale their ineffectual fires. This was Young Tom Morris, who soon proved himself quite a royal and ancient Samson by metaphorically standing head and shoulders above his compeers of the green.'

Any towering on Tommy's part was indeed metaphoric, since he stood five foot eight, a jot more than his father but well short of Fergusson and Dunn, the gangly Musselburgh men. Still, he overshadowed them and every other golfer, and his popularity changed professional sport for good. Before Tommy won the Belt, the only respectable sportsmen were country gentlemen whose wealth bankrolled their amusements. The word *sport* reeked of decadence; as a verb it still suggested sex. For a tradesman's son to make a career as a sportsman and hold his head high was unthinkable, and yet here he was, the academy-trained son of a greenkeeper, drawing a crowd to the links. His brother Jimmy, now fifteen, was only one of the boys who trailed Tommy the way gulls chase after a fishing boat. Andra Kirkaldy was another. Ten years old in 1870, Kirkaldy recalled his boyhood hero in his 1921 book *Fifty Years of Golf*. Tommy Morris, he wrote, had 'the gift of golf . . . We were all his worshippers.'

Part of Tommy's appeal was the way he exuded pleasure in motion. The Scots word is *kithe*, meaning to express or to reveal. The exhilaration of the boy who raced up and down dunes was kithed in the young man as what golfer J.R. Gairdner called Tommy's 'easy confidence and perfect optimism'. It took optimism to swing hard at a solid rubber ball with a nineteenth-century driver, a thick-handled hickory switch with a concave head that measured less than an inch from top to bottom. Still the champion golfer made perfect contact more often than not. You could tell from the billiard-ball *clack* at impact, ever so slightly louder when he swung all out. Everard noted how easily Tommy added 'just another half-ounce of pith where something extra was required . . . the enemy were never safe with him'.

Twenty years earlier, he would have been a minor, local figure. It was Tommy's good fortune to arrive as the machine age began churning out one of its most important products, leisure time, without which there would have been no golf boom. Workdays were getting shorter in the 1860s, for many in the middle and working classes the Sabbath rest day was now preceded by a free afternoon called the Saturday half-holiday. That unpaid afternoon off was a first step towards the work-free weekend of the late nineteenth and early twentieth centuries. It gave people time to make railway trips to the seaside, particularly when the occasional Monday off for a local or national holiday followed the Sabbath. Traditionally, however, seaside towns had little to offer but muddy beaches and shallows that smelled faintly of sewage.

Circuses and fairs might come around once a year. Ladies and gentlemen spent their resort holidays promenading, showing off their holiday finery, the men tipping their black silk top hats, the women averting their eyes from passers-by because a lady did not acknowledge anyone to whom she had not been introduced. Children ran to the beach to build sand castles and climb aboard what passed for thrill rides – donkeys that trudged up and down the sands. Another prime recreation was bathing, which meant wading. Seawater was thought to promote circulation and aid digestion, so bathers made a point of swallowing a few mouthfuls. One joke told of a bumpkin who treated his wife and daughters to a fortnight in St Andrews. He left his wife and daughters at high tide, went home to work the farm and returned when the tide was out, the beach dry for a quarter of a mile. 'Good Lord,' he cried, 'they must ha' drunken well!'

Professional golf provided drama that donkey rides and wading couldn't match. Men bet on it; boys hailed their towns' heroes and dreamed of being like them, and even women were intrigued by the deeds of a young hero who swung so hard that his hat flew off. Golf became a spectator sport in the 1870s as hundreds and then thousands of spectators came out to follow professional matches and tournaments. Like the football and rugby lovers of the time, they were called 'fanatics', a term that was later shortened to 'fans'.

Now that Tommy owned the Belt, professionals had little to play for but money. There was seldom much of it. He was the only golfer in the Open who didn't need to caddie during Prestwick's autumn meeting to cover his expenses. But the money was improving: research by Peter Lewis of the British Golf Museum turned up two dozen professional tournaments in the 1860s with an average purse of £12.92. There would be twice as many in the 1870s, when the typical purse nearly doubled to £23.87 with an average first prize of about ten pounds. Fatter purses were one of the first signs of the late-century phenomenon Bernard Darwin would call 'the golf boom'. This first boomlet did not make anyone rich, but it did vastly improve the lot of one member of the Young Men's Improvement Society of St Andrews: by winning more often than anyone else, Tommy put more than £200 into his bank account before he turned twenty. Two hundred pounds was a bonny penny, equal to about £15,000 today and by some measures his savings were still more impressive.

Houses and horses, for example, were far cheaper then. With £200 he could have bought a respectable house and put a horse in every room. Of the 1.4 million workers in Scotland in 1870, fewer than half of one percent had incomes of £1,000 per year. Tommy was not yet at that level, but then he was only nineteen.

He made much of his money in foursomes matches. When an R&A member and a professional played against another member-professional duo, the club men bet with each other and gave the cracks a fee. Occasionally Tommy partnered a member against two professionals – a tall order in foursomes, in which his amateur partner hit half their side's shots. All these professional-amateur games were for the amusement of the gentleman golfers, who would give their professional partners what amounted to a gratuity at the end of the match. A gentleman who had won might give his professional ten or twenty percent of the bet; one who had lost might give his professional less, or give him nothing at all if he thought the cur had cost him the match.

The most sought-after player dared to change the ground rules. To the surprise of R&A members, and to the consternation of his father, Tommy demanded payment upfront: a fair fee for his time. And, being Tommy, he got it.

His spirit was infectious. Even nervous jabbers like Maitland-Dougall made braver strokes when they teamed with the champion golfer. It was hard to fuss and fidget when he was rolling putts and then pointing at the ball, ordering it to 'Duck in!' Even his father made more short putts when he played with Tommy. 'Rap it, Da,' Tulloch heard Tommy say. 'The hole's not coming to you.'

While the champion's iron play was 'uniformly magnificent', in Darwin's words, 'by all accounts it was his putting that, as it were, put the coping stone on the rest of his game, and gave him that inside turn against all his rivals and particularly his nearest competitor, Davie Strath.' As a foursomes team Tommy and Strath were practically unbeatable, with Davie's elegant game complementing his Rose Club friend's bold strokes. But though he and Strath were friends, more often than not Tommy would turn to his father when he chose a foursomes partner. Newspaper accounts of money matches in the early 1870s are peppered with references to the team of 'Tom Jr' or 'Young Tom' and the golfer now known as 'Old Tom'. But filial loyalty had its costs. It cost Tommy money and injured his father's self-respect, for this loyalty was a form of charity. As Hutchison wrote, Tom hurt his son's chances: '[A] spell of the most utter bad play, lasting four or five years, took possession of him: and this was the more provoking, inasmuch as it occurred when his son Tommy was at the very zenith of his powers, and father and son were in the habit of playing other professionals.' To use Hutchison's five damning words, Tom was 'a drag upon his son'.

Tommy was willing to be dragged. He carried his father in dozens of foursomes matches, knowing that the money match – the thrill of the hunt on the links – was in his father's blood. Like many sportsmen before and since, Tom felt most alive when a wager hung in the balance. Tommy, who played more for self-kithing, was shrewd enough to see that his father's decades of winning bets, paying bills and wrestling with whins had given him, Tommy, the chance to play for love and money. This was the luxury of being a striver's son. 'During these years of phenomenal success he lived with his father at St Andrews, and many a great match they played,' wrote fulsome Tulloch. 'Often, too, they would be out on the links at the same time, playing in different matches with some of the members of the Royal & Ancient Club and their visitors, who were proud to enjoy alike their play, their talk and their friendship. And, at night, father and son would talk over their matches ... The father was proud of his son, and the son was full of affection and reverence for the father, though he could chaff him when he missed one of the short putts that would have been easy of negotiation to the lad.'

Tom needed no help in his roles as greenkeeper, shopkeeper, husband and father. His greens were as smooth as suede after he spent £8 for the game's first lawn-mowing machine in 1872. In the shop, where the smoke from his pipe mixed with steam and sawdust, Tom oversaw Jimmy, who was always dying to run out to follow his big brother Tommy, and Jack, whose sandbag legs grew fat, but whose eleven-year-old arms and hands were so strong that he won Indian-wrestling bouts with Tom's assistant James Foulis. The four of them and a crew of hired men made gutties and clubs, using shafts and clubheads that came from club-maker Robert Forgan's shop next door. Forgan was the white-bearded nephew of Hugh Philp, the woodworking Stradivarius who made niblicks, spoons, drivers, putters, lockers and even a wheelbarrow for his R&A patrons. In 2005 a Philp putter would sell at auction in Edinburgh for £70,000. Before his death in 1856, Philp passed his secrets down to Forgan, who was a better club-maker than his neighbour Tom Morris, but less famous, which led to an uneasy alliance: Tom paid Forgan for half-finished clubs, which Tom's workers assembled, polished and stamped TOM MORRIS, the one name that was known wherever golf was played. One day an order came from Bombay, where British colonists had founded a golfing society: 'Send 180 sets of golf clubs.' Tom hired extra men who worked in shifts around the clock until 1,440 clubs were finished, stamped and packed into 180 boxes that went by horse-drawn cart, train and clipper ship to India.

Forgan was said to envy Tom Morris' fame, and Tom may have felt a little guilty about their arrangement. The only side of his house without a window was the one facing Forgan's shop.

On the links, Tom contended with weeds, heather, divots, grass-killing salt spray and drunken caddies. Most of all he fought whins. The thorny shrubs were pretty in spring when they were garbed in clusters of yellow flowers, but in the summer they grew hairy black seed pods. One shrub could produce some 10,000 seeds in a year; seeds that could lie dormant for forty years before springing to life. In his seventh and eighth years as keeper of the St Andrews links Tom was still coming home with scrapes on his arms and whin thorns in his jacket and beard. Eighteen-year-old Lizzie plucked out the thorns for her father. Nancy, fifty-five years old, was often ill. Her heart raced, her stomach ached and she suffered from a stiffness the doctor called 'congestion of the spine'. She lay in bed with the curtains drawn to protect her from miasmas, the palls of bad air that were thought to carry illness. At night, Tom would sit by her bed reading the Bible aloud until she fell asleep.

Tom was devout, dutiful and successful. But a nagging disquiet was growing in him. The former King of Clubs wasn't ready to settle for keeping the green, paying bills and playing the occasional twenty-pound foursomes match. All he needed, he thought, was a big-money match to prove there was still some life in Old Tom. He got his wish when Willie Park offered him a sucker bet.

Twenty-one miles as the rook flies, the distance from
St Andrews to Musselburgh was far greater by rail and
ferry. There was no straight way over the sheep-dotted
fields of Fife and the wide Firth of Forth. The trip
could take half a day. Musselburgh was a weathered
Roman-built port five miles east of Edinburgh, where
the links shared space with a horse-racing track and
a dirt path that coal miners took on their way to
the pits. The Musselburgh links were also home to the
Honourable Company of Edinburgh Golfers, a fact
that made for some clashes of manners. Once, when
an Honourable Company player in his golfing jacket
and leather breeches drove a ball that conked a
passing miner, the victim charged the golfer, waving
his fist.

'But my dear fellow,' the gentleman explained, 'I
shouted "Fore".'

'Then *five*,' said the miner, dropping him with one
punch.

Musselburgh had been a hub of golf for a century, but the Morrises had lately moved the focus
northward. This insult lodged in Willie Park's craw.
Park was often described as 'his own man', being too
cussedly independent to serve as anyone's greenkeeper
or lesson-teacher. Like every other Musselburgh
loyalist he believed that he, Willie, was a better golfer
than Tom Morris, and he was right. Park was longer
off the tee than Tom, stronger if less accurate with his
cleeks, and a far better putter. Over the years he had

beaten Tom more often than Tom had beaten him. Still, St Andrews had cast a pall over Musselburgh ever since Tom swore off tobacco and topped Willie in their marathon of 1862, almost a decade ago. Now Musselburgh's golf-fanatics were riveted by talk of a rematch between the warhorses – single combat over four greens for £100. The stakes, as usual, were put up by gentlemen, with the winning player expecting a cut of ten percent, plus any side bets he won. As the stakes rose to £125 and then £150, Tom's pulse quickened.

There were several gloomy omens for Tom, who had publicly sworn off marathon matches back in '62: the thirty-seven-year-old Park was in his prime while Tom was in his fiftieth year; Park seldom missed a short putt, while Tom had days when he couldn't make one; and plans for the 144-hole match called for the last thirty-six to be at Park's home links at Musselburgh, the lion's den. Still, Tom's yearning for a restorative victory was so strong that not even Tommy's warnings about finishing on 'Willie's dunghill' could sway him. When the stakes reached £200, he said yes.

In London, the editors of *The Field* framed the issue: 'During the past fourteen years the two players who have stood forth most prominently in the golfing world are Tom Morris, the custodian of the links at St Andrews, and Willie Park, the professional at Musselburgh. The great question as to who is the best player has never been definitely settled.' The fact that Tommy Morris was now golf's best player may have dampened interest in the opening rounds between his father and Park, who took a one-up lead during the first day's play before a small gallery at St Andrews. The contest resumed three days later at Prestwick, where Tom's putter regained the flash it had shown in his youth. He made everything under three paces and sent one long sidewinder bounding and curling more than thirty feet until it dropped into the hole. 'Morris, driving in great style and playing both his quarter-strokes and his putts with beautiful precision, drew ahead of Willie,' read the next issue of the *The Field*. 'A very lucky but withal well-played long putt turned the tables.' Winning the day by two holes put Tom a hole ahead at the marathon's halfway point. When his Prestwick cronies said he had seized the advantage, Tom shook his head. Were he in Park's boots, he said, he'd be delighted to be one-down after seventy-two holes on Tom Morris' two home courses, heading east to decide the matter at North Berwick and Musselburgh.

North Berwick was technically neutral, but the briny resort on the Forth's south bank was only half an hour by train from Musselburgh. Three days after Tom's victory at Prestwick, a host of backers applauded his demolition at North Berwick. Park won six of the first nine holes to go five ahead overall. By then he was walking like a hunter stalking a wounded deer, hurrying forward. Tom responded by slowing his pace. He paused to tap a dollop of tobacco into his pipe. He lit it, breathed blue smoke and only then followed Park through the throng to the next teeing-ground. In the following hour, Tom ground out fours and fives, inching his way back into the match, looping pinpoint drives while Park swung ever harder. He whittled Willie's lead down to sawdust and then, while spectators whistled and hissed at him, took the last hole to regain the lead. One hundred and eight holes in the books and thirty-six to play, he was one hole ahead. The train took him towards the setting sun, towards Musselburgh.

Spectators arrived in force on Saturday, the last day. After some early rain, the sky cleared enough to let silver-white bolts of sun fall through the clouds. Spectators paced, gossiped, laughed. Some sipped from pocket flasks. Some were there not only to cheer Park and hoot at Morris but to bat Tom's ball out of the air if they got a chance. Interference by spectators was a growing problem, most of all at Musselburgh. Andra Kirkaldy, a St Andrean who would wage his own wars with Musselburgh's rowdy crowds, called them 'unruly bullocks' and 'damned miners'. Every important match had a referee who could declare one golfer the winner if spectators misbehaved, but the referee who ruled against a hometown player might trigger a riot. So players often dealt with interference as a rub of the green, a twist of fortune that was part of the game. A rub of the green could be good fortune – a crow snaps up your ball and drops it into the hole

– or bad. At Musselburgh, golfers from St Andrews could count on getting rubbed the wrong way.

The nine-hole Musselburgh course erupted in hoots and cheers when the golfers appeared. Willie Park was joined by his brother David and Bob Fergusson, while Charlie Hunter and Bob Kirk stood on Tom's side. Hunter, one of Tom's Prestwick cronies, had been greenkeeper there since Andrew Strath's death. Kirk, the son of Tom's long-time caddie and one of the game's leading players, would act as Tom's caddie today. A peppery fellow with a short fuse, Kirk watched with mounting annoyance as the spectators pressed in around Tom. They pushed so close that Tom's first backswing nearly ruffled one Park-backer's beard. Tom stopped his swing and stepped away from his ball. Referee Robert Chambers, an Edinburgh publisher and an R&A man, waved the crowd back. Tom took a breath, then hit a low fade into the widest part of the first fairway. The next sound was applause, but it wasn't for him. It was for Park, stepping up to take a practice swing.

'The weather was showery,' *The Field*'s report began, 'and a high wind interfered with play. Eight thousand spectators were present, and crowded in on the players, there being great excitement over the game.' Over twenty-seven holes neither player gave an inch. With nine holes to play, Tom still led by one.

By then the town's artisans had finished work – Saturday was a half day. They dashed to the course. Many had already placed bets on the match; others made last-minute wagers as the final nine began. The crowd was feverish – men and boys charging onto greens before approach shots landed. Park stood whispering with the tall, quiet Fergusson, while men in the crowd shouted, 'We're with you, Willie' and 'Musselburgh forever!' One writer called the multitude 'disgraceful ... the players were pressed in upon in a very rude manner and were scarcely allowed room to use their clubs freely.' Kirk, Tom's caddie, irked the crowd by shouting, 'Keep back, keep back!' Park could have calmed his followers but left that task to the referee, who called in vain for order, while spectators pressed so close that they could have picked the tobacco out of Tom's jacket pocket. On the second hole a man kicked Tom's ball sideways. Tom played it as it lay and lost the hole. Soon another spectator kicked Tom's ball into high grass. Then, 138 holes into the 144-hole contest, the golf devolved into farce. Tom missed a short putt. Spectators laughed and cheered. Referee Chambers, raising his hands, appealed to the crowd's sense of fair play. He looked to Park for help, but Willie was on his way to next tee with a one-up lead.

Tom stood watching Park's boosters crowding the green. Some waved to him. Some swung their feet to show what they'd like to do to his next shot. 'The crowd, anxious for their favourite, the local man, to win, transgressed all rules of fair play,' Hutchison wrote, 'and repeatedly injured the position of Tom Morris' ball to such an extent that the latter declined to continue.'

Tom had longed for a victory over his old enemy, but this was chaos, not golf. He walked past his ball and kept going, past the bellowing spectators, past the putting-green and through the door of the nearest pub, Mrs Forman's Public House, where he found a chair and sat puffing his pipe while referee Chambers faced down the jeering crowd. 'The match is postponed,' Chambers declared. 'We will finish tomorrow.' He was threatened, spat at.

Willie Park said no, the match was still on. According to *The Field*, Park maintained 'that the referee had only to do with disputes as to holes, and could not postpone the play'.

So Park went on. With his brother and a pained-looking Fergusson walking behind him, he played the last six holes alone and claimed victory. The stake-holder, a gentleman named Dudgeon whose role was to hang onto the backers' money until there was an official winner, was nowhere to be found. He was holding at least £200; some reports suggest that late betting by the gentlemen sponsoring the match boosted the stakes to £500. Given the customary ten-percent share for the winning golfer, Tom or Willie stood to have a career day.

At eleven the next morning, Tom and Chambers returned to the fourth hole. Park was there, too – without his clubs. Chambers invited him to play, but Willie refused. 'I finished yesterday,' he said. He watched while Tom played alone, taking twenty-six strokes over the last six holes, four more than Park had taken on the same holes the day before. After Tom putted out on the final green, referee Chambers declared him the victor. The crowd hissed and booed. Backers of both players claimed victory. There were lawyers among the backers on both sides, and stakes-holder Dudgeon was soon served a court order instructing him to keep the money safe pending legal action. Finally, six months later, the courts declared neither Tom nor Willie the winner. The riotous Musselburgh match was nullified. The backers got their money back and neither player got a penny. By then, poor Dudgeon had suffered a nervous breakdown.

After eight rounds of golf and more than a thousand swings the only winner was Mrs Forman, whose pub became famous as the spot where Old Tom Morris nursed a blackstrap while crowds outside sang for his hide.

The game was in constant flux, inventing itself on the fly. In 1871, the Edinburgh University professor Peter Tait had a brainstorm: night golf! Rather than illuminate the course with lanterns, Tait proposed to paint golf balls with glowing phosphorus. He headed for St Andrews along with two colleagues: Thomas Huxley, the biologist, whose grandsons included Aldous Huxley, the writer, and Nobel Prize-winning physiologist Andrew Huxley; and the great German physicist Hermann von Helmholtz. Joined by Tait's brother-in-law, the chemist Alexander Crum Brown, the scientists teed off in the dark and watched their drives rise and fall like shooting stars. They cleared Swilcan Burn with glowing approach shots. 'The idea is a success; the balls glisten in the grass,' wrote Sir John Low of the R&A, who got off his pony long enough to record the event. 'All goes well until the burn is passed, and Professor Crum Brown's hand is found to be aflame; with difficulty his burning hand is unbuttoned, and the saddened group return to the professor's rooms, where Huxley dresses the wounds.'

Golf grew despite being limited to daylight hours. Within days of Tommy's victory in the 1870 Open, the *Fifeshire Journal* was looking towards the future: 'As Young Tom carries off the Belt to St Andrews and retains it, a new champion trophy will require to be furnished . . . We understand that it is the intention of the Prestwick Golf Club to order another Belt, but we have not learnt what the design will be, or the probable cost.'

Time was short. If the next Open was to coincide with the autumn meeting of the Prestwick Golf Club, like previous Opens, it had to be organized by the spring of 1871. There was talk of allowing the R&A and the Honourable Company of Edinburgh Golfers to share the tournament with Prestwick, with the three clubs splitting expenses and the Open rotating among their home links. Perhaps North Berwick and the English club Westward Ho! would join in as well. Gilbert Mitchell Innes, a prominent Prestwick member, said his club would be foolish to pay for a new Belt or other trophy before such matters were resolved. He proposed a motion at Prestwick's spring meeting in April 1871: 'In contemplation of St Andrews, Musselburgh and other clubs joining in the purchase of a belt to be played for over four or more greens, it is not expedient for the club to provide a belt to be played for solely at Prestwick.' Why drain Prestwick's coffers when other clubs might split the cost?

Harry Hart could not believe what he was hearing. The diminutive secretary of the Prestwick Club said it would be foolish to give up control of the Open to save fifteen or twenty pounds. Feisty as a terrier and not much taller, Hart countered Innes with a motion calling for the club to go forward alone. But he was wasting his time. For many Prestwick members the Open was a trifle, far less urgent than their own medal competitions. Stuck in a smoky room after the long winter of 1870–71 had finally thawed into April, they were dying to get out on the links. Their vote was quick and decisive: Innes' motion passed. For the price of a horse, Prestwick gave up control of the Open.

Where would Tommy Morris defend his title? One day the likely site was Prestwick, another day St Andrews or North Berwick. After their spring meeting, the Prestwick members scattered to their homes and estates. They could only vote on Open matters at their spring and autumn meetings or by returning for what was called an extraordinary general meeting; the fate of the Open was not deemed critical enough to warrant one. Spring and summer passed; the hourglass ran out. The Open Championship of 1871 was cancelled.

Every ten years the Scottish government undertook a census. In the census of 1871, Thomas Morris Jr of St Andrews, asked to provide his occupation, answered that he was a golf-ball maker. Later, a clerk in the local census office crossed out those words and wrote 'Champion Golfer of Scotland'. Open or no Open, everyone knew who Tommy was.

'This youthful hero having thus effectually swept the board, matters came rather to a deadlock,' wrote Everard, 'and for a year there was an interregnum.' While the officers of the Prestwick Club, the R&A and the Honourable Company debated the Open's future, the champion entered one of the busiest stretches of his career. Downing all-comers in money matches, he found himself earning more in a good month than his father earned in a year and when strokes and odds were no longer enough to lure challengers, he dreamed up other stunts. In one match he played his own ball against the best ball of Davie Strath and Jamie Anderson, two of the best professionals in Scotland, and beat them. Later he spent a solid week playing high-stakes golf alone. He did it by backing himself – betting that he could play the St Andrews links in 83 or better. That gaudy number enticed many R&A members. Their own Sir Robert Hay had recently won the club's Royal Medal with a 94. All week the stake-holder's pockets were packed with coins and banknotes the members had bet against Tommy, and each day Tommy took the money home. Playing in sunshine, wind and rain, he won for six days in a row. After a rest day on Sunday he felt a surge of Christian charity, or so he said, and offered the bettors a chance to recoup. They were reluctant to try him again. He convinced them by dropping the number to 81, a mere four shots above his course record. That spurred a flurry of wagering. He shot 80, capping what some called the first perfect week since Genesis.

He must have felt invincible. Otherwise he would not have agreed to play against a man armed with a bow and arrow.

The R&A golfer James Wolfe Murray was also a member of the elite Royal Company of Archers, the queen's ceremonial bodyguards in Scotland. He and

Tommy squared off in a ballyhooed match in which the young champion hit golf balls while Wolfe Murray played true target golf, shooting arrows around the links. Dogs and boys scampered ahead of the players, the boys taking care to stay out of bowman's range. Golfers could only dream of hitting balls that tunnelled through the wind like Wolfe Murray's arrows which soared on long, 300-yard arcs. From closer range he could make an arrow come almost straight down, a literal bolt from the blue. He had nothing to fear from bunkers, though he looked comical standing chest-deep in a pot bunker, pulling back his bowstring and letting fly. Tommy's sole advantage was on the greens, where his opponent found it hard to shoot an arrow into the hole from more than two or three yards. His efforts left arrowhead-divots around the hole on every green and when he finally sank a 'putt' it often caved in the hole on one side. Tom Morris, walking along with the spectators, puffed his pipe and shook his head. Was this what the old game had come to – a circus act? In the half-century of Tom's life, golf had grown from local pastime to national sport. In the past five years it had grown so swiftly that otherwise sane men were willing to bet on a match between a golfer and an archer. God only knew where the game was going next, but Tom knew one thing: it would be his job to repair the caved-in holes.

Tommy won most of the short holes, but as the match wore on and they turned to play against the wind, the bow's power proved too much for him. Wolfe Murray pulled ahead on the inward nine and, for once, Tommy was out-shot.

# EIGHT

## *The Better Ball*

JOHN BLACKWOOD STOOD on the teeing-ground at eight a.m., the hangman's hour, dressed in his red jacket and white leather breeches. The new captain of the Royal & Ancient Golf Club was up early for his ceremonial Driving-In on the last day of the club's autumn meeting. Surrounded on this cold October morning by a red-coated brigade of fellow members, he waited while Tom Morris teed him up. Tom, still red-cheeked from his morning dip in the sea, dropped to one knee, made a thumb-sized sand tee and placed a ball on top. Blackwood waggled. A few yards away another R&A officer stood beside a little Prussian cannon, watching Blackwood's every move, for timing is everything in cannonry, as in golf.

Blackwood swung – a booming drive, thanks to the cannon's boom at the moment of impact. He was now the 'winner' of the R&A's oldest prize, the Silver Club, which had once been competed for in the R&A's first century, but which now went automatically to the newly elected captain, who claimed it with this one symbolic swing. In later years the Driving-In ceremony would inspire another tradition: the caddie who retrieved the captain's ball got a gold sovereign that was worth a fortnight's pay. When a duffer-Prince Albert, the future King George VI, drove in one year, the caddies were accused of standing 'disloyally close to the tee'.

Later on Medal Day the new captain led R&A golfers to the links, where Tom Morris waited. Tom doffed his cap to each one, then gave a little speech. They were about to play for the Royal Medal, he said, donated by His Late Majesty King William IV. The club's Gold Medal would go to the man with the second-best score. The format was stroke play: he who finishes eighteen holes in the fewest strokes wins. They would play by St Andrews rules, of course.

Tom started each twosome on its way, saying, 'You may go now, gentlemen.' Later he stood by the Home green to greet the players as they came in. After the last group holed out he pulled the flag from the Home green and waved it over his head, signalling the cannoner. Another cannon blast signalled the end of Medal Day.

At a lavish dinner that evening, the captain presented the medals to the winners. The highlight of the week, however, was the following night's Royal & Ancient Ball, sometimes called the Golf Ball. Starting at ten p.m., carriages delivered many of Fife's leading citizens to St Andrews town hall, a turreted Scottish-baronial castle that glowed from within, its keyhole windows lit up like jack-o'-lantern eyes. Few commoners passed the attendants at the doors; no one would have dreamed of inviting the greenkeeper. Worthies from Edinburgh and London handed their canes and black hats to the attendants while their wives and daughters rustled past in long dresses of silk and satin. Under the dresses, corsets ribbed with whalebone pinched the women's waists as near as possible to the ideal of twenty inches around. These pinched women smiled behind fans made of ostrich feathers.

Moving from the doors to the town hall's cavernous ballroom, revellers passed relics of St Andrews' long history: a wooden panel showing the town's coat of arms and the date, 1115; a rusted set of handcuffs; a headsman's axe that cost the town treasurer six shillings 'for shairpine the aix' before a 1622 beheading. In the ballroom, guests danced in groups of four couples, the couples changing partners as they moved in measured paces from the corners to the centre of a six-pace square. Quadrille dancing was the latest fad from France. A forerunner of square dancing performed to the music of a small string ensemble plus a trumpet or French horn, the quadrille mixed and matched couples as they traded partners, stirring the social stew.

The Ball lasted long into the wee hours. The *Citizen*

always carried a long account of it, listing dozens of dignitaries who attended. For weeks no one in town spoke of anything else, or so it seemed to Tommy. The twenty-year-old champion golfer could not help noticing that the Royal & Ancient, which had dickered over ten or fifteen pounds when the issue was sponsoring the Open, threw banknotes at a caterer and a confectioner and bought a quadrille band from Edinburgh when the R&A Ball came around.

November frosts hardened the links. In December the sun set at four in the afternoon. Tommy played an occasional match to keep his muscles loose, but as the year without an Open wound down, there were no matches or tournaments to kindle his interest.

Perhaps there was another way to remind the gentlemen he was still alive.

'On Friday night the town hall was the scene of a gay and brilliant assemblage on the occasion of the first ball given by the St Andrews Rose Golf Club,' the *Citizen* reported on 6 January 1872, three months after the latest R&A Ball. 'Over the civic chair in the centre of the platform hung a large sized group [photograph] of the members of the club, on the right of which was the medal of the club, and on the left the beautiful champion golfer's belt, won by Young Tom Morris three years in succession, which entitled him to retain it ... At the front of the hall was a large cross, with a garland of evergreens and the words "Rose Golf Club". The orchestra, which was occupied by an efficient quadrille band, was hung with scarlet cloth and ornamented with garlands of evergreens ... the whole being overhung with a beautiful new flag of the club. Refreshments were served in the council chamber, and purveyed by Mr G. Leslie of the Golf Inn, and Mrs Thomson, confectioner. The ball was opened at about half-past nine by the captain of the club, Mr James Conacher, and dancing was kept up with the greatest spirit until about half-past four in the morning.'

Tommy and the enterprising Conacher had chipped in to rent and decorate the same ballroom where the mighty Royal & Ancient cavorted every autumn. Now it was dark winter, but the place was even brighter than on the night the wheezing ancients had gathered here to try to dance. The Rose Club Ball was a livelier affair for a younger crowd; its quadrille dancers moving on nimbler limbs, changing partners in kaleidoscope patterns while the buckle of the Championship Belt reflected light from half a dozen chandeliers.

Someone tapped Tommy's shoulder and put a glass of champagne in his hand. He took a gulp, thinking perhaps of Dom Perignon, the French monk who added yeast to wine in 1668 and exclaimed, '*Je bois des etoiles*' ('I am drinking the stars'). Holding his glass in a white-gloved hand, Tommy felt stars percolate down his gullet. A moderate drinker, he was willing to temper his moderation tonight. Looking around the ballroom he saw his brother Jimmy trying hard to look older than his years, telling anyone who would listen that he'd be sixteen next week; and Jamie Anderson, whose precision game Tommy admired; and Davie Strath, less funereal than usual, lifting a glass.

According to the *Citizen*, 'The company present numbered over a hundred.' Heads turned as Tommy slipped between celebrants in cigar-scented air, shaking hands and patting friends' backs under an oversized flag festooned with the club's petalled emblem. He wore his finest suit and a pinstriped waistcoat. Dozens of lasses and ladies must have wished they could dance with him, and many would get their wish. 'The thing about quadrille dancing,' one St Andrean said, 'is that you may start with your auntie, but soon you find yourself with the girl you spotted across the room. Imagine gazing at her as everyone changes partners until finally your hand is on her hand and your other hand is on her waist.'

The following week, newspapers including the *Scotsman* informed the nation that the first Rose Club Ball in old St Andrews had been a sensation, surpassing even the annual ball of the Royal & Ancient.

Only Tom Morris realized what bad news that was. Tom knew that the town's gentleman golfers would not appreciate being upstaged by a pack of foolhardy young men.

With a population of only 6,000, dwarfed by Edinburgh's 200,000 and Glasgow's half a million, St Andrews was a small town with the surface calm and subterranean strife of other small towns. The busybody pastor A.K.H. Boyd liked to quote a visitor who said, 'Hell was a quiet and friendly place to live in, compared with St Andrews.' Early in 1872 the town hummed with talk of the Rose Club while Tom's employers sat in their clubhouse, muttering over the newspapers. As Tommy would have expected had he had a politic bone in his body, he and his friends had angered the men who ran the town – the R&A men who put up the money golf professionals played for and controlled the businesses Tommy's friends hoped to enter. An apology from the champion golfer might have helped, but he was not sorry. It was left to Tom to spend weeks assuring his employers that the lads meant no offence. In the end, the success of the first Rose Club Ball had assured there would never be a second one.

In March 1872, a dozen golf professionals met for a stroke-play event in Musselburgh, the scene of Tom's riotous match with Willie Park. Tommy coasted home six shots clear of Jamie Anderson and seven ahead of local heroes Park and Bob Fergusson. As the *Citizen* saw the Musselburgh tourney, 'none had hitherto succeeded in anything like the steady play for three rounds now added to Young Tom's credit.' The win added twelve pounds to Tommy's bankroll; his father finished eighth ... and won nothing. A day later, Tommy teamed up with Davie Strath in a foursomes match against Park and Fergusson. The Rose Club duo took the first of three rounds by the thinnest margin, one-up. Tommy and Strath also won the second round by one hole, spurring Park to swing so hard in the last go-round that he *huffed* with the effort, which Tommy found funny. Willie may as well have ducked into Mrs Forman's Public House; the boys from St Andrews closed out the contest on the seventh green. After that Tommy accepted one more challenge: facing Fergusson in singles. One hole down at the midpoint and out-driven on almost every hole, he rallied to beat the quiet man and went home from Park's dunghill unstained – three wins in three tries in two days.

In April, the Royal Liverpool Golf Club spent an eye-popping £103 to give Scotland a run for its money. The golfers of Royal Liverpool were merchants who had made fortunes turning their rusty port city into England's 'maritime metropolis'. Now they wanted to put their club on the map by hosting the grandest professional event ever seen. Their course in Hoylake was no gem, but a record-setting purse would attract what newspapers called 'Scotland's golfing celebrities'. Even then the way to a golfer's heart was through his pocket.

The event's purse of fifty-five pounds would more than quadruple the Open purse of twelve pounds, with forty-eight pounds more paying for railway tickets and lavish dinners for the golfers – astounding luxury to professionals of Tom's generation, who had never been treated as a club's guests. Willie Park, Davie Strath, the Rook and other players took fast trains south to Liverpool, where horse-drawn coaches took them across the River Mersey to the links. Spectators watched for the coach carrying the golfer one writer called *primus inter pares* – first among equals.

Stepping down from his carriage at the Royal Hotel, a stone box with the Irish Sea at its back, Tommy saw the course – a patchy waste nibbled by rabbits, with a horse-racing track running through it. He had won an informal tournament there a year before. Now he joined the other players for a long, loud dinner hosted by barkeeper John Ball, whose son would win the 1890 Open. Ball kept the drinks flowing while the golfers sang and toasted bonny Scotland.

Sixteen golfers gathered in front of the hotel on Tuesday morning, 25 April 1872. According to a newspaper story, the Grand Professional Tournament would be 'a rare treat' for those 'who have never had an opportunity of seeing the "far and sure" strokes of the leading professionals'. It would be the first major professional tournament held in England. Tommy teed off first, his drive sailing over a corner of the racetrack.

He set off after it, trailed by more than a hundred spectators, in spitting rain.

The first hole was 440 yards of sandy turf and marshes pocked with reeds. The wooden rails of the racetrack were in play. So was the track itself: you might find your ball in a hoof print. Tommy struck a low second shot to safe ground, knocked an iron to the green and rapped in the putt for a four. He had an edge already – nobody would beat four on that hole that day.

The second hole ran along a hedge. The racetrack's railing cut the fairway in half. Tommy's drive was 'successful', *The Field* reported, but his next shot 'went into a ditch which caused a bad stroke'. His recovery veered out-of-bounds and he made eight on the hole – the first sign that the champion might struggle today. One newspaper quoted him in dialect as saying it was 'no' my day oot for stealing long put[t]s'.

Tom and Willie Park also stumbled. In a turn of fate *The Field* called 'rather unfortunate', Kirk hit three balls out-of-bounds and made a seventeen on the first hole. His 97 in the first of two rounds left him fifteen strokes behind Davie Strath, whose 82 gave nervous Davie a three-shot edge on Tommy and the Rook.

By now the rain was pelting the links. The golfers waited out the downpour inside the hotel. Perhaps Tommy had a small beer with his cousin Jack, Royal Liverpool's resident professional. This walking Jack

Morris, with the same name as Tommy's crippled brother, lived in a converted horse stall in the hotel's stables. His father, George – Tommy's uncle – was still living down his long-ago thrashing at Willie Park's hands ('For the love o' God, man, give us a half!'). In 1869, George Morris went to Hoylake with Robert Chambers, the wealthy amateur who had umpired the riotous, nullified match between Tom and Willie Park. At Hoylake, Chambers and George Morris laid out the Royal Liverpool links. It was not a task modern golfers would recognize as course design: they walked the links, picking out spots that looked like putting greens. When they found one, George cut a hole with his penknife. They left a stick or a seagull feather in the hole to show golfers where to aim.

Now, three years later, the players filed out of the Royal Hotel to finish the tournament in mist and drizzle. Tommy didn't mind the rain; he rubbed up his grip with the lump of pine tar in his jacket pocket.

Strath was tired of losing to Tommy. 'He swung high, and came through well with a sweeping stroke, driving a higher ball with more carry than Tommy's,' one contemporary wrote, 'but his putting was not so dangerous as his rival's. Nor had he so even a disposition. He was excitable, talked quickly, was readily elated or depressed.' Strath nursed his three-shot lead while the course meandered to the beach and turned back towards the hotel. Tommy gained a stroke, then another, until they were all-square.

The last hole was only 218 yards from the tee to a green beside the hotel. Tommy, aggressive as ever, knocked in a final putt and Strath – working the tobacco in his cheek, chewing, spitting – failed to match him. Tommy had come from behind to win by a stroke.

'Tom Morris Jr increased his already very long list of achievements by carrying off the first prize, consisting of a medal and fifteen pounds,' one reporter wrote. 'The members of the club regard this, the first golf tournament held in England, as a complete success.'

The next day brought a foursomes match between England and Scotland, with national pride and five pounds at stake. Two professionals from English clubs challenged Tommy and Musselburgh's Bob Fergusson. The Scots won in a rout, eight-and-seven. Then the champion golfer headed home to St Andrews, his triumph in England complete.

A letter to *The Field* congratulated Royal Liverpool for staging the golf show of the season: 'Here the young champion added another leaf to his laurels; here England's professionals fought and lost against Scotland's, here they stayed together as brother golfers, and parted in the best fellowship, without jealousy or discontent, satisfied with their own performances, the prizes and the links, anxious only again to meet, and in friendly fray swing the hickory wand.'

The money and the medal Tommy won at Hoylake meant less to him than another piece of silver he received that spring. On 20 April 1872, Tommy's twenty-first birthday, his sentimental Da handed him a pocket-watch. The watch had a heavy silver case, a silver fob and a palpable heartbeat. Tick-tock, like his father's swing. From that day Tommy carried the watch in his vest pocket, near his heart.

At a meeting of the Royal & Ancient the following month, 'the secretary read a letter which he had received from the honorary secretary of the Prestwick Club as to the desirability of reviving the "Champion Belt" competition.' This is the first reference to the Open in the minutes of R&A meetings. A committee was directed to explore co-sponsorship of the Open, 'and they were authorized to contribute a sum not exceeding fifteen pounds from the funds of the club.'

That spring two of the club's best gentleman golfers hit upon a clever bet. Robert Clark and Gilbert Mitchell Innes – the same Innes who had pushed Prestwick to share the Open, and who happened to belong to the R&A as well – challenged any professional to beat their best ball. The amateurs won every time. Still they were two-to-one underdogs in spirited betting the day Tommy Morris took their dare. Innes and Clark held a one-up lead through sixteen holes as the golfers and a bevy of bettors and spectators reached the Road Hole. The amateurs' backers were mentally doubling their money until Tommy won the Road Hole, then ran in a putt on the boneyard Home Hole to pick their pockets.

By then Queen Victoria sped from England through Dundee in a royal-blue railway car that ate the rails at fifty miles per hour, heading for Balmoral Castle, west of Aberdeen. She suffered from the heat and travelled with a bucket of ice rattling under her seat; a footman replenished the ice faster than it could melt. The Queen had fled London for Balmoral twice a year ever since her husband, Prince Albert, died of typhoid fever in 1861. She wore widow's weeds for the rest of her life. 'A cold, dark country,' she called Scotland, a place to match her mood. The second-youngest of her nine children was Prince Leopold, England's first royal haemophiliac. After doctors told the prince that golf might aid his fragile health, a short course was laid out on the grounds of Windsor Castle. Nineteen-year-old Leopold looked forward to playing golf on real courses in Scotland, though he would need to watch out for whin thorns.

Tommy rode a slow train coughing eastward from Leuchars. Golfers crowded the links ahead. Dogs romped though dunes, yapping at a sky specked with herring gulls; courting couples strolled the path to the beach; bathers waded in the shallows. This was the busy town Provost Playfair had imagined when he opened the rail link twenty years before. 'A golf-mad town,' one writer called it. Tommy stepped off the train at St Andrews station.

When he looked up he saw the familiar spires and chimney pots of St Andrews. Stopping to drop his luggage at his father's house, he blinked while his eyes adjusted to the dim. Few Scots were wasteful enough to light lamps in the daytime; on sunny days a traveller going inside would be blind for a moment. He found his sister, said hello and went to look in on their mother. Nancy was confined to her bed. Her back and stomach ached. If she asked about Tommy's plans for the summer, frowning when he spoke not about working as a gentleman's clerk but about playing golf, he would cheer her with family talk and ask questions about her day. Tommy was a good listener, solicitous of his mother. When she tired of talking, he would kiss her forehead and leave her to her sewing.

Out again in first-of-summer light, he walked under white clouds stacked up to the sun. Just east of his father's shop was a wood-walled stall where old Kirky, the creaky-jointed father of golfer Bob Kirk, sat boiling chunks of gutta-percha in a stew pan. When the chunks were putty-soft he plucked them out with tongs and rolled them round in his hands that were spotted red from frequent scaldings. A longtime caddie who had lugged Tom Morris' clubs in Tom's Open victories, supplemented his caddie pay by fashioning new gutties from bits of old ones. He rolled his chunks of rubber until they were round, dropped them in cold water and spun them to make sure they cooled evenly. He dried and painted them and sold them as 'Kirky's Remakes'.

Caddies loafed around Kirky's stall, trading stories. One would grouse about the three-hour rounds he endured while carrying for Sir John Low, a notorious 'slow-coach' who played at such a glacial pace, despite his pony, that the caddies called him Sir John Slow. Another caddie might be telling the tale of two dour old-timers who never spoke. After two silent hours they were dead even on the Home Hole, where one sank a putt to win the match. The other said, 'Well in,' the only words either man had uttered. To which the first replied, 'Chatterbox!'

Tourists spilled down the steps of the Golf Inn beyond Kirky's stall. These holiday-makers, travelling in loud groups of three and four bachelors, came from all over to spend a few days a week at golf's Mecca. They scuffed up the links by day and played whist all night, eating and drinking like nabobs, sleeping like stones until noon.

As golf grew, the R&A's stone clubhouse grew with it. Built as a squat rectangle when Tommy was a year old, the grey hulk had always been an eyesore as well as a landmark. As one critic wrote, 'the architect is, happily for himself, unknown.' In 1866, the club replaced the front window with a grand oriel window that gave members a panoramic view of the links. Now the clubhouse was getting a new north wing. Canvas and scaffolding shrouded its seaward side. The building's hindquarters, long plagued by what club records call 'the evils as regards smell', were getting a new block of toilets and a billiards room. Architect David Henry's bill for that work came to £1,430, enough to fund the Open for half a century had the R&A chosen to do so. Instead the club negotiated with the Prestwick Club and the Honourable Company of Edinburgh Golfers in hopes of saving twenty pounds on the Open. Each passing month increased the chance that there would be no Open Championship in 1872.

Tom Morris stood at the first teeing-ground, his hands stuffed into his jacket pockets. He was pairing golfers with caddies, helping the golfers decide who had priority on the tee and telling tourist-golfers where to aim. Had he told them how to spit or scratch themselves, they probably would have obeyed. Tommy had long been amazed at how sheepish most golfers were. From the lowliest mechanic to the proudest nobleman, they all wanted a professional to tell them what to do. Tom Morris' gift was that he could tell any man what to do without giving offence.

After the men teed off and started after their bouncing drives, Tom climbed the steps at the southwest corner of the clubhouse. He walked to the club secretary's window and gave it a tap. He waited, tapped again. After a minute the window went up. The secretary leaned out and spoke into Tom's sun-burnt ear. It was the same every day: the club officer telling the greenkeeper which important gentlemen would be playing in the foursomes to come. Tom would nod and then go back around the clubhouse to the teeing-ground. In eight years as greenkeeper for the Royal & Ancient Golf Club he had often been inside the clubhouse, but had never once sat down there. A greenkeeper in that clubhouse, even a beloved one, would not sit without being invited to sit; an invitation that would never come. While Tom knew his place, he saw the course as his domain and bent it to his will with little interference from the Green Committee.

For centuries the first teeing-ground had been the only one that was not on or near a putting-green. To play the second through eighteenth holes, players teed off within a few club-lengths of the hole on the previous green. The distance had tripled since Tom's youth, from four club-lengths to twelve, as golfers realized that stamping around near the hole was no favour to the putting-green. Now Tom was building a separate teeing-ground for each hole. He was following the lead of Tommy and his Rose Club friends, who deemed the twelve-club-length rule ridiculous and teed off from flat spots nearby. Some R&A men objected: who were these lads to make up their own rules? But Tom saw the wisdom of the new approach. The pace of play quickened and the greens suffered less. By 1876 every hole at St Andrews would have its own teeing-ground. In time every course in the world would make the same change.

Tom's own troubles on the greens were harder to correct. Bernard Darwin might have had Tom in mind when he wrote, 'A man may miss a short putt and yet be a good husband, a good father and an honest Christian gentleman.' Not that such virtues made the misser feel any better. Tom tried putting with his right forefinger wrapped tight around the putter's grip, to no avail. He tried putting with the same forefinger extended down the shaft, and when that didn't help he joked about having that finger amputated. Everard recalled a day Tom tried putting with a cleek, made several long ones and went home delighted, 'happy in possession of the magic secret.' But the magic didn't last. Five years after winning the 1867 Open, Tom was missing most of his four-foot putts.

In July he and Tommy played as a team in what the *Citizen* called 'the first great professional match of the season'. Their opponents were Davie Strath and another young St Andrean, a jut-jawed powerhouse named Tom Kidd. Four years older than Tommy, Kidd wore his side-whiskers so bushy that the wind ruffled them. Unlike his black-coated partner, Kidd was a dandy. On Sundays he dressed 'like a peacock', one St Andrean wrote, 'with tall hat, blue socks, lavender trousers, yellow kid gloves and a cane.' He sported a silk top hat he called his 'Whar-ye-goin'?'

hat, so splendid it made people ask what destination could be worthy of such a hat.

Tommy may have shaken his head at Kidd's plumage, but he admired the way the man whacked drives well past 200 yards. Kidd and the painstaking Strath were such a well-matched foursomes pair that bettors made them even money against Tommy and his faltering father. According to *The Field*, which recounted the event for readers all over the empire, 'Old Tom led off at half-past eleven with a fine tee shot, in the presence of a large company of spectators.' Twenty holes later, with Strath and Kidd two-up Tom left a putt two paces short. With Tommy facing a dodgy putt to save four for their side, Kidd tried a defensive ploy. He left his team's third shot on the edge of the hole, blocking Tommy's putt. In those days a ball on the green could not be marked unless two balls were touching, so Kidd and Strath's ball served as an obstacle. Kidd and Strath were sure to make four on the hole while Kidd's ploy, called a 'stymie' (sometimes spelled *stimy*), blocked the Morrises' shot at four.

There were two ways to foil a stymie. You could go around the other ball or chip over it. You had to take care not to knock the other ball into the hole, for if you did it counted – your foes went from lying three on the lip to writing three on their scorecard. There wasn't room to putt around the other ball, so Tommy tried flipping his gutty into the hole, a shot he had practised countless times in his father's workshop. This time he failed.

The stymie was already controversial – some said it was 'no' golf' and called for a ban – but it would last for almost a century. Bobby Jones would stymie an opponent while winning his Grand Slam in 1930. The tactic was finally banned in 1952, eighty years after Kidd's perfectly legal stymie at St Andrews put his side another hole ahead. Tom botched another putt at the Road Hole and the Morrises lost, three-and-one.

Summer days stretched towards midnight. In July you could read your pocket-watch at half past ten at night while shadows lengthened and the broad expanse of the first and last fairways looked as rippled as water. Tom had a particularly long day on 10 August 1872, when the caddies went on strike. R&A members called it communism, a word popularized by Marx and Engels' *The Communist Manifesto* in 1848. Some also blamed William Gladstone, the liberal prime minister who tolerated trade unions. Organized labour was seen by the gentry as a first step towards revolution. Right here in Fife, coal miners had threatened to strike unless their workweeks were cut to sixty hours. The *Citizen* reported that some of the colliers' wives were offering to replace their men in the mines, 'stating that they neither cared for the union nor their husbands.'

The caddies' strike put Tom in a delicate spot. It was his job to ride herd over the caddies, but some R&A members doubted his loyalty. Tom Morris was a former caddie, after all, and a famously soft touch for any sod with a sob story. And perhaps they were right to doubt him: Tom may have believed that society's ladder was part of God's design, but he knew how poorly treated the caddies were.

He quietly supported them, letting them know they could count on a coin from Old Tom if they needed one. The strike ended when club members agreed to pay all caddies at least a shilling per round, the price of a gutta-percha ball.

There was news from Prestwick. On 11 September 1872, the Prestwick Club agreed to share the Open with the R&A and the Honourable Company of Edinburgh Golfers, with the clubs taking turns hosting the event at Prestwick, St Andrews and Musselburgh respectively, starting with Prestwick that autumn. The purse would be twenty pounds, the most ever, with eight pounds for the winner and four other cash prizes. Perhaps there would be a new Championship Belt as well, but that matter was tabled because time was short; the tournament would take place the day after tomorrow.

The Open Championship was reborn on Friday, 13 September 1872. Only eight players entered. Willie

Park, Bob Fergusson and the Rook opted to stay home rather than chase Tommy Morris around the links he grew up playing.

It rained hard all week, flooding grainfields the *Citizen* described as 'terribly lain and twisted'. The wind rolled off the Firth of Clyde as golfers slogged through puddles to Prestwick's first teeing-ground at the foot of Station Road. The defending champion had the right to tee off first, an honour Tommy had held with growing impatience for two years. He uncorked a drive that drew shouts from the crowd. For much of the day, however, he putted more like his father than himself, missing three- and four-footers on rain-sodden greens. An ugly shot in the second round came to rest no more than three inches from the chin-high stone wall behind the fourth green. This was the Wall Hole where he'd made a seven two years before. The wall, flecked with yellow moss, was no more than a stride from the back of the putting-green. With no room to make a normal swing, he turned his back to the green and tried a cannon shot, hoping to bounce the ball off the wall towards the hole. To his horror the ball sprang straight up and went over the wall into a muddy field full of tall grass and black-faced sheep. The sheep, chewing cud like Davie Strath with a chaw of tobacco, watched Tommy climb the wall and jump down on their side. From there, he faced a pitch over the wall to a green he couldn't see. An error now could cost him any chance to win.

Instead, what *The Field* called 'a well-directed stroke with his niblick' lofted his ball to a soft landing on the green. He had dodged disaster, giving Davie a chance to lose.

After two rounds the markers turned their score-cards over and kept the last round's scores on the card's blank backs. Strath led by five strokes. Bettors rejiggered the odds, making him a five-to-four favour-ite over Tommy, who had not been an underdog in an important event since winning his first Open.

Tommy was out of miracles. Still he kept the ball out of the Sahara Bunker on the Alps Hole and well short of the wall at the fourth. Playing three pairings ahead of Strath, he kept up the pressure on his friend, who lost two shots with what the newspapers called 'an unfortunate iron' at the Alps Hole. With three holes left, his lead pared to a single stroke, Strath's swing and his nerves were fraying. The bulge of tobacco in his cheek bobbed as he chewed and spat, chewed and spat. On the 417-yard final hole, he watched his drive splash in Goosedubs Swamp. His shoulders sagged. After a graceful 52 in the second round, a horrid third-round 61 left Strath three strokes behind Tommy, the winner and still champion golfer.

The first player to win three consecutive Open Championships was now the first to win four. Even today, no other golfer has won four Opens in a row. In addition to the eight-pound first prize, Tommy was handed a gold-plated medal inscribed *Golf Champion*

*Trophy*. There was no trophy, but the gentlemen running the event promised that his name would be engraved on the Open trophy when they got around to buying one.

Leaving Prestwick, Tommy was smiling about one of the tournament's surprises: Tom had made enough putts to tie for fourth, good for two pounds ten shillings.

At the R&A's autumn meeting a fortnight later, Major Boothby announced that per its recent agreement with Prestwick and the Honourable Company, the club would allot ten pounds towards the purchase of a thirty-pound prize for the Open champion. The prize would not be a belt but a proper trophy, engraved with young Morris' name as the first winner, but not subject to his ownership. As *The Field* reported, 'This trophy can never become the absolute property of any winner.' The champion golfer would keep the trophy for a year, then return the trophy to the site of the next Open, and so on for as long as the tournament lasted.

Alexander Kinloch, newly elected captain of the R&A, drove himself in during the same autumn meeting. Sir Robert Hay won the Royal Medal with a 94 that day, while Dr Douglas Argyll Robertson claimed the Gold Medal with a 97. Captain Kinloch, wearing the Queen Adelaide medal that signified his captaincy, presented their medals at the club's annual dinner that evening. Applause followed Hay and

Robertson to the head table where the 118-year-old Silver Club, ensconced with silver golf balls donated by past captains, was draped in blue and white, the colours of the Scottish flag and of the R&A. Since 1839, when the first Silver Club was fully covered by silver-plated balls, there had been two Silver Clubs. Now the R&A members stepped forward one by one to kiss them. Wine slid from bottles into goblets and quickly down gentlemen's throats. Some men preferred gin, brandy or whisky, though whisky was thought to be a commoner's drink.

Most of the gentlemen at the R&A dinner stopped well short of falling down drunk, for the dinner was a warm-up for the next evening's annual R&A Ball. Captain Kinloch had promised the grandest ball in memory, a night to make everyone forget the previous winter's cheeky effort by the Rose Club. He had even hired the man who'd decorated the hall for the Rose Club Ball.

In the town hall ballroom the following night, gaslight flickered over table settings so lavish that guests filed by to spectate. A quadrille band from Edinburgh played under crossed swords, wreaths, banners and floral arrangements of paper and cloth, as Scottish flowers had already lost their petals to October frosts. 'The walls of the large hall were entirely covered from floor to about nine feet high with white calico,' read the *Citizen*. 'The spandles of the roof being supported by Corinthian pilasters, while the spaces between were filled with fluted panels of various coloured cloths, the whole being surmounted with a grand festoon of evergreens and artificial flowers. At the south end of the hall were placed the silver clubs and golf medals of the club on a stand with a background of scarlet, fringed with ivy leaves.'

Captain Kinloch, resplendent in a red golfing jacket with a blue collar and gilt buttons stamped with the cross of St Andrew, liked what he saw. The wealthy Kinloch had paid for it all, the decorations as well as a feast for a crowd of more than 200: sheep's head broth, oatcakes, heaps of salt herring, onions, radishes and peas, grouse, ox feet, lobsters and scallops, winkles, whelks, haddock and skink, flounder roasted alive over a fire, slabs of good Fife beef, sweet flummery, brandy and snuff. Club members toasted the Queen's health and Captain Kinloch's as drinks before supper led to drinks with supper, the meal starting at one in the morning, followed by dancing and drinks.

Around three a.m., R&A members began leaving the town hall, some staggering, for their carriages, homes and hotels. At four, music and voices still drifted from the town hall.

A week after the great R&A Ball, more than forty golfers vied for a fifty-pound purse in Aberdeen. Davie Strath led at the midpoint, but folded in the face of a late charge by Tommy. They were essentially touring professionals now, earning enough to make their expenses and a comfortable living besides. Tommy and Strath were planning a series of singles matches for the following year, duels that would draw golf-fanatics by the thousand. Tommy thought they could get town councils to put up purses for both players, an idea that was sure to scandalize old-timers who believed the only pure match was winner-take-all.

Back home in St Andrews, he was on his way to the links when he passed Alexander Kinloch. According to a story still told in St Andrews, Tommy paid the R&A captain no attention.

'Stop,' the captain said. 'You'll tip your cap to a gentleman.'

Tommy stopped. He examined the captain, a man with mottled skin and grey whiskers, wearing a red golfing jacket and white leather breeches.

'I would if I saw one,' he said.

# NINE

# *Surprises*

LATE IN NOVEMBER 1872 the heavens put on a rare show. First the Merry Dancers appeared and, within an hour, those eerie red and yellow-green lights were pierced by buckshot – clusters of meteors that made white scratches in the northern lights.

Townspeople hurried to watch. They pointed at the sky. They stood on the beach and on the Scores, the seaside road that runs along the bluffs east of the links, families with small children riding on their fathers' shoulders, young couples with maiden aunts in tow as chaperones, schoolboys running and laughing. The Morrises came out, all but Nancy, stuck in her sickbed. Thirteen-year-old Jack was stuck on his wheeled trolley, his head at waist level in the crowd, Tommy and Jimmy making sure no one bumped him or blocked his view of the falling stars, which appeared in clusters, each one making what the *Citizen* called 'a trail of mellow light in the sky'. Tom Morris, looking up, may have recalled other meteor showers in other years when looking up didn't make his neck ache.

Townspeople talked about the Merry Meteors for weeks. Many said they were surely an omen for the coming year of 1873. The trouble was that no one could decide what they portended.

Tom had every reason to regard the new year with suspicion. He would have been aghast at what his son had said to the captain of the Royal & Ancient. *I would if I saw one!* Such an insult would be repeated on the links, in the streets and in the pine corridors of the R&A clubhouse. Such an insult called for an apology, but Tommy would sooner bite through his tongue. If Captain Kinloch ever received an apology, it would have been Tom who made it. As St Andrews' best diplomat, he would have spent months deflecting and de-emphasizing the insult, saying again and again how proud Tommy would be to defend his Open title here at home in the coming autumn of 1873, for the greater glory of St Andrews and the R&A.

Tommy escaped the resentments of his hometown by taking a job fifty miles away. He had turned down offers to be a resident professional at Blackheath, Westward Ho! and North Berwick, but when the officers of a fledgling club in Stirling, a two-hour train ride from St Andrews, offered him such a post a few weeks before Easter, he surprised them by accepting. According to the club's records, 'His terms were thirty a week and travelling expenses. His duties were to teach and play with the members.' Thirty shillings was a relative pittance, less than a fifth of the eight pounds he'd earned in a day at the last Open. He often won twenty pounds in a match, more than three times what Stirling would pay for a month's work. But there were few money matches in early spring, and he'd be free to leave at the end of April. While dreaming of life as a touring professional, he could try being a club professional, teaching lessons to gouty gentlemen, setting their handicaps and selling them clubs and balls. It wouldn't be hard work. It would please his parents. And if the champion golfer tired of his duties he could always look up at the castle.

Stirling's seven-hole course, ringed by wooded hills, looped through sun and shade under the stone walls of Stirling Castle, which rose from a 250-foot shelf of mottled black rock overlooking the course. Tommy remembered his father telling him that Mary Queen of Scots had been crowned up there when she was an infant, too young to sit on her throne. The gentlemen of Stirling Golf Club told him another bit of local lore: in 1507, the Queen of Scots' grandfather, King James IV, employed a royal alchemist, John Damian, at Stirling Castle. The great Damian weaved himself a pair of wings made of chicken feathers, and one day he mounted the castle wall and flew off, straight down the wall to a crash landing in a dunghill.

Tommy may have seen his time at Stirling as a

reiteration of Damian's trajectory. The club members were not bad fellows, but they were dreadful golfers. As their professional he needed endless patience, and his month in Stirling may have increased Tommy's regard for his father, who spent long hours with men whose idea of a golf swing included clenched eyes and dancing feet. When a gentleman golfer swung twice before popping the ball fifty yards, Tom Morris would smile and call the shot 'a clout, well played!' When the Stirling golfers held their first tournament, it took all the tact Tommy could summon to tell a newspaperman that he was pleased with the zigzag spectacle. The subsequent item in *The Field* told of the new club's 'competition for the silver Challenge Cup ... was won by Mr Robert Shand (Stirling) with 99 strokes ... Tom Morris Jr, from St Andrews acted as umpire and expressed himself satisfied with the play.'

On May Day, the traditional start of summer in Scotland, Tommy took an eastbound train from Stirling station, leaving the life of a hireling behind.

In summer, dandelions and half-inch daisies spring up on a links already dotted with golf balls. Fast-moving clouds cast shadows that pass over golfers like premonitions. Tommy was glad to be home, winning matches on the St Andrews links where he would soon defend his four Open titles. His insult to the captain forgiven, if not forgotten, Tommy was golf's leading citizen, a hero with a leonine moustache and Balmoral bonnet, swinging all out in the style every local boy copied: right knee knuckling inward as his back-swing began, trunk twisting to its limit as his left shoulder turned under his chin. 'Every muscle of his well-knit frame was summoned into service,' one writer recalled. 'He stood well back from the ball, and with a dashing, pressing, forceful style of driving, which seldom failed, sent it whizzing on its far and sure flight.'

R&A golfers crowded the links until grouse season opened in August and they went shooting on the moors. In July and early August they played high-stakes golf matches. Tommy often joined them. He could only shake his head at their occasional club-throwing, foot-stamping fits, wondering how a man could hit two awful shots in a row and then curse fate when, wrapping his elbows around his ears on the backswing, he hit a third. 'The Links,' wrote Pastor Boyd, 'are sometimes a place of awful language: such are the temptations of golf.' Boyd recalled a 'peppery' match during which the Reverend John Tulloch, head of divinity college at St Andrews University and one of the queen's chaplains, offered his partner a swing tip. The man shook his club in Reverend Tulloch's face and cried, 'No directions! I'll take no directions!' Another golfer was so profane that his R&A brethren, who called him Mr Dammit, joked that rather than driving himself into the club, he swore himself in.

Unlike other professionals who were paid at the gentlemen's whim at the end of a match, Tommy insisted on getting his couple of crowns before he hit a ball. He knew his worth, as they said. Other professionals would send a friend through the crowd with hat in hand, begging, 'Silver, if you please, sir?' Tommy was too proud for that – entirely too proud for a greenkeeper's son, some said. Did he not personify the greed, gall and common ambition that were the ugliest aspects of modern life? As the preacher James Baldwin Brown said of Tommy's generation, 'Nothing is more detestable ... than the air of self-assertion and independence in the young.' Tommy, who was better educated than many R&A members, was known to correct them when they misspoke, as if being right could undo the social defect of his birth. The gentlemen preferred his father, who never spoke out of turn or looked them too hard in the eye. Old Tom had a genius for tact. He had a way of lowering his head to the perfect degree when speaking to a gentleman, showing deference without being slavish about it.

Tom's diplomacy was tested again when Tommy and Davie Strath capitalized on a kind of golf that gentlemen scorned. The young professionals began staging their own events, singles matches that drew large, raucous crowds. Their matches made for good theatre because they were perfect opposites: Tommy's brio versus Strath's cool technique, fire versus ice.

And to the dismay of the men who had controlled the sport, young Morris and Strath were not content to perform for their bettors' amusement, giving gentlemen something to bet on and then passing the hat for themselves. Instead Morris and Strath launched a sort of road show, a series of matches like the great boxing bouts of the next century. Such matches had always been winner-take-all, but Tommy and Davie demanded – and got – what would come to be called 'appearance fees'. North Berwick paid them twenty-five pounds each to play a match there. The North Berwick town council tried to keep the payment secret, but news leaked out and gentleman golfers huffed as if the boys had robbed a bank. One red-coated curmudgeon called such events 'a deadness' that deprived the players of 'their honour'. Tommy seemed to enjoy causing the tumult, which left his father stuck in the middle once again, humouring the R&A men who held his future in their soft, pink hands. And while Tom did not admit it, he was on Tommy's side in this matter. Tom Morris might have been old, but he was modern enough to believe that even a greenkeeper's son had a right to bargain for his work.

For a week that summer, St Andrews was packed with golf-fanatics who spoke of little but the latest skirmish between Morris and Strath. Even R&A officers came out in the rain to watch Tommy and Davie play for an eye-catching £200. Side bets added hundreds more. Tommy was a five-to-four favourite in what *The Field* called 'the most important golf match played since 1870'. On the morning of the first day's play, Tommy pointed to a boy caddie named David Ayton. 'Here, lad,' he said, handing over his clubs. 'Put these under your oxter.' Young Ayton did as he was told, stowing the clubs under his armpit, and followed the champion golfer to the teeing-ground.

Strath was coming off a victory over Tommy in a celebrated match at St Andrews that spring. As Everard would write, Strath's 'style was the very poetry of swing, the most perfectly graceful'. Davie had been swinging a bit harder since his last-round collapse in the 1872 Open, his driver making a louder clack on the ball. He surprised spectators and reporters by out-driving the champion on the early holes. Still, Tommy had Strath's backers fearing a rout ten minutes into their three-day, 108-hole contest. He won the first two holes, one with a stymie. But at the simple sixth Tommy lashed a long drive that found wet sand in one of the Coffin bunkers. He flailed twice without escaping and surrendered the hole. Strath gained another hole coming in and the first of the day's two rounds ended even. After a rainy luncheon break and another eighteen holes – Tommy sinking a pair of long putts, Strath answering with two of his own – they were still deadlocked with two days and seventy-two holes to go. 'Considering the wet state of the grass, better play has seldom if ever been seen on any course,' the *Citizen* declared.

The next day Tommy led by a hole with one to play in the morning round, but stumbled at the short Home Hole, where he always expected to make three. With his gutty in an iffy lie, he chose valour over discretion. He swung hard, the ball squirted to a worse lie, he made six and they were tied again.

In the afternoon round, beginning the second half of the 108-hole contest, the black-clad Strath outdrove and out-putted the champion to take command of the match. His supporters sent him off the Home green with a round of hoorahs. With seventy-two holes played and thirty-six to play tomorrow, Davie Strath went to sleep that night with a four-hole lead.

'Strath and his backers were in high spirits from yesterday's success, he being four-up,' *The Field* observed. 'Put upon his mettle, the champion went to work with a will and secured the first two holes.' Tommy took the first hole the next morning with a chip that nearly kissed the flagstick. When Strath's chip went bouncing sideways, his backers had to wonder: was Davie funking again? Not yet – Strath took a long breath and matched Tommy shot for shot as they neared the Eden in a gentle rain. The players' scores on the ninth through fourteenth holes were identical: 4–4–3–5–5–5. Then Tommy pressed harder, smacking in putts from all over his father's greens. When his putt to win the Home Hole ducked in, the £200 battle was all-square with eighteen holes left.

The skies went from grey to blue. Bees hummed in the heather under a fat July sun. While Tommy and Davie made their way to the turn, St Andrews' streets emptied as everyone went to the links. 'The male population of the city appeared to have turned out en masse,' the *Citizen* reported. 'It was with the greatest difficulty players kept from being completely surrounded.' The town had seldom seen such excitement since a circus passed through thirty years before, dazzling St Andreans with dancing dogs, fire eaters and acrobats. The golf circus of '73 found Auld Daw Anderson hawking ginger beer and lemon crushes from his wicker cart by the ninth hole, wealthy travellers trading calling cards, bettors shouting offers in a crowd half a dozen deep, pressed so close in the sudden heat that there were sweat stains in the oxters of the finest ladies and gentlemen. The players didn't disappoint: from the moment Tommy sank a curling putt on the first green, the golf was inspired. He led by two at the turn. Then, just as Strath's backers began to lose hope, their man won the tenth hole with a tidy four and squared the 108-hole contest with a three at the short eleventh. Strath took the next three holes with a flawless run of 4–5–5. Now Tommy was reeling, three down with only four holes left.

At the long fifteenth, Cartgate In, both players drove safely to the right of the Cottage Bunker, aiming for the church steeple between shapely knolls called the Bosoms. Both had chips to the whale-shaped double green. Strath, waggling over a shot that was worryingly similar to the one he had foozled earlier, bumped his chip with a firm stroke that sent it skipping towards the pin. The ball died near the hole. He looked up at his rival and for once, perhaps, there was defiance in Davie Strath's hollow-set eyes. *Top that.*

Tommy tried, but his ball ran past. They halved the hole, leaving the champion three holes down with three to play. Strath's supporters erupted in what the *Citizen* called 'loud and prolonged cheering'. Their man had entered that state of grace in which he could win but could not lose: he was dormy.

'It is doubtful whether golf, or indeed life, has any sensation to offer equal to that of becoming dormy,' Bernard Darwin wrote. Reflecting on 'the ultimate poignancy of dorminess', he called it 'a blessed relaxation after strain ... a moment of almost delicious bliss'. A match-play golfer leading by the same number of holes left to play can stumble, lose them all and have to settle for a draw, but he is immune to defeat. The word 'dormy', wrote Darwin, 'is the only one in our language which signifies that for one transcendent moment we can snap our fingers under the very nose of Fate.'

Strath's transcendent finish dealt Tommy a newsmaking blow. When another halved hole made Davie the victor, three-and-two, Tommy offered a handshake. Strath had won the £200 for his backers, enough cash to buy a hundred tweed jackets, 200 bottles of fine claret or a thousand dozen of Kirky's remakes. His own cut of about twenty pounds was more than twice what Tommy had received for winning the last Open. '[A]fter another volley of cheers the crowd began gradually to disperse,' reported the *Citizen*, whose correspondent, keeping track of strokes played as well as holes won, noted that Davie had shot 40 over the final nine to Tommy's 47. As *The Field* warned, 'the young champion will require to look to his laurels.' The stage was set for a rematch.

Tommy issued his challenge the following week. Strath accepted and the rematch was made: another three-day, 108-hole contest at St Andrews, this time for £100. 'The golf mania will reach its climax next week,' *The Field* predicted, 'on the occasion of the return contest between Tom Morris Jr, the champion golfer of Scotland, and Davie Strath. The betting is at evens.' The duellists met late in the forenoon of 27 August. Again the air was festive, with gamblers bickering over odds that eventually favoured Strath by three-to-two. As the previous winner, he had the honour. He cracked a long, straight drive. Tommy matched it and off they went, pursued by a boisterous crowd. At the head of the mob were well-dressed correspondents from the *Daily News* and the *Times*, sent north to follow 'The Great St Andrews Golf Match' between 'these two young Scotchmen'.

On the short, treacherous eighth hole, which Hutchison dubbed 'that slantwise little catchy-hole', Strath stymied Tommy, who tried to chip over and in, but overshot. The day went to Strath by four holes.

A hard-fought third round the next morning ended with thunder and a cloudburst that soaked the golfers and spectators. Tommy waited out a forty-five-minute luncheon break while the rain drummed the roof of his father's house, where he still lived with his parents and siblings. Having dropped another hole, he stood five behind at the marathon's midpoint. Davie's backers were giddy, patting each other on the back, while Tommy's looked as glum as the weather. But that afternoon, playing in steady rain, Tommy found his stroke. He would start a putt rolling and walk off the green, telling his boy caddie Ayton to fetch the ball from the hole. As one observer wrote, 'It seemed to us all he was simply invincible with his wooden putter.' Tommy made putts long and short, straight and twisting. Some banged the back of the hole and popped upward before they fell, some crawled over the hole's front edge, but nearly every putt he struck ended its journey underground. Tommy took back four holes of his five-hole deficit, then returned for the next day's play on a links jammed with spectators including rival professionals. 'As was to be expected, the number of onlookers was larger than on the previous two days,' reported *The Field*, 'and golfers were present in strong force from the principal clubs in Scotland, who enthusiastically watched the play of our two best professionals.' Swinging from his heels, Tommy 'almost invariably out-drove Strath'. By noon, 'the crowd was larger than on any previous occasion ... All classes were represented, hundreds of strangers being present from all parts of the country, even England contributing its quota.' Captain Maitland-Dougall, acting as umpire, came to the players' rescue several times, holding back the bumptious mob, calling for quiet when Tommy or Davie putted. Over the final eighteen, Tommy reclaimed his spot at the top of the game: 'Strath did not gain a single hole in the last round.'

Tommy Morris and Davie Strath helped legitimize professional golf in that summer of 1873. By staging the golf show of the year at a time when the game was becoming a spectator sport, they helped blaze a trail that Arnold Palmer, Jack Nicklaus and Tiger Woods would follow, and their battles were as remarkable as any in golf history. Over the twelve rounds of their two 108-hole marathons, covering six days, Tommy finished three holes ahead overall. But in total strokes, astonishingly, he and Strath were even: 1,027 to 1,027. As Everard put it: 'For brilliant and steady play combined with absence of mistakes, the golf that those two exhibited day after day has never been surpassed.'

Now Tommy's generation ruled the game. In Musselburgh, the ex-prodigy Willie Park, who turned forty that year, was not amused. Young Morris may have got the best of him a time or two or three, but Park reckoned he could thrash Davie Strath, a known funker. In September the two of them squared off at Park's home links for stakes of £100. Musselburgh's rowdy golf-fanatics turned out in such force that 'a rope cordon was drawn up immediately behind the players', the *Citizen* reported. What may have been the first gallery rope in golf history was not the only drawback for the home crowd. Park, whose power had awed Allan Robertson twenty years before ('He frightens us with his long driving!') swung as hard as ever, only to see Strath, who seemed half asleep, unfurl that smooth motion of his and out-drive him on the fly. Davie closed out the match with ease, three holes to the good. 'Mr Blyth, the umpire, asked for three cheers for the victor,' the *Citizen* noted. 'He then announced that a subscription was open for the vanquished.' A subscription was a collection – a dignified way of passing the hat. Willie Park, described by the *Citizen* as 'the weaker and losing party', had been reduced to taking charity.

That autumn, for the first time, the Open was coming to St Andrews. Gossip centred on the town's leading players. Could Davie Strath win another clash with the four-time champion, or would Tommy claim his fifth Open in a row? Tom Morris, seldom mentioned as a contender, spent the summer's end preparing the links for the event his R&A bosses had finally brought to his hometown. Tom raked and re-raked his putting-greens. He seeded and top-dressed them, exhorting his assistant greenkeeper, David Honeyman, to pile on the sand. ('More sand, Honeyman!') Tom scythed heather; chopped the black arms off whin bushes; hired extra workmen to load beach sand into barrows and roll them to dozens of bunkers, each of which he filled and re-filled; supervised the men who ran his horse-drawn grass-cutter; and walked the course scores of times, bending his aching back to pull a weed or pick a bit of shell off a green. By the first September frost he was as close to satisfied as a perfectionist can be. The east bank of the River Eden had never looked more like the garden of the same name.

Two weeks before the Open, Prince Leopold rode the royal railcar thirty miles east from Balmoral Castle to Aberdeen. The prince waved to ten-deep crowds on his way to Royal Aberdeen Golf Club. Soon another young man stepped off a clattering railcar in the same city, where golf-fanatics and celebrity-watchers shouted when they glimpsed his Balmoral bonnet.

Tommy waved. He stopped to shake hands with his supporters before moving on to the Aberdeen links, where Prince Leopold and Davie Strath waited. Scotland's gentleman golfers may have been clucking at the way crass professionals were beginning to over-shadow the amateur game, but the press and public were captivated. Tommy and Strath played for fifteen pounds under the watchful eyes of the prince, while reporters and spectators followed them around the links. One correspondent called Strath's golf 'brilliant', though Tommy beat him handily, four-and-two. Cheers, applause and hats flew up from the gallery as Tommy removed his bonnet and stepped forward to meet Prince Leopold, who looked as wan as Davie, his moustache hanging over pale, thin lips.

The prince spoke, but it was hard to hear his soft voice with so many people hip-hoorah-ing and calling on God to save him; a cheer that carried more weight in light of his fragile health.

Prince Leopold, who had just turned twenty, shook hands with twenty-two-year-old Tommy Morris, who felt the pulse of royal blood in that delicate hand.

After twelve years at Prestwick the Open Championship made its first visit to the links at St Andrews on Saturday, 4 October 1873. It had all the makings of a disaster. A storm settled over the Fife coast that week and camped there, dousing the course for two days and nights, blowing tiles off roofs and shutters off windows, throwing sea spray over the dunes and flooding bunkers. This Open was supposed to be a showcase for the artfully sewn turf of Tom Morris' fairway and the putting-greens he had built for the first and last holes, but the tempest undid all his work. Rainwater sluiced off putting-greens and stood waist-deep in bunkers. Acre-wide pools covered three fairways. Even the holes in the greens were full of water, leaving Tom to shake his head and quote Burns' line on best-laid schemes. The storm was bad news for him, his links, the town, the R&A and Tommy, who, above all, wanted a fair fight. It was good only for ducks and Tommy's challengers, who hoped that ponds and mud puddles might turn the odds their way.

One did more than hope. Tom Kidd, the whiskery dandy known for his colourful waistcoats and Whar-ye-goin' hat, sat up late on the eve of the tournament, working on his clubs. While the rain poured down outside his window, Kidd used a file to cut grooves in the faces of his cleeks.

The sun came out on Saturday, glinting in pools of rainwater at every low point on the links. Much of the course was submerged. Ducks swam in the gulleys in front of several greens. Pot bunkers had turned into rain barrels. The gentlemen running the Open announced a local rule for the tournament: golfers could move a submerged ball to a spot no nearer the hole at a cost of one stroke. The so-called 'pick and drop' rule made its Open debut that day.

Twenty-six players entered, more than triple the turnout of the previous year at Prestwick. They would go twice around the St Andrews links for a total of thirty-six holes, the same total as three circuits of Prestwick's twelve-hole course. The winner would get eleven pounds, a medal and a new trophy, a silver pitcher the three sponsoring clubs had commissioned. Tommy was the bettors' favourite, widely seen as invincible, while Strath was the clear second choice. By the time play began at ten in the morning 'a large crowd had taken up their position on the ground', *The Field* reported. Tommy struggled from the start, slashing drives that skipped into puddles and missing more short putts in the first round than he missed in a typical week. His first-round score of 94 suggests that the course was practically unplayable. 'The driving was bad,' wrote *The Field*'s correspondent, 'but the putting was wretched.' Tommy's supporters took heart from the fact that no one else did much better. The three first-round leaders shot 91. One was Bob Kirk, the pug-nosed son of Kirky the ball-maker. Another was Jamie Anderson, the thirty-year-old son of Auld Daw, presumably raised on the ginger beer his father sold. Anderson's cautious, pinpoint game suited the day's poor conditions. His backers swore that Jamie had once played ninety consecutive holes without hitting a bad shot. Still, it was the other co-leader who had the gallery chattering: Tom Kidd, who had spent the previous night etching grooves into his irons' faces, was having the day of his life. His prodigious drives sailed past ponds that Anderson, Kirk and even Tommy couldn't carry, and his 'ribbed' irons, as he called them, added backspin that stopped his ball while other players' approach shots skipped or slid off the greens.

Kidd's tactic was nothing new, though purists considered it unsporting. Allan Robertson had tried scoring the faces of his cleeks twenty years before. Ribbed cleeks anticipated the square-grooved irons used more than a century later by Mark Calcavecchia, who won the 1989 Open Championship, but unlike Calcavecchia's controversial irons, Kidd's clubs were legal. Kidd left the other co-leaders behind by shooting 39 on the outward nine that afternoon, a jaw-dropping score given the puddles and mud on the course. Kirk fell back first. Jamie Anderson, flailing in a watery bunker on the Heathery Hole, made a nightmarish nine on the hole, but rallied on the inward nine as Kidd began labouring under the weight of the lead. While Tommy and Anderson crept into contention, Kidd was falling apart, sixes and sevens disfiguring his card. After that sparkling 39 going out, he would stagger home in 49.

That meant Tommy was still alive. The champion golfer, surrounded by St Andreans urging him on, wanted nothing more than a fifth Open victory. Five consecutive victories might never be matched. He would be halfway to the ten in a row his most confident backers predicted. Surely that shiny new trophy belonged in the house at 6 Pilmour Links Road. The title had been his since he was seventeen, and no one who wasn't named Thomas Morris had won it since 1867.

Tommy studied the putt he had left on the Home Hole green his father had made. The green was sodden; he could hear the *squish* of wet soil with each step he took. Tommy always played quickly from tee to green, but took his time on any putt of more than a foot or two, examining the break, settling into his stance with the toe of his right boot nearly touching the ball, gathering his wits before starting the ball on its way to the hole and willing it to go in.

He gave it extra force and overspin to make sure it reached the hole. Droplets of water spun up off the ball as it rolled. The crowd drew a collective breath, then let out a huge, glad roar as the ball struck the back of the hole and dropped.

Four twosomes back, Tom Kidd heard the noise. The dapper leader was still bashing drives and hitting ribbed-iron approaches that hopped and stopped on Tom's wet greens, but now he was missing putts left and right and short. By the time he wobbled to the teeing-ground at the Road Hole, Kidd was desperate for good news. It came in the form of a number: 183. Spectators relayed the number from the Home Hole green through the crowd that lined the last two holes. Tommy Morris had shot 89 in the second round and was in at 183, an astronomical two-round total for him, giving Kidd a bit of breathing room.

The other contender, Jamie Anderson, had fought back from his nine at the Heathery Hole until he stood at the last teeing-ground with a chance to finish at 179. All he needed was a standard four on the Home Hole that measured a jot more than 250 yards. Anderson drove his ball to a dry spot on the wide lawn that served as fairway to both the first and last holes, but his approach fell short, the ball trickling to a muddy lie. He could not control his chip, which squirted off at an angle, barely reaching the green. Two putts for five left Anderson at 180, three shots less than Tommy's score.

Tommy's reign was over. Spectators walked past him to watch bearded, bedraggled Kidd trudge up the last fairway towards town, clinging to his lead and a rib-faced iron niblick. His pitch shot plunked to earth, close enough. One last putt and the deed was done: Tom Kidd was the champion golfer of Scotland.

Tommy applauded him and shook his hand. Red-coated R&A officials brought out the new trophy, a silver pitcher made by the Edinburgh silversmiths Mackay Cunningham & Co. at a cost of thirty pounds. The Golf Champion Trophy, as it was named, was a claret jug, a familiar feature of nineteenth-century clubhouses. Gentleman golfers had long bet wine as well as money on their matches and had lugged their claret to the clubhouse in such jugs in case they lost. Twelve inches high, this new Claret Jug – as it was quickly, indelibly christened – would hold enough claret, champagne or whisky to get a happy Open winner and several friends singing. But what it held mattered less than who held it. The jug would be kept for a year by the reigning Open champion, whose name would be engraved on its curved surface and each champion would pass it on to his successor. In its time the game's most-prized trophy would share railway berths with Harry Vardon, J.H. Taylor and James Braid, the 'Great Triumvirate' who combined to win sixteen Open Championships. The jug would ride in cruise-ship cabins with Bobby Jones, the American amateur who won three Opens. It would accompany Open winners until 1928, when the R&A decided to keep the trophy in its clubhouse year-round. That year the R&A commissioned a Claret Jug replica that has travelled with the champions ever since, while the original stayed home in St Andrews, except in 1982, when Tom Watson, given the original by mistake, took it to his home in Kansas City, where a wild Watson practice swing dented it. Every summer the one true Claret Jug is hauled out and handed briefly to the Open winner, who is introduced as the 'Champion Golfer of the Year'. The winner kisses the Claret Jug and holds it aloft for the crowd to see. His name is engraved on its wooden base, the latest name on a list of champions that reaches back to the soggy Saturday in 1873 when Tom Kidd upset Tommy Morris.

Yet if you look at the original Claret Jug in its glass case in the R&A clubhouse, lifting your eyes from the square wooden base where the name of the 2006 champion Tiger Woods is engraved, you see that Kidd's name is not first on the list. Tom Kidd is listed second. The first line belongs to the 1872 winner, whose name was backdated when the trophy was made. The first champion listed on the Claret Jug was and still is Tom Morris Jr.

Seeing his name ahead of Kidd's on the trophy was no solace to Tommy, who spent the last weeks of 1873 seeing the *Citizen* and the *Fifeshire Journal* bestow on Kidd the title he had thought of as his birthright:

'Tom Kidd (champion) beat Mr Louden by five-and-four . . .'

'Tom Kidd, the champion golfer, announced his engagement . . .'

But Tom Morris was pleased to point out (for he so loved a proverb), 'tis an ill wind that bloweth no good. The storm that swamped the links, ruined all Tom's work and probably cost Tommy a fifth Open was a boon to some – and not just the men who took long odds on Kidd. As the whole town learned after the Open, Kidd's triumph was a boon for love as well. It made him solvent enough to propose to his beloved Eliza, who became the new champion's fiancée within hours of his victory. As Open champion Kidd took home eleven pounds, the richest purse of his career, and a gold medal that he promptly sold to pay for his wedding. He would have sold the Claret

Jug too if he hadn't been legally bound to return it.

Tommy Morris had his own affairs to think about. He spent much of that winter courting a woman who had come to St Andrews from Edinburgh. She was older than he, long of leg, dark of hair and eye.

She was called Margaret.

# TEN

# *Tommy and Meg*

SHE WAS TALL enough to look him straight in the eye. Her hair was black, or rather the darkest possible brown, showing the brown only in direct sunlight. Margaret Drinnen was older than Tommy and she was no innocent people said, but that was no sin as far as he was concerned. The St Andrews lasses he knew, stuffed into their crinolines and flounced multi-tiered dresses, resembled toy dolls and knew as much of life as a doll knows. Raised to be marriageable, they could play piano, sew and pray and many would be rudely surprised by the barnyard aspects of their wedding nights. But this was a woman of thirty, new in town, working as a maid in one of the grand houses on The Scores.

No one knows how she and Tommy met. It may have been at a dance. Margaret arrived from Edinburgh in 1872, too late to attend the Rose Club Ball that January, but there were other dances. As one Scotsman timelessly put it, 'the search for a mate and dancing go hand in hand.' Victorian mores set strict limits on contact between young men and women; dances were designed to subvert the limits. A young woman held her handkerchief a certain way to signal her willingness to dance with a particular fellow. He would bow and offer his hand. She moved to him and their left hands interlocked, his right hand on the curve of her waist. Scottish couples danced the faddish French quadrille, as well as such old Scottish reliables as the Gay Gordons and Strip the Willow. Tommy may have first seen Margaret across the town hall ballroom, a tall woman in a long, dark gown and white kid gloves that stretched to her elbows, her dark hair framing an angular face that turned his way for a moment before a crowd of dancers drifted between them.

She came from West Lothian, a region the journalist William Cobbett described in 1832 as 'a very fine county altogether; it has a due mixture of orchards, woods, cornfields and pastures ... butter and milk are the chief products of the soil'. Since then, coal and ironstone mines had turned farmland into a moonscape of coal pits and slag heaps, one of the most poisonous places on earth and one of the most productive, for the industry that blackened West Lothian helped build the British Empire.

Britain lacked the vast forests that pre-industrial iron-making required. For centuries, as Barbara Freese wrote in *Coal: A Human History*, 'Iron was still essentially a forest product; you couldn't make it without burning vast amounts of wood, which Britain simply didn't have.' Coal was plentiful, but it contained impurities that made for bad iron. Baking the coal yielded coke, which worked better, and in the 1780s technical advances helped smelters use coke and iron ore to make high-quality iron in unheard-of tonnages. Between 1830 and 1844, with steam-powered blast furnaces running day and night, Scottish iron production rose from 40,000 tons to 412,000. By 1850, Scottish iron accounted for ninety percent of Britain's iron exports.

Margaret Drinnen's father Walter, called Watty, was a coal-pit bottomer. He ran the cage that took men from the surface to the tunnels of a West Lothian mine owned by the Coltness Iron Company. Coltness had built a ramshackle town, Whitburn, atop the underground seams of coal and ironstone it owned. Watty Drinnen, a black-fingered, black-toothed man, lived with his wife and six children at number 5 Crofthead Road, Whitburn, one of 129 identical shacks facing a rutted dirt track. The eight Drinnens shared two rooms with a boarder, who paid a few pennies' rent. Margaret and the rest shared three water closets with more than a thousand inhabitants of the other two-room shacks on Crofthead Road. Some mornings the toilet lines were so long that people relieved themselves outdoors, adding to the stench of coal and sulphur that hung in the air until rain drove it into the muck.

According to David Malcolm, a St Andrews golf historian who uncovered many details of Margaret's life, her hometown was almost unimaginably foul. 'The hellish filth and squalor of mid-nineteenth-century Whitburn,' says Malcolm were 'entirely outwith the experience of present times.'

A generation earlier, women and children had worked in the mines, dragging coal up steep flights of steps. 'The mother ... descends the pit with her older daughters when each, having a basket, lays it down, and into it the large coals are rolled: and such is the weight that it frequently takes two men to lift the burden upon their backs,' goes one account. 'The mother sets out first, carrying a lighted candle in her teeth; the girls follow ... they proceed with weary steps and slow, ascend the stairs ... till they arrive at the pit top, where the coals are laid down for sale; in this manner they go for eight to ten hours almost without resting. It is no uncommon thing to see them when ascending from the pit weeping most bitterly.' Eleven-year-old girls dragged 100-pound loads and were 'hags' before they turned twenty. An 1853 law that barred females from working underground simply shifted the burden onto boys. In 1872, the House of Commons passed a bill cutting the daily shifts of boy miners – those under the age of thirteen – from twelve hours to ten; that left boys of nine and ten with six-day, sixty-hour workweeks. Men worked longer hours, including the occasional twenty-hour shift, sweating in darkness so heavy they could taste it.

The air in the mines was hot and thick with coal dust. It stung the eyes and blackened bread that sat out too long. Coal wagons rode rails through rat-infested tunnels to the pit in the Coltness mine, where Watty Drinnen ran the steam-powered cage that had replaced the stairs – an innovation that coalmasters considered a kindness to miners. The wagons sometimes crushed exhausted boys who had fallen asleep on the rails. Killed boys were buried on Sunday, the one day their relatives didn't have to work.

After women were prohibited from working underground, they sought other ways to supplement their husbands' meager wages. Many looked after the children of other miners' families as well as their own, calming the sick ones with watered-down ale or whisky. They would pour a week's worth of porridge into a pewter-lined drawer; after it hardened you could cut out a chunk and fry it for breakfast, or wrap it in a handkerchief to save for lunch. Margaret Drinnen probably cooked hundreds of drawers' worth of porridge while contemplating her one likely alternative to spinsterhood: marrying a miner and moving to another cramped shack in Whitburn. Even that honour was denied to many girls, since miners didn't always marry the girls they got pregnant. When Margaret was eighteen, her older sister, Agnes, bore an illegitimate son. The same fate befell another Drinnen sister, Helen, three years later.

Margaret, the tall, striking one, wanted none of that. She was literate, thanks to a school system founded on the belief that reading the Bible was vital to spiritual growth. Bright and capable, Margaret apprenticed as a lace tambourer, doing weaving that required quick, talented fingers. Lace tambourers occasionally landed work as ladies' maids, and Margaret won a post as a maid in Edinburgh, a triumph for a Whitburn girl. 'In those days you *dreamed* your daughter might get a job "in service",' says Malcolm. 'She'd be fed and clothed and live in a clean, well lighted house, a respectable house.' Margaret worked in the home of a prominent solicitor in Edinburgh's thriving New Town. She toiled like a dray mare for food, board and pay of about eight pounds a year.

Housemaids typically worked from dawn until half past ten or eleven p.m., cleaning floors on their hands and knees, feeding coal fires, sweeping and shaking out rugs, dusting, washing windows, serving meals, making beds, heating and carrying water for baths, polishing brass, blacking shoes. Maids worked seven days a week and had little time for social lives. Some were literally barred from courtship: in many of Edinburgh's better houses, the maid's bedroom was the only one with bars on the windows. Still, that did not always keep her virginal. Many maids were preyed on by men in the homes where they worked, men whose only other sexual outlet was paying prostitutes who themselves had probably fled the ranks of domestic servants. As historian T. C. Smout of St Andrews University notes, four-fifths of the prostitutes in the Edinburgh Magdalene Asylum had been maids.

Somehow Margaret thrived. Stiffer of spine than her ladylike manner suggested, she had a certain grace that set her apart. In 1872 she moved up in the world again. The Edinburgh solicitor's mother, who lived in St Andrews, needed a bright, reliable maid. The solicitor's wife recommended Margaret, who went to live and work in a grand villa on The Scores, facing the sea.

If she hadn't already heard of St Andrews' golfing celebrity, she soon heard plenty. Everyone in town knew 'our Tommy'. Girls found him dashing; matrons clucked fondly over his quick smile, his fine-but-not-fancy suits and his gallantry, for he was quite the young gent, despite being only a greenkeeper's son.

Like Margaret, Tommy had seen a bit of the world. He often visited smoke-shrouded Edinburgh with his Rose Club friends, some of whom spent time and coin in the city's brothels – there were more than a hundred – and came home with unmentionable itches. Tommy may have done some scratching of his own. Young men were not expected to stay virginal into their twenties, and he was almost certainly not a virgin at twenty-two. Yet he wasn't a wastrel, either. There was too much of his father's common sense in him for that. That left Tommy with a challenge: if whoring wasn't to his taste, and neither were innocent girls who lived to sew and pray, he would need to find an unusual woman.

It seems Tommy's parents were not pleased to hear that their son was courting Margaret Drinnen. They had doubtless pictured him marrying a wealthy gentleman's daughter. Never mind that Nancy had also been a maid in her day. This was different. Tommy was a celebrity, and his parents had reason to hope for a marriage that would secure all their futures in the middle class. But in love, as in other things, Tommy made his own choices.

At least courting Margaret wasn't sapping his strength. Tommy was in top form in 1873 and '74, winning singles and foursomes matches in bunches, filling the pockets of both Tom Morrises.

The 1874 Open, held in April to coincide with the spring meeting of the Honourable Company of Edinburgh Golfers, renewed the duel between the Morrises of St Andrews and the golfers of Musselburgh. The surprise was that Musselburgh's hero this time was not Willie Park or Bob Fergusson, but a man who had spent twenty years fishing.

A morning hailstorm turned the nine-hole Musselburgh links cold, bumpy and white. The hail left meltwater on the putting-greens, but a breeze off the Firth of Forth dried them before play began at noon. Tom Kidd's ribbed irons would do him no good today.

A field of thirty-two golfers, the largest ever, featured five prominent St Andreans: defending champion Kidd, sporting one of his colourful silk waistcoats, black-clad Davie Strath, and three Morrises – the famous two as well as Jimmy, a whip-thin young man of eighteen with even thinner hopes of finishing ahead of his older brother.

Most of the crowd followed Tommy and Willie Park, the marquee pairing. Golf had changed mightily in the seven years since Park turned to Tom Morris at Carnoustie and asked, 'What have you brought this boy here for?' Now Willie had strands of grey in his bushy side-whiskers. He still swung as hard as any man, but these days his driving frightened no one. Tommy, Strath and Kidd could all outdistance him. Park drew whoops from the Musselburgh crowd when he sank a long putt at the first hole, called The Graves to honour the sixteenth-century soldiers buried under the green. He wavered with a six at the next hole, a score Tommy was annoyed to match after a perfect drive and a second shot that sliced so far to the right that his ball rolled onto a road beside the course. From there Tommy chunked his approach, the heel of his cleek bouncing at impact, the ball blooping only halfway to the green – a shot as noisome as the Park-fanatics who applauded it. Matters did not improve for either player. He and Park both finished the first eighteen in 83 strokes.

A hum in the gallery told them that someone was

doing better. The crowd around Tommy and Park dwindled as spectators hurried to follow the surprise leader, who had fired a flawless 75 over the first eighteen holes. As *The Field* put it, 'onlookers who had been following other couples forsook their allegiance and attached themselves to the game of Mungo.' When Willie Park heard the news, he smiled. The leader was Park's younger brother Mungo, the golfer who had gone to sea.

In his youth, Mungo Park had been the best boy golfer in Musselburgh. Then he took work on a North Sea fishing boat, perilous work that seemed to offer a better future than that of a golfer. After twenty years at sea Mungo came home, tanned and fearless with scarred, corded forearms and a face creased by winter gales. He bought a set of hickories and began beating all the local golfers except his brother. And at the 1874 Open he shocked the crowd and probably even himself by taking an eight-shot lead on Willie and the player they both feared, Tommy Morris.

The more his gallery grew, the more Mungo squirmed. He gave five strokes back during his third circuit of the nine-hole course, while getting no challenge from Willie, who fell back stroke by stroke. But Tommy crept closer while Mungo's putter suffered from the shakes. *The Field*'s reporter saw the crowd yo-yo back towards Tommy: 'A goodly number of the spectators bethought themselves of reverting again to their old favourite ... towards the close of the match it was anticipated that he would at least "tie".' Mungo wrestled home a putt on the last green to finish his closing eighteen in 84 shots for a total of 159, a score that eliminated every contender but one.

Now Mungo's supporters charged out to join Tommy's gallery. Some went to watch, some to hoot and hiss, some hoped to kick his ball if they could. He disappointed them by spearing his drive into the fairway. As the *Scotsman* reported, he was 'swiping beautifully' with his driver. At the next hole, named the Gas Hole after the fuming gasworks behind the green, he struck an approach that fell on a shallow arc, skipped forward and sniffed at the hole. For an instant it seemed it would fall in, but the ball ran just past the flag. On his way to the green, he had the same numbers in his head as everyone else: if he made this putt, then a standard three at the short Home Hole would be enough to tie Mungo. This putt and a two at the Home Hole would win the Claret Jug.

Tommy spent almost a minute studying the putt. It wasn't long, no more than a yard, but he was careful with every putt. He took his stance, centring his weight over the ball, and spanked it at the hole.

It stayed out. There were cheers from the crowd. Willie Park, standing beside the green blinked. He could barely believe what he had seen: Tommy Morris botching a short putt.

Tommy still had one chance. A two at the Home

Hole would force a playoff. His target was starkly framed for him – the jostling mob packed tight around the putting-green less than 160 yards away. Tommy waggled his iron. He knuckled his right knee inward and brought the club back, twisting so far that he nearly lost sight of the ball, then jack-knifed downward and *clack* – the ball took off like a bullet.

It rose and kept rising. He had put too much steam behind it. The ball carried over the flag, over the green and over the crowd. It bounced and finally stopped on the far side of a railing behind and above the green.

This ball needed no kick from a Morris-hater. It was bad enough as it lay. The spectators cleared a path between the ball and the green. The shot was downhill; Tommy saw that he could putt it. He saw a hollow in the green, a shallow slope that would turn the ball towards the hole.

A long, smooth stroke got the ball started. It bounced onto the green and curved as it closed in on the hole, Tommy glaring at the ball as if daring it to miss.

It was close – a brave try that drew applause from the hostile gallery – but it stayed out. Shouts and a round of hip-hip-hoorays announced the news: Mungo Park was the champion golfer of Scotland. Willie Park bear-hugged his brother while Tommy missed his tap-in to finish at 161. He had made up six shots in the last eighteen holes to lose by two strokes. But the margin didn't matter. A loss was a loss. A loss was an ugliness; the collapse of the image he had in his mind of the ball going in. As *The Field* put it, 'the blue ribbon of the golfing green has fallen to the lot of an outsider. Mungo Park, a golfer previously unknown beyond his own green, has stepped forward and carried off the trophy.' The feud between the Morrises and the Musselburgh boys, which seemed settled in St Andrews' favour, was a hot war again.

A month later Tommy tested his supremacy on his father's links. He agreed to play Davie Strath at St Andrews during the R&A's spring meeting. The whins were in bloom, the old course in such pristine shape that the *St Andrews Gazette* judged Tom's work priceless. 'We suppose it is for the interest of Old Tom to keep the links in proper condition,' the *Gazette* allowed, 'but *con amore* he does more for it than can be compensated by any pecuniary reward.' Tommy, still stung by losing the Open at Musselburgh, showed his Rose Club friend no camaraderie that day. A match set for eighteen holes ended on the thirteenth with Strath routed, six-and-five.

During the humdrum summer that followed the *Citizen* complained that there had been 'no important golf matches in 1874'. One reason was the gap between Tommy and the other professionals. He may have lost the last two Opens, but Mungo Park and Tom Kidd, the champions, were still supporting players. Few bettors would back either man against Tommy without getting odds or strokes. The same went for Strath, who had not lived up to his dazzling play of '73 and seemed content with the lucrative role of playing Tommy's foil, the worthy adversary and second-best St Andrean.

Another reason for the slackening interest in golf was the calendar: with the Open at Musselburgh having been played in the spring, there wouldn't be another Open until the autumn of 1875. Yet another reason, if you credit the local gossip, was Tommy's rising interest in Margaret Drinnen, for he seemed to be spending as much time courting the pretty housemaid as he spent playing golf.

In small towns like St Andrews, courting consisted mostly of going for walks. The young couple was always supervised by a chaperone, in this case one of Tommy's aunts or another married relative. He and Margaret made a handsome couple, him in his trim, expensive suit, checking the time on the pocket-watch his father gave him, and Margaret in a sensible dress over crinolines and a corset that cinched her already-thin waist to twenty inches. Some girls fainted after too many hours in their corsets, but she was both thin and strong. Soon he would be calling her Meg, the nickname for most Margarets in West Lothian. Meg wore spotless gloves over hands that Tommy touched every chance he got, earning him smacks on the wrist from their chaperone.

Like most courting couples they would stroll the East Sands towards Crail, stopping at the moss-crusted basalt formation called the Rock and Spindle. A longer walk, one that would get their chaperone grumbling and give them a chance to outdistance her, took them through a countryside splashed with irises, daisies, celandines and meadow rue to Drumcarrow Hill, four miles from town. Looking south from the hilltop they could see the blunt-topped Berwick Law in the distance beyond the green and yellow fields of Fife. To the north was the sea, with the links in the foreground, flat, green land threaded with whins, golfers creeping antlike between the whin bushes. There were red ants and brown ants – red-jacketed R&A golfers and other players in plain tweeds.

Tommy and Meg also wandered St Andrews. While there wasn't much territory to explore in a town a mile long and half a mile wide, what little there was came with no end of baroque, bloody history. Tommy had never much cared for the lore of the town his father so loved, but he found that it meant more to him now that he was sharing it with Meg, whose hometown had coal and iron instead of history.

Passing Queen Mary's house on South Street, he told Meg about Chastelard, the French poet who spied on the Queen of Scots while she undressed. Walking east from there the courting couple passed the walls of the ruined cathedral. Grass grew where stone floors had once felt the boots of King Robert the Bruce, who consecrated the cathedral in 1318. Tommy had often walked to the cathedral cemetery with his family to visit the grave of the brother who died before Tommy was born. Now he showed Meg the tall white stone with its report of Wee Tom's brief life: DIED 9 APRIL 1850, AGED 4 YEARS.

Walking towards the bay they reached St Andrews Castle, once the palace of bloody Cardinal Beaton, who so enjoyed burning Protestant leaders at the stake that he would lean from his window high up the castle wall, clapping his hands while they burned, before returning to bed with his mistress. In 1546, seven Protestant spies sneaked into the castle when its drawbridge was down and surprised Beaton in his sleep. They gutted him and dragged him to the castle wall while alarms sounded and townspeople gathered outside. 'Incontinent they brought the cardinal dead to the wall,' reads a contemporary account, 'and hung him over the wall by the arm and foot, and so bade the people see their God.'

St Andreans recalled bloody Beaton with disdain. Pastor Boyd wrote of a dinner party at which a visitor asked where Cardinal Beaton had lived. 'He lived at the Castle,' another guest replied. 'In a quite literal sense, he hung out there!'

Pastor Boyd's church, Holy Trinity, was the sight of the 1559 sermon by Protestant reformer John Knox that called down the wrath of heaven on Roman idolatry. When he finished the congregation poured out onto South Street, ran two blocks east and set upon the cathedral with hammers, pick-axes and bare hands, tearing up bishops' tombs and stripping bishops' bones of gold and jewels. The cathedral that had been the seat of Scottish Catholicism for 250 years was destroyed in a day. A year later, Scotland was a Protestant country.

Below the ruined cathedral a long stone pier jutted into the bay. The pier was made of stones salvaged from the cathedral. On Sundays, the students of St Andrews University, the nation's oldest, walked to the end of the pier in their crimson robes, looking like a procession of cardinals. Or gentleman golfers.

A left turn led to Holy Trinity church, where pastor A.K.H. Boyd carried on the tradition of Knox by giving sermons that seemed three days long. It was here that Tommy took his first holy communion in June 1874. His younger siblings Lizzie and Jimmy had already had their first communions two years before; his late acceptance of the sacrament signalled a change in Tommy, who was not particularly devout. Taking communion was a concession to propriety, probably for Meg's sake. It was a step towards a church marriage. He might not have given a whit about ritual, but she did. She had proved it back in Whitburn, where Margaret Drinnen learned that church membership was the hard-won reward of a redeemed sinner. The town's gossips were right about one thing: Margaret Drinnen was no innocent. She was what they called a woman with a past.

In Whitburn, where her father's pit-bull fighting dogs tore up live rabbits and rats for practice, she grew up cold and hungry. Coal bings – black heaps of mining waste as tall as the town church – blocked the horizon. The niceties of middle-class propriety had little to do with Whitburn, where Margaret's sisters nursed the bastard sons they'd had by local miners.

Meg did somewhat better. Aged twenty-five, she got pregnant by a Coltness mine official named James Stark.

James Stark would not marry Margaret (or perhaps it was the reverse), and so she faced a choice: have the baby or abort it. Many girls chose abortion, a hazardous internal stabbing with a whalebone speculum. But Margaret chose to have her baby. Her daughter, Helen Stark Drinnen, was born in 1866, six years before Meg appeared in St Andrews. That hard choice led to another, for if an illegitimate child was to be baptized, the mother must do public penance for the sin of fornication. 'Naming and shaming' the rite was called.

Margaret submitted. Whatever the congregation thought of her, she was determined to keep her child sinless in the eyes of God and the church. And there was no time to lose. The stub of the child's umbilical cord had become infected; baby Helen was in danger of dying unbaptized.

Three consecutive Sundays she sat on a stool in Whitburn Parish Church, facing the congregation, her sickly child in her arms. Sunday after Sunday after Sunday the minister spoke Margaret Drinnen's name and the name of her sin. She bowed her head and nodded to the term the minister used, admitting that she was a fornicatrix.

Yet, even in her shame, there was something special about Watty Drinnen's third daughter. 'There can be no doubting that Margaret Drinnen was an exceptional woman,' insists David Malcolm, who found an entry, dated 8 July 1866, in the parish's minute book: 'Margaret Drinnen residing at Crofthead compeared before the session acknowledging guilt of fornication and was very affectionately rebuked and exhorted to walk worthy of her spiritual vocation, her child was at the same time baptized.'

Affectionate rebuke and immediate baptism were a rare sequel to naming and shaming. This was clearly someone who made a memorable impression. Reverend Boyd of St Andrews, Meg's next pastor, would call her 'a remarkably handsome and healthy young woman: most lovable in every way'.

Less than a month later, the baby died of septicemia. Soon after that Meg fled Whitburn for Edinburgh and, later, St Andrews.

The old seaside town was paradise compared to Whitburn – a meadow dotted with wildflowers and golf balls. Its residents tended to live out their Biblical span of threescore and ten rather than dying at forty or fifty. By the time Margaret met Tommy Morris, her father Watty, too ill to work, was stuck in his bed, wheezing and spitting black phlegm, while Tommy's father still splashed in the bay every morning and worked six days a week on the links, merrily smoking his pipe and joining his son in golf matches. When she arrived in St Andrews, Meg knew little about golf, a game that seemed to consist largely of men cursing and handing Tommy money. But like almost everyone in St Andrews, she soon knew all about it.

In 1874, the year Tommy and Meg began discussing marriage, the *Times* looked north to Scotland and saw a nation falling in love with golf: 'There are districts and burghs where every second inhabitant is a golfer. It is the game of the country gentry, of the busy professional man, of the bourgeoisie of flourishing centres of trade, of many of the artisans, and even of the roughs . . . It is the one amusement which any "douce" man may pursue . . . and lose neither respect nor social consideration.' If Tommy lost some social consideration by courting a woman of doubtful repute, his standing as golf's leading figure was secure. No one saw Davie Strath or any other golfer as his equal. Still, he was vulnerable in foursomes, stubbornly teaming with his father. In August, after Willie and

Mungo Park challenged the Morrises to a match for twenty-five pounds, Tom and Tommy made a half-day trip by train and ferry to a North Berwick links swarmed with Park-lovers from nearby Musselburgh. Tom's putter sputtered as usual that day. 'Willie and Mungo . . . played a fine game,' *The Field* reported, 'as likewise did Young Tom, but the senior Morris was not in his usual fettle.' In fact he was missing putts left and right. Tom shook his heavy head as the Parks closed out the match on the sixteenth green and the umpire, a gentleman named Mr Virtue, called for applause for both sides. Tommy looked around at the Musselburgh rowdies, who could now claim that their boys held both the Claret Jug and the unofficial foursomes title.

This was too much losing for Tommy to stomach. He challenged Willie Park to play singles for twenty-five pounds. Willie, never one to turn down a bet, agreed.

In the early holes, the greying Park, having regained some of his old power through practice or sheer cussedness, took a two-hole advantage. But Tommy wasn't fettered to his father as he had been in four-somes. Two down with four to play while Willie's fanatics howled at him, he squared the match, then took the last hole to send them shuffling home. Later that autumn, he faced Willie Park for another twenty-five pounds at the same links, again with a raucous crowd tracking their every move. This time Park held a two-hole edge with only three to play. According to the *Fifeshire Journal*, 'It was the general impression that he had the game in hand, but Young Tom made a brilliant finish, won the three holes, and gained the match by one.'

The marriage banns of Thomas Morris Jr and Margaret Drinnen were announced from the pulpit of Holy Trinity church for three consecutive Sundays in November. The wedding was set for 25 November 1874. As tradition dictated, it would be held at the bride's home church, the parish church in Whitburn.

It is telling that Tom did not go to Whitburn for the wedding. His wife Nancy was bed-ridden, but Tom could have made the trip in half a day. The fact that he missed his son's wedding suggests his disapproval, suggesting in turn that the bride's past was no secret to the Morrises. Tommy may have answered gossip about her by telling his parents everything. To him, Margaret was brave as well as beautiful. Their marriage would serve as a mutual rescue, with Meg saved from servitude, sin and disrepute, while Tommy was delivered from a frilly army of timid, devoutly Presbyterian piano-playing virgins.

While their parents stayed home on his wedding day, Tommy rode the train into coal country with his sister Lizzie and his paraplegic brother Jack, who had to be lifted onto the train along with his trolley. It was hard work getting Jack through Whitburn's muddy streets. He could pull himself along in the flat, dry parts, propelled by his muscled arms and gloved hands, but mud foiled him and he had to be carried – heavy work now that Jack was fifteen years old – up the church steps and eased into a pew where he sat beside Tommy, across the aisle from the bride's family. Among the Drinnens was Meg's father Watty, turned out in his shabby Sunday best, his skin tinged with coal dust. Watty was proud of his Meg and he had every right to be, even if his pride was mixed with puzzlement, seeing his pretty daughter marrying a well-to-do lad, academy-educated – a golfer, of all things.

Lizzie Morris served as Meg's best maid. Jack, helped forward from his pew, was his brother's best man. The service was straightforward, with the bride and groom saying their vows and the minister pronouncing them man and wife. There was no kiss. After the ceremony, Tommy and Meg signed the parish register. He signed as *Thomas Morris, Golf-Ball Maker, Bachelor*. She signed as *Margaret Drinnen, Domestic Servant, Spinster*. A spinster no more, she left the church as Margaret Morris, wife of the world's best golfer. Soon she would have a respectable house and a maid of her own.

Back in St Andrews, Tom Morris proposed a toast. A born conciliator, Tom never held a grudge in his life. What he wished above all was to keep things running: the links, the shop and the partnership of the golfing Morrises, father and son. That partnership would last even if they disagreed on something as vital as Tommy's choice of wife. And so that evening, while Tommy and Meg enjoyed their first hours as husband and wife, Tom hosted a supper in Tommy's honour at the Golf Hotel.

There were echoes here for Tom. The Golf Hotel stood on the former site of Allan Robertson's cottage, where Tom had made featheries with Allan and Lang Willie thirty years before. Now Tommy's Rose Club friends and Tom's workshop employees gathered to eat, laugh and drink the newlyweds' health. The *Citizen* described 'a substantial repast and the usual toasts being drunk', including a toast to 'the health of Tom Morris Jr, who they must no longer call Tommy, remarking on his distinguished career as a golfer, and the many victories and trophies he had won. These marked him out as the champion par excellence. He had carried off the "Belt" in three successive years against allcomers notwithstanding that he was then not out of his "teens". His performance had not in the least abated, as shown by his having twice this autumn defeated Willie Park ... No doubt much of his success was due to that amiability of temper, together with fixed determination, which made him so much a favourite both on and off the green, and which would be carried into the new relationship he had that day formed.' With Tom and company hoisting drinks, the night careened pleasantly towards a final toast to the club-maker's craft and one, obligingly, to 'the health of "The Bride"'.

## ELEVEN

# *A Telegram*

THE NEWLYWEDS SETTLED into a two-storey house on Playfair Place, 200 yards from the Morris place on Pilmour Links. The rent was twenty-seven pounds a year. Some St Andreans thought the house a bit ostentatious, though Tommy could have afforded a bigger one. Without quite flaunting his money, which would be a sin in his father's eyes, he was demonstrating his and Meg's desire to be a respectable couple in a respectable area of old St Andrews.

According to the Rose Club member George Bruce, Tommy was 'united, both in the bonds of affection and wedlock, to a young woman for whom he had the strongest love'.

Meg furnished their half-dozen rooms in a style that would have suited a house in Edinburgh. As custom required, she consulted Tommy's mother before buying anything for the house, though Meg knew more than Nancy about fabric and furniture. Meg put up Venetian blinds and tasteful wallpaper. She put a new cast-metal bed in the bedroom and stocked her well-lit kitchen with tin-lined saucepans and Staffordshire crockery. On a kitchen counter sat Mrs Beeton, a sturdy book titled *Beeton's Book of Household Management*. Isabella Beeton's 1,014-page Bible of middle-class domesticity advised Britain's wives on everything from cooking, cleaning, making social calls and renting a flat to whipping up a batch of home-made hair tonic. Mrs Beeton had died in 1865 during childbirth at the age of twenty-eight, but her advice lived on. It was a measure of how far Margaret Morris had risen in the world that she now had her own Mrs Beeton, a prized wedding gift.

Along with recipes for broiled partridge, stewed rabbit in milk, baked apple pudding and 2,000 other dishes, Mrs Beeton gave Victorian wives advice on how to hire a maid. That was a section Meg could skip. She had little patience for the conventional wisdom that saw maids as lazy, though they worked up to twenty hours a day, and greedy, though they dined on table scraps and paid for the clothes they worked in. Meg hired a local girl and gave her crisp direction on cleaning, washing, dress, manners and other matters, from walking behind the lady of the house when they went out to making sure that Tommy's boots were clean before he went to the links to muddy them. After leading the girl to the grocer's on Market Street to shop for tea and peas, Meg would open wooden drawers stocked with nuts, spices and dried fruit, each drawer holding its own strong scent. She'd leave the grocer her instructions and off they went to the next shop, the golfer's wife with her maid trailing behind her and whispers trailing the maid. The whispers had to do with Meg's fast rise in status. After all, she had been a maid in this very town only months before, unable to say good morning to St Andrews' high-hatted matrons without giving offence, and now she walked down Market Street with her head held high. On social calls she left behind a calling card with Tommy's name on it and another with her own: 'Mrs Thomas Morris Jr'.

Meg and Tommy must have known what a stir their marriage would cause. She was no blushing bride, rather a test case for social mobility, a thirty-year-old from coal country. How had she landed young Tommy Morris? By being quick to lift her crinolines? Despite the gossip, Meg did what she could to fit in. She greeted other wives in the street and spoke knowledgably about the latest fashions from London and the Continent when someone stopped to chat. Tommy's sister Lizzie became a particular friend. Lizzie, who had begun taking chaperoned walks with a Rose Club member named James Hunter, may have joined Meg and other women in one of the town's more comical social experiments of the season, the Flagpole Curriculum.

The well-meaning wives of several R&A members wanted to teach the youngest caddies to read and do figures. That way the boys might rise above their illiterate fathers. After recruiting young women like Meg to be teachers, the R&A wives convened early-morning lessons at the flagpole beside the R&A clubhouse. To keep the lads alert, the ladies served coffee. Unfortunately, the coffee was a stronger diuretic than the tea the boys were accustomed to drinking. They were willing to learn, but their bladders were weak. To the ladies' horror, and Meg's likely amusement, the boys put the flagpole to what was delicately termed 'an ignoble purpose'. They peed on the flagpole; then ran like collies. That spelled the end of reading lessons by the links.

On Sundays, when the links were closed by order of Tom Morris, drums called the town to worship at half past ten. Tommy and Meg, looking stylish but not showy, linked arms and walked up North Street towards the seven-storey tower of Holy Trinity church. A thousand was a middling turnout in St Andrews, a devout town in which the *Citizen* chided those who missed Sunday services. The congregation generated enough body heat to warm the coldest Sabbath, while in the summer, parishioners carried a posey to ward off the thickening scent of all those bodies.

In church, Tommy and Meg mingled with local swells and their wives, professors from the university, bankers, butchers and bakers; the coal-pit bottomer's daughter worshipped within sniffing distance of R&A members. With God's eyes on them, even better-born townspeople were likely to be civil, even friendly. 'Tommy, I hear you've a match coming up,' a gentleman might say. 'You're in fine form. We must have you and your wife over for tea.' Yet no invitation to tea would follow. Tommy was no more welcome in a gentleman's parlour than Meg would be in the sewing circle of the gentleman's wife.

Tommy still had his Rose Club allies. The lack of an annual ball hadn't kept the Rose Club from 'flourishing', according to the *Citizen*, 'yearly adding to its membership and popularity.' In March of 1875 the Rose Club's James Hunter married Lizzie Morris at Holy Trinity church. Tom Morris, who had passed up Tommy and Meg's wedding, was delighted to attend this one along with the rest of his family. Hunter was a favourite of all the Morrises, a bright young businessman who had made a fortune in timber. After an 1865 fire ignited fifty tons of Civil War gunpowder and levelled much of Savannah, Georgia, Hunter sailed to America and helped rebuild the town. Tom was thrilled to see his only daughter wed such a clever and prosperous young merchant. He joked that he and Hunter were in the same business: turning sticks of wood into money.

Hunter repaid Tom's regard for him. As part of his wedding-night revels he threw a party for his new father-in-law and Tom's club-makers. 'On Thursday evening last week,' the *Citizen* reported, 'the workmen in the employment of Mr Thomas Morris were entertained along with a few friends to supper in the Golf Hotel (George Honeyman's) by Mr Hunter on the occasion of his marriage with Miss Morris. Among a variety of suitable toasts "The Newly-Wed Pair" was pledged.' James Hunter would be the Morrises' financial bulwark from this time forward, transforming Lizzie from greenkeeper's daughter to rich man's wife, paying for a new gravel path for Jack to ride from the Morris house to the workshop and easing Tom's lifelong fear of going broke.

In the summer of 1875, the R&A rejoiced at word that Prince Leopold had agreed to be the club's next captain. The following year the prince himself would stand waiting while Tom Morris teed him up, then drive himself into office with a royal cannon boom. Take that, Perth and Prestwick and Musselburgh! There was no longer any doubt as to which club was the hub of golf or which town was the game's true home.

Summer also brought Lammas Fair. A throwback to medieval times, the fair began as a feeing bazaar: men from the countryside would come to town, offering their labour to landowners who needed help at harvest time. The men signalled their availability by walking with pieces of straw in their mouths. By the nineteenth century, Lammas Fair had become a summer festival featuring gypsy caravans, music, dancing, sweet treats and free-flowing beer. A confectioner's stall held rows of pink sugar hearts, gifts for a young husband to offer his wife in exchange for a kiss. Tommy and Meg strolled past jugglers, acrobats, contortionists and dancing monkeys. Perhaps they had their fortunes told in the tent emblazoned *Gypsy Queen*. If the palm-reader was cunning she foretold a happy event, a child coming to the young couple. A baby boy. There was no magic to this. The uncorsetted middle under Meg's dress gave her pregnancy away, and predicting a male child was just good business, a way to snag an extra coin from the happy parents-to-be. A son was said to be a 'double blessing'. The customary gift to new parents was a bottle of whisky if the child was a girl and if the child was a boy, two bottles.

When the Park brothers offered to renew hostilities at North Berwick, Tom welcomed the challenge. There was a tournament coming up in North Berwick on 3 September; he agreed to a foursomes match for twenty-five pounds to be played the following day. Tommy promised to partner his father in the match. For him it was one match among many, but for Tom, another shot at Willie and Mungo Park was a chance to restore his good name. The Parks' supporters claimed that Musselburgh ruled the world in foursomes, thanks to Willie and Mungo's victory the previous autumn – a win they owed to Tom's horrendous putting. Tom knew that golf-watchers were calling him a liability in foursomes, a drag on his son. He knew they said Tommy and Davie Strath made a well-nigh unbeatable duo, while Tommy and Tom were eminently beatable. Bettors made Tommy and Strath heavy favourites in any match they played, but the two Morrises were often underdogs. Like many an aging athlete, Tom was driven to prove his doubters wrong. He was sure he could play as well as ever on a given day. All he needed was the chance. All he needed was the day.

He needed the money, too. Not to live or even prosper – his son-in-law Hunter had eased the fear of penury that spurred men of Tom's generation – but to measure his success or failure. Despite all his progress in the world, Tom was still a crack at heart. He was a gambler, and like most gamblers he knew exactly how his wagers stood. He and Tommy were twenty-five pounds down to the Parks after losing the previous autumn. Tom looked forward to September with a gambler's hunger to get even.

But Tommy was torn. The timing was wrong. Meg was in her ninth month of pregnancy. Her belly was as big and tight as a drum, with the occasional drum beat from inside. The portly town midwife, nicknamed Clootie Dumpling, said Meg's time was at hand. Meg was nearing her confinement, when men were banished while females boiled water, gathered up linens and enacted the bloody drama of childbirth. There had been progress in Clootie Dumpling's time: by 1875 only five women died for every thousand live births. Yet labour and its aftermath, when infections took many more lives, were fearful events.

There was no reason to think Tommy was any more inclined to witness childbirth than any other Victorian man. His view would have matched that of Kipling, who wrote, 'We asked no social questions, we pumped no hidden shame, we never talked obstetrics when the Little Stranger came.' But Tommy was unusually devoted to his wife, whom he showed what Pastor Boyd called 'the strongest possible affection'. Tommy wanted to be with Meg at the onset of her confinement, before she was shrouded in female commotion. He wanted to see her afterwards, to embrace his wife and greet the Little Stranger the two of them had made.

The North Berwick tournament and the foursomes to follow would take him away for three days. But he could hurry home if needed. Meg may have encouraged him to go, placing his hand on her belly and saying, 'Go on. You've done your part here.' Still, ultimately, it would have been Tommy's choice. He decided to honour his pledge to his father.

The journey took more than six hours. The Morris men – newspapers dubbed them 'sire and son' – rode the train from St Andrews to Leuchars, changing there to a train that huffed between fields dotted with sheep. They caught a ferry at Burntisland. The boat was loud, packed elbow to elbow with travellers, some heading for North Berwick to see the golf. They crossed the Firth of Forth to Granton and boarded a train that rattled into Edinburgh's Waverly Station, where they switched an eastbound train that rolled past Holyrood Palace and the rugged brown-green cliff called Arthur's Seat, through humpbacked fields of turnips to the end of the line.

North Berwick is a seaside resort of red sandstone walls and grey tile roofs. Its year-round population of one thousand was less than a good Sabbath turnout at Holy Trinity. The town had two sandy bays, panoramic sea views and a brand-new telegraph office that had recently moved from the foyer of the Dalrymple Arms Hotel to a proper storefront. Town fathers called their burgh 'the Biarritz of the North', though without golfers and the crowds that came in their wake, the beaches and the Dalrymple Arms might have been as lively as Pompeii. The caddies of North Berwick were known for what one golf writer called 'superfluous dress and infinite capacity for fiery liquors', but that was true of caddies everywhere, except for the superfluous dress. The links lay at the foot of Berwick Law, the 600-foot hill that loomed over the town. Visible for miles around, Berwick Law was a long-dead volcano, sculpted into a blunt arrowhead shape by ancient glaciers. Above the tree line the arrowhead was rock patched with grass. From its rounded summit rose an odd relic, a twenty-foot arch that resembled a huge croquet hoop. The arch was the gaping jawbone of a whale, planted up there by early whalers. Over the years, while the world changed and the whalers were replaced by holiday-makers, waders, telegraph operators, golfers and caddies, the jaw went on casting its hungry shadow down the hill. Today its shadow fell on Scotland's best golfers and hundreds of spectators.

'The professional tournament,' *The Field* told its readers, 'has this year been on a more extended scale than formerly, and has on the whole been highly suc-cessful.' In the tournament held on Friday, 3 September, Tommy outgunned a strong field that featured both Park brothers, Bob Fergusson and Davie Strath as well as Tom Morris. Once again Tommy pipped Willie Park by a single stroke, leaving Willie gritting his teeth, cursing his luck. Then came a sudden protest. Another golfer came forward waving his scorecard, claiming he had beaten both Morris and Park. The *Fifeshire Journal* described the card, 'which bore that a Musselburgh professional named Cosgrove had accomplished the three rounds of the green in one less stroke than Morris'. Bob Cosgrove, a decent player but no threat to the leading professionals, was the sort of crack Colonel Fairlie had worried about when he and Tom organized the first Open – the sort who needed a gentleman scorekeeper to keep him from cheating. Cosgrove had tried this trick before. He would shave strokes, turn in a low score and hope to make off with a few pounds. Now Cosgrove waved his scorecard, demanding the seven-pounds first prize, while a mob of his fellow Musselburghers cheered him on. Kindly Bob Fergusson tried to make peace, while his townsmen shouted at the umpire for disqualifying Cosgrove, touching off a row that threatened to become a brawl.

Tommy slipped away with his seven pounds, enjoyed a celebratory dinner with his father and made his weary way to their hotel room for a good night's sleep before their battle with the Park brothers.

Saturday, 4 September 1875 broke clear and cool, a hint of autumn. Beachcombers padded through the sands beside the North Berwick links, pausing to grab for crabs skittering in tide pools. Behind them was Craigleith, a grassy rock 500 yards from shore. Farther out sat Bass Rock, a steep-sided crag protruding from the sea a mile and a half out. Then, as now, the white sides of Bass Rock itched and moved – the motion of tens of thousands of gannets, the snowy sea-birds that nest there. Male gannets fly off to hunt for fish while females stay behind to sit on eggs.

The water at North Berwick may be bluer than the roiled grey of St Andrews Bay, but it is just as cold, as Tom discovered during his morning dip. He met Tommy for breakfast and then they ambled to the links to meet the Musselburgh boys. Newspapers were calling it the 'Morrises' Return', a grudge match pitting the Parks of Musselburgh, who had staked a claim to be foursomes champions of Scotland against the Morrises of St Andrews, who aimed to take back that title along with twenty-five pounds and pocketfuls of side bets. They would go four times around North Berwick's short, quirky nine-hole course where the outbound holes slanted towards beach dunes bordering a defunct old rock quarry overgrown with reeds. Two stone walls angling through the course, could send low approaches caroming backwards. A stand of firs jutting into the links tempted golfers to try to drive over the trees, risking what one prolix golf guide called 'that bourne from which no traveller returns – for if you cannot carry it, the penalty is that for a lost ball, viz., stroke and distance'.

The Morrises and Parks teed off at eleven, encircled by 'a very large number of spectators ... whose numbers were, despite the use of a long rope behind which they were kept, at times rather difficult to manage'. What *The Field* dubbed 'golfomania' was on the rise. Hooligans from Musselburgh tugged at the rope and hooted at the Morrises, while female spectators – another sign of the game's growing popularity – applauded by tapping gloved fingers to their palms. 'The prevailing enthusiasm may be guessed from the fact that in the throng the young lady visitors to North Berwick were numerously represented, all of them resolutely sticking to their posts abreast of the rope.'

The Parks drew first blood when Willie knocked in

a putt and Tommy's bid to answer stayed out. Tommy evened the match at the seventh and the St Andrews men took the eighth as well. The Morrises were one-up. Willie and Mungo struck back with a pair of booming, wind-assisted clouts at the long ninth to pull even. In the second round, the Morrises held a one-hole edge when Tom found a bit of old music in his putter: 'By a clever long put[t], Old Tom increased the lead to two,' said the *Scotsman*. He and Tommy boosted their advantage with help from Mungo, who kept knocking the Parks' ball into bunkers, leaving his fuming brother to slash it out. Then Mungo flubbed a short putt. 'By missing a put[t],' the *Scotsman* grumbled on Willie's behalf, 'Mungo failed to secure a half of the next hole, and through his brother's short-comings Willie had the pleasure of seeing the eighth also go to the Morrises, making their lead "three-up".' After two nine-hole rounds – the midpoint of the match – the Morrises led by four holes. Tom tapped sweet tobacco into his pipe and breathed blue smoke during the luncheon break. He was well pleased. A four-hole lead with eighteen to play wasn't safe, but the day was shaping up nicely. He had already contributed more to the cause than in a dozen other tries as Tommy's partner. Two dozen. Perhaps even more than that. As Hutchison wrote twenty years later, 'never but on one occasion at North Berwick was old Tom much better than a drag upon his son.' That occasion was today.

The third round began at two o'clock. The long Sea Hole, a three-shotter that called for a carry over a jagged, shoulder-high boundary wall, became a six-shotter for the Morrises when Tom duck-hooked a drive: 'On the way to the second hole,' the *Scotsman* reported, 'fortune changed sides. Here Old Tom swerved to the left in his "tee" shot, and brought his son into using the niblick.' Tommy slapped the Morris ball from a bad lie to a worse one, and Tom's next swing barely moved it. Meanwhile, the Parks' gutty flew to the green. When Tommy's aggressive approach 'came to grief in a bunker', his father picked up the ball. The hole was lost, but they were still four-up.

Tommy's bold play cost his side again when he tried to putt through the long, rocky bunker on the Trap Hole, a play the *Scotsman* deemed foolish: 'Young Tom gave the hole to his opponents . . . the youngster had an easy iron lift to the green, but taking his putter, and trying to run the ball across the bunker, he failed.' The shot skipped into the sand and died short of the green.

Willie and Mungo were whittling away at the Morrises' lead. They looked certain to pull within two at the next hole, where Tommy flailed at a bunkered ball only to see it catch the lip, pop straight up and roll between his boots. Tom had to get the next one close to keep the Morrises alive on the hole. 'This the veteran did beautifully,' the *Scotsman* reported. With his coat tails flapping, Tom sent a spray of sand towards the pin, the ball floating through chunks of flying sand to a skidding halt inches from the cup.

Tommy grinned, clapping his hands. The Parks could still claim the hole by getting down in two, but after Willie ran a thirty-foot putt to tap-in distance, Mungo blew the tap-in.

Tom's bunker shot had reversed the tide. Mungo, desperate to redeem himself, knocked an approach at the eighth hole over the flag, over the green and half the beach, 'overshooting . . . and running down to the seaside'. Willie hit a skilful pitch from there, but Mungo's putt stopped four feet short and Willie missed from there. Mungo, the current champion golfer of Scotland, must have wished he were on a boat to Zanzibar. When the sides matched perfect fours at the ninth, the third round finished the way it began. With nine holes to play, the St Andrews men were four to the good.

In the last round, the Parks got one back at the first hole and stole another at the second when 'the Morrises found luck against them, as Old Tom had to play . . . from a bunker, while a promising swipe of his son's was afterwards caught and spoiled on the top of a knoll'. Tom and Tommy won the fourth hole to go three-up with five to play, but saw the fifth snatched away by 'an admirable long put[t] of Mungo's, which somewhat redeemed the champion's character'. At the next, where Tommy 'played into a nasty hazard to the left of the green', the Parks sliced their deficit to a single hole. Now the course swept downhill, with the outward holes to the left and a seven-foot wall protecting the seaside villas to the right. 'The excitement among the onlookers was now intense, and it was doubly increased at the next hole, where Willie holed from fully a dozen yards' distance, making the match "all even".' Park-fanatics cheered and threw their hats. Bettors called out odds for new wagers on the duel of the year, a thirty-six-hole contest that was deadlocked with two holes to play. The crowd bubbled around the golfers as they stepped to the teeing-ground at North Berwick's eighth hole. Few noticed a boy moving through the gallery, a messenger from the telegraph office.

The Parks had the honour. Willie spoke to Mungo, who nodded. Tommy stood alone, staring at the green.

The messenger pushed through the crowd. He held a slip of paper, a telegram addressed to Thomas Morris. Which man was that? The spectators pointed and said that there were two Thomas Morrises, father and son. But leave them be, they are busily engaged, playing golf for twenty-five pounds.

The messenger couldn't wait. The telegram was urgent. He handed it to Tom, who read it while the others were playing.

Come home, the telegram said.

It was from St Andrews – probably sent by a frantic Jimmy Morris. Margaret's labour had begun, the telegram said, and she was struggling. *Come home post-haste.*

The bleeding would not stop. Meg lay in her new cast-metal bed, swaddled in sheets soaked with sweat and blood. Her sister-in-law Lizzie squeezed her hand. Clootie Dumpling, the midwife, ran for fresh rags to soak up the blood. An external cut might be cauterized with a red-hot iron from the hearth, but there was nothing to do about blood from inside but soak it up and pray. Clootie Dumpling brought rags and when the rags were full of blood she took fine new linens and bunched them between Meg's legs and Meg wailed, for her hopes must surely be gone if they were using her wedding linens to soak up her blood.

The midwife sent for Doctor Moir.

Tom Morris stood in the hubbub on the North Berwick links, reading the telegram from St Andrews. *Come home post-haste.*

If he and Tommy left now they would lose. They would lose the match, the twenty-five-pound stake and side bets of more than that, and Tom's field day would amount to nothing.

On the other hand, difficult births were common. Margaret might be cradling her child in her arms by now. In any case, time was surely not the issue. He and Tommy were six to eight hours from home and the match was almost over. Walking in from here would save a few minutes at most, and the next train wouldn't leave for hours. How much difference could a few minutes make?

Tom put the telegram in his pocket.

On the penultimate hole, Willie Park hooked his drive into a bunker. The ball ran up the face and stopped. All Mungo could do was chip out sideways. The Parks would be lucky to make six while the Morrises, 'who took a capital road for the pin,' lay twenty-five feet from the hole in three. Tommy could have cozied one close for his father to tap in. He probably should have; instead he tried to make the putt. He set up over the Morrises' ball, drew his putter back until it nearly touched his boot, and sent the ball barrelling across the green.

'Duck in!'

Now there was no ball. It had fallen in, knocking all the wind out of the Parks' loud, fist-waving crowd.

The mob wasn't quiet for long. According to the *Scotsman*, 'The Morrises were in this way "dormy", but the game for the last hole was watched with the greatest closeness by every one on the green, the spectators crowding in at times and giving expression to their sympathies in a not very becoming way.' From the last teeing-ground the golfers aimed for the far-off green between Bass Rock and the left flank of Berwick Law. 'After the "tee" shot things did not look too well for the Musselburgh players, as their ball lay rather badly.' But Willie's recovery put the Parks' ball near the green and Tommy overcooked his approach. The ball came flying in like a hornet, headed for trouble only to take a crazy, lucky bounce, a rub of the green that led the Parks' supporters to wonder why heaven so favoured Tommy Morris. '[H]ad it not been for a lucky "rub" which his ball came in for, it would no doubt have been into a bunker, and the result of the game might have been different. As it was, both holed out in five, the match consequently being gained by the Morrises by one hole.'

The crowd gave the winners a grudging round of applause for what the *Fifeshire Journal* would rate 'one of the best-contested matches ever seen'.

Tom pulled his son aside. 'We must go,' he said. 'Your wife is ill.'

They couldn't go home the way they came. There would be no train out of North Berwick until seven o'clock, almost three hours hence. They could take a horse-drawn coach to Waverly Station in Edinburgh, catch a train to Granton and reach the ferry dock around sundown, but by then the last ferry would be gone. Ferries from Granton couldn't cross the Firth of Forth after dusk; there were no lights at Burntisland on the other side.

Tommy looked across the Forth with mounting

fear. He saw the low hills of Fife blue in the distance, fifteen miles away.

'I'll take you,' said J.C.B. Lewis, a gentleman golfer who kept a yacht in North Berwick's little harbour. 'We'll sail across.' Lewis pointed to a twenty-eight-foot ketch bobbing in choppy water at the foot of the links.

He rounded up a two-man crew and off they went – Lewis and Tom chatting, Tommy with nothing to do but watch the sun sink over Scotland.

A myth would grow up around their journey. In the myth the yacht races across the firth as if it were a river, the Morrises' hobnailed boots clanking from the North Berwick dock to the St Andrews pier in an hour or two. In fact it was a long night's voyage, thirty-two miles in a ketch that made four knots in calm seas. Such a trip would take at least eight hours, which means that they could not have reached St Andrews before one in the morning.

The sun was already falling when Lewis' crew hoisted sail and the boat swung out of North Berwick's little harbour. Behind them a handful of Tommy's friends waved from the pier, wishing him Godspeed.

The yacht glided past white-faced Bass Rock and made for the Isle of May, a grey paving stone in the water to the north. Hours later, it slid past the isle on its way to the eastern tip of Fife, and northwest from there towards Crail and St Andrews.

'A long, weary crossing,' Tom recalled years later,

remembering 'the frozen look Tommy had on his face'. The boat rolled as the crew trimmed its sails. Perhaps Lewis cracked open a bottle of porter for his passengers. The stars were thick and clear, the yacht's lanterns the only other light. Midnight came and went. They heard the hull slapping the water. They kept watch for the Bell Rock lighthouse that would give them a line to their target. At last they saw it: three long beats of light followed by two short ones, the signature of the lighthouse at Bell Rock.

The yacht curved left like a putt on the Home Hole. Soon it found its way to the long stone pier. The town was pitch dark, the lamplighter having snuffed out the last streetlamp hours ago. The time was between one and four in the morning.

They heard Jimmy's voice. 'Father! Tommy!' The telegraph office had closed just after word arrived from North Berwick saying that Tom and Tommy were coming home by boat. Nineteen-year-old Jimmy had gone to the pier to wait for them.

At the end of the pier a set of stone steps rose out of the water. Tommy clambered out of the yacht, splashed onto the lowest step and hurried up to the pier. His father thanked Lewis and followed. The stars cast a pale light, just enough to keep a man from stepping off the pier into the black water. Jimmy spoke to Tom for a moment, saying something Tommy didn't hear.

Tommy walked 300 yards up the pier to the corner

of town where the fisher-folk lived. The air smelled off fish. He set off towards North Street.

The next day's *Scotsman* would tell of a second telegram that had gone from St Andrews to North Berwick on 4 September, arriving moments after Lewis' yacht departed: '[T]hey had just cleared the harbour, and were hoisting sail, when a messenger reached the pier bearing another telegram stating that Mrs Morris had given birth to a son, but that both mother and child were dead. The purport of the message being made known to a number of [Tommy's] friends who had been seeing him off, they agreed, although the yacht was within easy hailing distance, to allow it to sail without acquainting those on board with the distressing news, fearing that the shock to the unhappy husband would be too great.'

Jimmy had whispered the news to his father. Now Tom had to say it aloud.

'Tommy, it's over,' he said. Margaret was dead, he said. The baby was dead. He was sorry, he said.

Tommy started home. He walked past the fisher pubs, the Auld Hoose and the Bell Rock Tavern. It was a mile from the pier to the house where he and Meg lived. Their house was at the western end of town, the links end, where the air smelled of grass and seaweed. The houses he passed were all dark, but yellow light leaked through drawn blinds at the house ahead of him, 2 Playfair Place, Tommy and Meg's house. The front door was darker than the street, recessed by six inches, hidden from starlight. Inside he found his mother propped in a chair, his sister Lizzie and brother Jack and the country parson himself, the Rev A.K.H. Boyd, all waiting for Tommy to come home.

'There was a pathetic event here at the beginning of September,' Pastor Boyd wrote. 'On Thursday, 2 September, father and son went together to North Berwick to play a great match on the links there. Tommy left his wife perfectly well ... But on Saturday afternoon that fine girl ... ran down and died. A telegram was sent to Tom, who told his son they must leave at once ... I was in the house [when] they arrived. What can one say in such an hour? I never forget the young man's stony look: *stricken* was the word: and how all of a sudden he started up and cried, "It's not true!" I have seen many sorrowful things, but not many like that Saturday night.'

Tommy hurried to the bedroom.

# TWELVE

## *Winter*

THE BLOOD WAS gone, soaked up in sheets that were soon to be burned, but the scent of blood hung in the room. Meg lay in bed as if she were asleep. Beside her was a bundle no bigger than a cat. Male, the doctor said. A son. Stillborn, the doctor said, meaning that the child had not died in the womb but in the struggle to be born, a struggle that lasted four hours according to Dr Moir, who reduced Meg's dying to two crisply penned lines in the town's death registry: *Ruptured uterus, four hours.*

Tommy sagged. 'It's not true.' After that night, wrote Tulloch, 'He went about like one who had received a mortal blow.'

In the coming days, he let his father do most of what had to be done. It was Tom Morris who signed the death registry on behalf of the family. It was Tom who handled many of the funeral arrangements. There was whisky to buy, for one thing, for custom called for everyone visiting a house where a death had occurred to be offered a dram. Tommy roused himself enough to take a sip from time to time, feeling it warm his gullet like hot tea. He had little energy for choosing an elm coffin for Meg; or for buying a white linen mortcloth to wrap around her body and a smaller mortcloth for her stillborn child; or for hiring a hearse and a team of black horses to pull the hearse to the cathedral cemetery; or for selecting a Bible verse for Meg's memorial cards, the black-bordered reminders that urged recipients to remember Margaret Morris and to pray for her soul. Such matters were better left to his father, the diplomat. Tom Morris was a gracious host, shaking hands, offering each visitor a drink, making solemn small talk while Tommy did his best to nod hello.

The blinds in Tommy and Meg's house stayed shut until the hearse came later that week to carry her away. The Morrises gave Meg a funeral like no Whitburn girl could ever have expected. Nothing signalled respectability like a fine funeral. Whitburn's poor, like the poor everywhere, dreaded getting a pauper's burial, a hurried ride to the cemetery behind a drunken coachman singing, 'Rattle his bones over the stones, he's only a pauper nobody owns.' Tenement-dwellers paid a penny a week to burial societies that provided decent funerals for three or four pounds. A successful tradesman could be laid to rest for twenty pounds, his wife for ten pounds. But Meg's funeral was a fifty-pound affair. No one put the price in the newspaper or even said it aloud, but the point was made by the hearse, the team of horses pulling it and the coachmen with their silk scarves and top hats with black silk hatbands. The point was that the deceased was no sinner and no housemaid but a respectable wife, her soul recommended to heaven by the Reverend A.K.H. Boyd.

For Tommy, still staggered by Saturday's events, Meg's funeral was likely a blurred parade of black-clad mourners on green turf, Meg's relatives filing past in the same clothes they had worn to her wedding a few months before; the pastor mumbling prayers beside Wee Tom's old white stone and a pile of porridge-coloured earth. The grave went more than ten feet down into the cathedral churchyard. Cemetery plots were expensive, so families dug deep and sometimes buried as many as ten family members in a vertical queue. Meg's elm coffin held two bodies, for she was buried with her stillborn son in her arms.

If Tommy blamed his father for hiding the truth from him at North Berwick, he also loved his father enough to forgive him, or at least to try. In fact he moved back into his father's house. Tommy gathered up his clothes, razor, pocket-watch and Championship Belt and carried them the short distance west to 6 Pilmour Links Road, where he slept in a drafty room in the attic.

Everyone wanted him to play golf. The game had not stopped to mourn Margaret. Willie Park won the Open at Prestwick that autumn while Tom and Tommy grieved in St Andrews. 'It was a matter of much regret that severe family bereavement should have caused the absences of the Morrises,' *The Field* noted. 'During the entire day the links presented a scene of gaiety and animation.' Tommy's friends kept saying a match would take his mind off his grief, if only for a few hours, and wasn't that what he needed? His father thought so. 'Just when you want to lay down and die, a good tight match will clear your brain,' Tom said. Tommy was more inclined to take late-evening walks or to sit and drink, a habit he indulged in more often as the days grew shorter. But in early October, a month after Meg died, he agreed to play. Along with Davie Strath, Mungo Park and Bob Cosgrove, the Musselburgh stroke-shaver, he entered the 1875 St Andrews Professional Tournament. 'Tommy ... had been out of practice,' *The Field* reported, adding that he lacked 'his usual force and brilliancy' off the tee, but swung with his usual flair 'whenever the iron or cleek was put into his hands'. Wearing a black armband that marked him as St Andrews' youngest widower, he shot a tepid 93 and finished fifth.

Next he joined his father in a foursomes match against Strath and another professional, Bob Martin. With hundreds of spectators in his wake, Tommy showed flashes of his old form, drilling balls into the wind and rapping putts that thudded into the back of the cup on their way down. He and Tom took a four-hole lead to the fourteenth tee. 'The match seemed to be finished,' according to Tulloch, 'when Tommy broke down.' Suddenly he could do nothing right. He bunkered his drives, foozled approach shots. Too weak or half-hearted to summon up a rally at the end, Tommy plodded through the Valley of Sin to the eighteenth green. 'They lost every one of the remaining five holes and, consequently, the match.'

On the night of 27 October the ship *Fantee* ran aground in heavy seas just north of St Andrews Castle. The *Fantee* turned sideways and began to break apart in rocks a hundred yards offshore. Sailors lit torches to signal their distress. Few of them could swim, for knowing how to swim was thought to be unlucky in sailors, a sort of hubris that dared the sea to sink their ships. But even the most accomplished swimmer would have struggled in that night's thundering waves. The St Andrews lifeboat fought the storm for several minutes before turning back.

Like the meteor shower of '72, the wreck of the *Fantee* brought townspeople flocking to the shore. Tommy was probably among them, watching. If he was out walking that night, he may have been among the first to see the ship's torches. Soon the town's rocket brigade set up two cannons in the castle ramparts. The rocket brigade was the sailors' last chance. With blasts that shook the castle walls, its cannons launched rocket-driven lifelines towards the ship. 'Port fires and blue lights were burned,' the *Citizen* reported, 'which illuminated, with an almost unearthly light, the surroundings, the vessel as well as the castle ruin, and lit up hundreds of pale anxious faces of those who clustered on its walls.' After several tries, one of the lifelines found its target. Sailors lashed it down and began pulling themselves hand over hand through waves and rocks to the beach. 'As man after man was brought safely to land, a cheer rent the air.' Cheering would have echoed oddly in Tommy's ear. Aside from a few shouts during his failed outings of the past month, the last cheering he'd heard was on the day he and his father played the Park brothers at North Berwick.

The next morning, men with axes rowed out to the *Fantee* and chopped it up for salvage. By nightfall there was nothing left of the ship but its men, drinking and singing in St Andrews' pubs. They were the lucky ones. A month later a storm took down three ships and thirty-seven men.

'At this time there was a great golfing family from Westward Ho! playing splendid golf,' Tulloch wrote, 'winning great victories wherever they went.' The golfing family's patriarch was Captain George Moles-worth, a wealthy amateur who played with only three clubs: a driver he called Faith, a cleek known as Hope and a putter called Charity. Captain Molesworth took out advertisements in *The Field* challenging any other father-and-son pair to play him and one of his three sons, the best of whom was eighteen-year-old Arthur. Tom and Tommy had never responded to Molesworth's challenge. They had nothing to gain by playing English dabblers who would want strokes or odds in a match against professionals. Then, in the autumn of 1875, Arthur Molesworth challenged Tommy to single combat.

The men of the Rose Club were all for it. What better tonic than demolishing a teenaged golf celebrity from England? 'Tommy's friends readily entered into it with the view of rousing him,' wrote George Bruce, 'trying to infuse new life and vigour into his withered feelings.' Tommy's friends pushed him to play the lad, whose victory in the club championship at Westward Ho! made him an amateur prodigy, at least in his father's eyes. *The Field*, parroting the captain's claims, informed readers that young Arthur 'has been successful in matches against a professional player from St Andrews'. That player was, happily for himself, not named. Whoever he was, he was nowhere near Tommy's level and the Molesworths, knowing as much, set daunting terms: Arthur would play Tommy Morris only if he got six strokes per round in a punishing six-day, twelve-round match. Tommy would thus be giving young Molesworth seventy-two strokes. The bait: fifty pounds.

Tommy said yes. 'Young Tom has not been in robust health for some time, but he is now steadily at work and seems to be regaining his wonted vigour,' the *Citizen* declared, adding that the local hero was 'not playing such a strong game as he did in his great matches against Strath ... but on the other hand, he has generally been able to play well at the proper time, and the occasion may bring the play.'

On the last morning of November, Arthur Molesworth arrived at St Andrews' first teeing-ground for his moment in golf history. Six years younger than Tommy, he had the high forehead and wispy moustache of a university man. He shook Tommy's hand in weather *The Field* described as 'exceedingly cold, a strong breeze prevailing off the sea with occasional blasts of snow and hail'. Little David Ayton, shivering as he cradled Tommy's clubs under his arm, teed up a gutty and stepped back, giving his man room to waggle. Thus began a match that would feature what *The Field* would call the worst weather the game had ever seen.

Molesworth announced that he would take his strokes at the second, fifth and eighth holes of each nine. He made them count in the early going. Tommy fell behind in the first round, hitting drives that fell short of his usual distance, but revived himself enough to take the last three holes. After a luncheon break he had a lapse at the fourth hole, Ginger Beer. Tapping in to win the hole while Molesworth's ball sat on the lip of the cup, he misfired. His putt brushed the other ball and both balls fell in. The hole was halved. Still he finished the day two holes up despite his six-stroke handicap. The next day, Wednesday, began with a half after Tommy chipped to the first green from an ice-crusted puddle. He kept his two-hole lead until they reached the short twelfth, which had bedevilled him on and off since its scab-turfed days as the Hole o' Shell. 'Mr Molesworth secured the hole, reducing the lead against him to one,' *The Field* related, using 'Mr' to signify Molesworth's status as a gentleman. 'After this, however, the game went steadily in favour of Young Tom, who had warmed up into his usual style.' On the long fourteenth, where the challenger got a stroke, Molesworth topped his drive into a pot bunker. Soon Tommy was seven holes ahead. That afternoon, Molesworth nearly drove the green with a gust-aided drive at the 300-yard Heathery Hole, but Tommy kept the pressure on, halving the holes on which Molesworth got a stroke, winning more than his share of the rest. At the end of two days' play he led by twelve holes. A third of the way through their wintry marathon, the Englishman looked beaten.

On Friday, *The Field*'s correspondent telegraphed an account that must have pleased his London editors, who had puffed the event as a 'Great Golf Match'. Molesworth's tidy 45 on the outward nine that day beat Tommy's 47 straight up, and with his strokes he chopped three holes off his deficit. The golfers were trading blows like equals. 'That an amateur from England, a stranger to the green, should have ventured into golfing Scotland,' *The Field* gushed, 'required pluck, and Mr Molesworth is not deficient in this quality.'

On Saturday, 4 December, the links were top-dressed with snow. White golf balls would be invisible, so the players used gutties that had been painted red. Tom Morris dispatched workmen with shovels and brooms to clear the putting-greens. Tom, puffing his pipe, followed the players while the tall, stiff-backed Captain Molesworth peered over smaller members of a gallery that would number a thousand before the day was out. Young Arthur Molesworth led early. Making a show of playing in shirtsleeves while everyone else wore jackets and wool hats, he capitalized on his handicap strokes while Tommy struggled to navigate icy greens and bunkers decked with snow. The challenger had a putt to win the Home Hole, but three-putted from point-blank range, his ball skidding twice around the cup. Tommy's edge stood at nine with four rounds remaining.

On Sunday they rested, watching the sky. Dusk came early, a sign of a storm on the way. Most of St Andrews was asleep when the first flakes came down, followed by more and more until the night sky was as pale as Tom's whiskers. 'On Monday ... it was doubtful if the match could be proceeded with,' *The Field* reported. 'A heavy fall of snow had taken place during the night and had drifted into wreaths of considerable depth, while overhead the sky hung thick.' Tommy wanted to stay inside. Chasing a red ball through boot-high drifts was 'no' golf'. Several friends urged him to play, hoping that victory would bolster his spirits, while others told him to sit by the fire with a cup of tea to warm his hands, and perhaps a drop of something stronger to warm the inner man. Tommy had brought a new caddie with him, none other than Davie Strath, and Strath had no desire to see Tommy risk his health to finish off Arthur Molesworth. When the umpire declared the links unplayable, Strath made ready to lead his friend home. But the Molesworths objected: 'Mr Molesworth and his father, Captain Molesworth, stated it would inconvenience them to delay.'

'I'll play,' Tommy said.

In *The Field*'s account he 'waived his objections, and, under a protest from the umpire, who gave it as his opinion that it was not weather for golf, the match was at once proceeded with'.

Why play on frozen links with bunkers full of snow? According to George Bruce, Tommy felt a duty to friends who had bet on him and who would lose their money if he quit. 'He repeatedly remarked to his friends and backers that but for them he would not have continued.'

Even with Tom's workmen shovelling and sweeping, the greens were unputtable. The players chipped on and then chipped their 'putts', trying to flip them into the hole as if they were stymied. That should have given Tommy an edge, but he lost the third hole when Molesworth's long chip bounced into the cup. The challenger had his own misfortune at the next, the Ginger Beer Hole, where his tee shot found a patch of snow 'and in driving out the ball split'. It was trouble enough hitting a frozen gutty that stung your hands with every full swing: worse still to try chipping and putting with two-thirds of a ball.

'The next hole was played amid a blinding shower of snow. Mr Molesworth's ball was buried in a snowdrift, and it took him two to get out; but Tom being short in putting, the hole was halved.' This was comedy, but Tommy looked heartsick. Reaching for the lump of pine tar in his pocket, trying to keep his hands on the club as he swung, he was on his way to a score of 112 – thirty-five strokes over his course record. Molesworth was struggling even more, falling thirteen holes behind, but Tommy seemed not to notice. 'His heart was not in the game,' Tulloch wrote. 'It was, indeed, not very far away – in the snow-clad grave in the old cathedral churchyard, where his wife and baby had been so lately laid.'

Molesworth's best hope was that Tommy would

collapse, as he had in his last foursomes match, or simply give up and leave the challenger to claim the stakes. Instead, Tommy rallied. To his friends it seemed he was emerging from the shadows, regaining his powers. On Wednesday, 8 December, he and Davie Strath made their way to the first hole through ranks of applauding spectators wrapped in wool scarves and fur hats. The novelty of watching golf in curling weather had attracted such a teeming crowd that the umpire called for a rope 'to prevent crushing'.

Strath, lugging Tommy's clubs to the Eden and back, did his best to help his friend through the last two rounds. He urged Tommy on. He picked Tommy's ball from the hole, teed it up and handed Tommy a driver that he swung without a word. They were in accord now, dead-set on finishing, snow and ice be damned. 'The snow still covered the green,' *The Field* noted, 'and frost being very heavy the play, especially putting, was rendered even worse than on the previous day.' Molesworth's handicap stroke got him a hole at the long Hole o' Cross, where both players made nine, but he lost the High Hole when his drive hopped into 'long grass and snow, where he lost two strokes, and his fourth landed deep in a bunker among snow, and it took another two strokes to get the ball fairly *en route* to the hole'.

Tommy had one burst of brilliance left. He took the short tenth and treacherous eleventh 'with four and three respectively, play which could not be excelled even with the green in its best condition'. The match ended on the eighth hole of that day's afternoon round, the 206th hole of the match. By then the greens had thawed. Tommy fired a 150-yard bolt to the Short Hole green and banged in the putt for a two on a day when other holes were won with sevens. His backers hooted and shook their fists. What a finish! The last hole of the year's last match was vintage Tommy – perfectly played.

All evening his friends drank to his victory and his health. Tommy smiled for their benefit, but seemed no more festive than Davie at his most sepulchral. He had hit some clever shots and felt some delight in doing that, even now. But what he felt most of all was cold. He was spent.

'After the match,' Tulloch wrote, 'he continued to be seen on the links and in his old haunts, looking ill and depressed.'

Those who loved Tommy worried that he had risked his health by playing for a solid week in bone-chilling cold. But later in December he showed signs of life. Instead of drinking alone he would meet his brother-in-law James Hunter, Davie Strath, George Bruce and other Rose Club members for dinner at the Criterion or the Cross Keys. He ate boiled beef and potatoes, showing an appetite that heartened his friends. This rally was in character, they thought. On or off the course, in sickness or in health, Tommy's spirit rose to the occasion.

Just before Christmas, he spent two days in Edinburgh. Returning to St Andrews in time to take communion during Watch Night services on Christmas Eve, he met his hometown companions. Perhaps Hunter or Bruce offered a holiday toast to the coming year of 1876. It would have been a muted toast, softly spoken, all of them mindful of Tommy's regrets.

It was near eleven when Tommy came through his father's front door that night, bringing the cold in with him. He went to look in on his mother and found her awake. Nancy, now sixty years old, was so ill with back and stomach ailments that she struggled to sit up in bed. Still, she brightened at the sight of her eldest, her 'extra gift from God' grown up into a man. Tommy sat and talked with her for a time before going upstairs to his bed. A few minutes later his father poked his head into Tommy's room to say goodnight. Then Tom went around the house snuffing out the last lamps and the Morris place was dark until morning.

Tom was up early as always. Soon the fire was lit, a tea kettle whistling. He and Nancy had their breakfast. So did Jimmy and Jack. An hour passed and Tommy still hadn't appeared. Tom went upstairs to wake him.

Tommy was still in bed. His father stood beside the bed, gazing down at his son's handsome face. Tommy looked peaceful, as if he were in a dreamless sleep. There was a spot of blood at one corner of his mouth.

'On the morning of Christmas Day they found him dead in his bed,' Pastor Boyd wrote. 'And so Tommy and his poor young wife were not long divided.'

The *Citizen* was blunter. 'Retiring a little after eleven o'clock on Friday evening, he was found in bed next morning a lifeless corpse,' the newspaper reported. 'A little blood had oozed from his mouth, and the doctor who was called said that death had resulted from an internal haemorrhage.'

Tommy Morris was twenty-four years old.

Generations of Scots have claimed that Young Tom Morris died of a broken heart. 'It makes a nice story, but it's s****,' says David Malcolm of St Andrews, who is a scientist as well as a golf historian. 'He died of a pulmonary embolism due to an inherited weakness. He could have gone at any time.' And yet Tommy died at a particular time, three months after sailing home too late to be with his wife when she died in childbirth, three months in which he drank more than he had before, walked St Andrews' cold streets late at night and played a week-long, 200-hole match through a snowstorm. Grief, drink and the cold may have weakened him until his pulmonary artery ruptured, filling his lungs with blood and drowning him in his sleep.

'The news spread like wild-fire over the links and in the city,' Tulloch wrote. 'Christmas greetings were checked on the lips by the question, "Have you heard the news? Young Tommy is dead!" or the whispered, "It can't be true, is it, that Tommy was found dead in bed this morning?'"

Now it was Tom who was stricken. When John Sorley, the town registrar, came around with the death registry, it was Jimmy, not his father, who signed on the family's behalf. The census of 1871 had identified Tommy as 'Champion Golfer of Scotland'; the death register of 1875 cast him as 'Thomas Morris, Widower'. And now his father had a new round of funeral arrangements to make. Most woeful of all was the chesting service on the Tuesday after Christmas. Friends and relatives gathered in Tom's parlour to talk and pray over legs of lamb and glasses of claret. They wrapped Tommy's body in a pure white linen mortcloth. Then Tommy rode the men's hands, including his father's callused, wavering hands, into his coffin. After a last prayer they screwed the coffin shut. They buried him the next day.

'I have a picture in my mind of the popular young Tom,' the golfer Edward Blackwell wrote of his youth in St Andrews. 'I remember, too, his sad and sudden death, the gloom it cast over St Andrews and, in some respects, the most imposing funeral that has ever taken place at St Andrews.'

Tom Morris, who never wasted a penny in his long life, spent more than £100 to bury his son. He hired a gleaming hearse pulled by black horses festooned

with long, black ostrich feathers. Top-hatted attendants in silk scarves walked ahead of the hearse as
it carried his body to the cathedral cemetery. Half
the town followed the hearse. The cortege was led by
black-clad Morris men: Tom, Jimmy and sixteen-year-
old Jack, pulling himself down South Street. Tommy's
brother-in-law James Hunter was there along with
other Rose Club members, R&A gentlemen, professional golfers, caddies, fisher-folk and hundreds
of others, many carrying wreaths of evergreens and
artificial flowers. Scottish families had been ruined
by less lavish rites, and Tom would soon turn to
Hunter for a £200 loan. But, in these last bitter hours
of 1875, Tom was determined, even desperate, to
give Tommy a champion's funeral, a farewell that
the town would never forget.

'The remains of poor Tommy were yesterday followed to the grave by a large cortege of persons from
all quarters,' the *Citizen* reported on 30 December,
'and the city, usually dull at this season, wore its
gloomiest as the mournful procession deployed
through the streets.' At the cemetery, where the Morris
plot had been dug up yet again, Pastor Boyd prayed
and spoke of resurrection. Tom watched as the coffin
was lowered into the grave that held Tommy's wife
and stillborn child and, below them, the bones of Wee
Tom, buried twenty-five years before.

For months afterwards, Tom wore a black armband
to show that he was in mourning for Tommy. On

Sundays, he kept the links closed and spent much of the day in church, the armband over the sleeve of his Sunday-best jacket while performing his duties as church elder, one of which was to pass around the money bag that functioned as a collection plate, another was to hear parishioners' confessions. It is fair to ask whether Tom second-guessed himself while he listened to the Sunday whispers of truants, blasphemers and impure thinkers. Did Tom Morris feel that he too had something to repent?

# THIRTEEN

## *Grand Old Man*

'A QUARTER OF A century is a very little thing in this city's thousand years,' wrote Pastor Boyd in *Twenty-Five Years of St Andrews*, 'but it is a great thing, and a long time, to us who have lived through it. It has changed those who survive.'

During Tommy's lifetime, the most pivotal quarter of a century in golf history, Tom Morris became the first true golf professional and Tommy became the game's leading man. Now that time was past and Tom, walking uphill from the cemetery, felt the weight of his fifty-four years. He was often quoted in dialect in those days, once by an English writer who heard the mourning father say of Tommy's death, 'It was as if ma vera sowle was a'thegither gane oot o' me.'

Did Tom regret letting the North Berwick match go on while Margaret died? If so he took solace in his faith. *Thy will be done*. And there was at last some good news in the first months of 1876. His daughter Lizzie was expecting a baby. Perhaps Tom would have a grandchild after all. He felt a pang when Lizzie sailed with her husband to America but, in March, he received a telegram announcing the birth of his grandson, born in Darien, Georgia. Lizzie and James Hunter named their child Tommy Morris Hunter.

Lizzie's son was never healthy. He died in May, only two months old. This news was another blow to Tom, but he carried on. What else was there to do? Each morning he changed into his swimming longjohns. He padded out to the dunes, hung his jacket with its black armband on a whin bush, steeled himself and waded into the bay, which was icy in May, merely frosty in June. After his dip he dried off, dressed for work and spent another day supervising workmen ('More sand!'), inspecting caddies, tapping the club secretary's window, replacing divots (a visitor was amazed to see the great man 'taking up bits of cruelly cut turf and placing them in blank spaces with a press of his foot') and partnering R&A golfers as if his soul were intact.

Tom played a leading role that autumn when Prince Leopold drove himself in as captain of the R&A. This was the Royal & Ancient's proudest moment, the first royal visit to St Andrews in more than 200 years. Crowds surged towards the prince's royal railcar at every stop it made on its journey east through Fife; in one village a thousand people turned out to see the train speed by without stopping. On the night of the prince's arrival in St Andrews, townspeople lit every lamp in every building in St Andrews, giving the town a glow that outshone the half-moon that came out that night. At eight the next morning the haemophiliac prince, surrounded by his fretful retinue, stepped from his carriage to the first teeing-ground. Prince Leopold was terrified. How could he hit a golf ball with so many of his subjects watching – and so many caddies, hoping to grab the royal gutty, crowding so close to the tee? Tom Morris came to the rescue. He bowed, tipped his cap and told His Royal Highness to take a smooth, steady swing with his eye fixed on the ball. Tom teed up a ball, using a bit more sand than usual to add height to the shot. Prince Leopold waggled. He swung, the cannon sounded and the ball sailed over all the caddies – it was a drive worthy of the crowd's surprised, delighted applause.

The prince blinked. 'How was that done, Tom?' he asked. 'I never got the ball off the ground before.' After luncheon and a fox hunt, he and Tom beat two R&A golfers in a six-hole match.

Later that week came the second Open ever held at St Andrews. Davie Strath led for most of the day and had the Claret Jug within reach as he played the Road Hole. Unluckily for him, the R&A had failed to reserve the links for the tournament, leaving the professionals to share the course with the usual four-somes of gentleman golfers. Playing the Road Hole in semi-darkness at the end of a long, slow round, Strath saw a crowd around the green. Spectators, he thought.

He let fly and watched his approach shot bean a local upholsterer named Hutton who was lining up a putt. Mr Hutton keeled over as if he'd been shot. He was still rubbing his head as Strath, shaken, putted out for a six and then made another six on the Home Hole to tie Bob Martin for first place in the Open. But tournament officials questioned Strath's score. He may have played out of turn, they said, and skulling Mr Hutton may have saved him a stroke. If he won his playoff with Martin tomorrow morning, they might still disqualify him.

Strath, who had defied another red-coated committee the day he declared himself a professional, refused to play under such a threat. 'Settle it now or I won't be here in the morning,' he said. The officials refused, Davie stuck to his word and Martin claimed the Claret Jug by walking the course the next morning.

Tom Morris came in fourth, his best Open finish since 1872, then went home to help tend his wife in the stone house at 6 Pilmour Links Road. Nancy, sixty-one years old, was in constant pain. A white bedpan called a 'slipper' was a boon to her. The slipper was a ceramic wedge that slid under a patient who could not sit up. Nancy lamented the indignity of using such a thing. She lamented the loss of her children and grandchildren and on 1 November 1876, All Saints' Day, she joined them in heaven, as Pastor Boyd put it, leaving Tom to arrange yet another funeral. After which he returned to his duties in his shop and on the links. Old Tom was a marvel, people said. In little more than a year he had buried Tommy, Tommy's wife, their stillborn son, grandson Tommy Morris Hunter and now Nancy. Five dead and Tom was still standing. When a writer asked about the cause of Tommy's death, Tom said he didn't believe that grief could kill a man. 'People say he died of a broken heart,' he said, 'but if that was true, I wouldn't be here.'

Two Septembers later, Tom, Jimmy and several hundred others gathered around the Morris plot in the cathedral cemetery. Sixty Scottish and English golf societies had commissioned a Tommy Morris monument. It was a sign of golf's growing importance that a representative of the Crown, John Inglis, Lord Justice General of Scotland, presided over its unveiling. The monument, which still stands in the south wall of the churchyard, shows Tommy in his tweeds and his Balmoral bonnet, preparing to drive a ball over the cemetery to the sea. 'In memory of "Tommy", son of Thomas Morris,' reads the plaque at his feet. 'Deeply regretted by numerous friends and all golfers, he thrice in succession won the Championship Belt and held it without envy, his many amiable qualities being no less acknowledged than his golfing achievements.'

'Ladies and gentlemen,' said Inglis. 'We are met to inaugurate a monument to the memory of the late

Tommy Morris, younger.' With that the Lord Justice General nodded towards the honoree's father. 'You will allow me to say that we have some consolation still, for we still have a Tom Morris left – Old Tom – and I may venture to say that there is life in that old dog yet.'

After Tommy died, Tom cut back on the money matches he had lived for. He devoted more time to promoting golf and making sure that golfers remembered what Tommy had done. Tom went on to lay out more than sixty courses, including County Down, Dornoch, Macrihanish and Muirfield. Building a course – clearing whins, digging and filling bunkers, turfing greens – could cost £100 to £300, but Tom's fee for designing one never varied. He charged one pound per day, often completing his work in a single day. And, wherever he went in Scotland, England, Ireland and Wales he spun tales of his famous son.

Old Tom's rustic charm played well on the road. After hiking some barren, wind-burnt heath for half an hour he would turn to his hosts and say, 'Surely Providence meant this to be a golf links.' Each course he laid out was 'the finest in the kingdom, second only to St Andrews', at least until he laid out the next one. Tom showed novice greenkeepers how to top-dress and rake putting-greens. He pioneered inland golf by introducing horse-drawn mowers for fairways and push-mowers for greens. Beyond that his work as a course-maker consisted largely of walking and pointing. 'Put a hole here. Put another over there,' he would say, leaving plenty of time for a free lunch before he headed back to the railway station. If he stayed all day it was often to be feted as a visiting dignitary. After a singer serenaded him at one lavish lunch, Tom said, 'I did no' think much of her diction.' No one had the heart to tell him she'd been singing in French.

Still, the old greenkeeper was sly enough to have some fun with an Englishman who saw him rolling putts one day.

'What! Do you play the game?' the man said.

'Oh, aye,' said Tom Morris. 'I've tried it once or twice.'

In 1886, Tom went to Dornoch in the Highlands, 110 miles north of St Andrews, a cold whisper from the Arctic Circle, to extend the links there to eighteen holes. The Dornoch Golf Club's junior champion was a boy named Donald Ross, a carpenter's apprentice who tagged along while the old man hiked the dunes overlooking Dornoch Firth. Five years later, Ross left home to work for Tom at St Andrews. He may have helped Tom build a new course on the ancient links. Called simply the New Course, Tom's layout was in some ways better than the original, which has been known ever since as the Old Course. Ross returned to Dornoch for a stint as the club's greenkeeper before moving to America in 1899, his head full of pictures of Tom's links: elevated greens, grassy hollows and hungry bunkers; subtle deceptions that rewarded local knowledge. Over the next half-century he would design Pinehurst #2, Seminole, Oak Hill, Oakland Hills and more than 500 other courses that made Donald Ross the most important golf-course architect of all. Even if Tom Morris had never seen Prestwick or planted a flag at County Down, his influence on Ross would still make him a crucial figure in the game's evolution. But Ross was only one of his disciples. Charles Blair Macdonald kept a locker in Tom's shop before he crossed the Atlantic to build America's first eighteen-hole course at the Chicago Golf Club and the National Golf Links of America, a bit of Scotland in Southampton, New York. Alister Mackenzie studied Tom's handiwork before designing Cypress Point in California, Royal Melbourne in Australia and, with Bobby Jones, Augusta National; Mackenzie titled his book on course design *The Spirit of St Andrews*. Albert Tillinghast, who learned the game from Tom, went on to lay out Baltusrol, Bethpage and Winged Foot. Harry Colt, who spent boyhood summers at St Andrews, improved Tom's Muirfield links before working with the American George Crump to fashion Pine Valley, a course many regard as the world's finest. In the last analysis, Tom Morris' chief contribution to the game may have been in course design, a multi-billion-dollar business that grew from the barrow, spade and shovel he used at Prestwick and St Andrews.

Not far from Alister Mackenzie's locker in Tom's workshop was another wooden locker, a relic that held Tommy's clubs and club-making tools. 'Undisturbed since he last touched it,' Tom said. But he often disturbed it. While showing a visitor around the shop, filling the fellow's ears with well-worn stories, Tom would open the locker and pluck out a club. 'This was Tommy's last putter,' he would say, or 'Tommy's last niblick', placing the stick in the visitor's hand. 'Take it – keep it.' Of course, his workshop turned out putters and niblicks by the gross; this so-called relic, part of a growing supply of 'Tommy's last clubs', could be replaced tomorrow. Cynics would call him a showboat, but Tom wasn't showing off. He knew that every golfer who left with one of those clubs would spread the gospel of Tommy Morris.

Tom surprised himself by playing better as his beard turned white. He couldn't drive the ball 180 yards anymore, or even 150 – 'I can no' get through the ball,' he told Andra Kirkaldy – but his yips disappeared. Tom Morris was now the maker of short putts. 'I never miss them now,' he said. After winning a tournament at Hoylake, he celebrated his sixty-fourth birthday by shooting 81 at St Andrews, only four strokes off Tommy's famous course record. He did it with ten fives, seven fours and a three – the only time Tom ever went around the old links without a six on his card. 'No' that ill for an old horse!' he crowed.

By then Old Tom had another nickname. He was golf's 'G.O.M.', short for grand old man. The term was borrowed from Prime Minister William Gladstone, who had been the original G.O.M.. (His rival Disraeli said the letters stood for 'God's only mistake'.) Twelve years younger than Gladstone, Tom was no less grand to golfers, though his latest honorific puzzled one grumpy old Musselburgher. The aging, ailing Willie Park had outplayed Tom through most of their careers only to see his rival hailed as the game's patron saint.

In 1879, at a tournament in haunted North Berwick, Tom and Willie had finished far behind younger professionals while drawing the day's biggest crowds. Three years later, Tom did his fellow warhorse a favour: he agreed to play Park for £200. Tom was sixty years old, Park was forty-nine. Their last battle was, in effect, the first senior golf event. 'No match of recent years has created anything like the excitement attached to this,' proclaimed *The Field*. Tom had little to gain, but made the match because it would bring one last week of headlines as well as a hefty fee. Still, Tom's sympathy ended at the first teeing-ground. With more than a thousand spectators following the match, he stung the hole with sharp short putts and beat Park by four.

Soon a man whose sole vice was his briar pipe saw his photograph on cigarette packages. Pictures of Tom seemed to be everywhere. Thomas Rodger, the calotype artist who had photographed Tommy in the Championship Belt, superimposed an image of Tom over an image of a river to make a postcard showing Tom walking on water. Its subject wanted no part of such blasphemy . . . the card was a bestseller.

Golfers from as far off as India and America wrote to the venerable Morris, whose word was law wherever the game was played. One summer, a St Andrews boy named Freddie Tait, son of the professor who had painted golf balls with glowing phosphorous, hit a drive that tore a hole in a bystander's hat. Tom told young Tait to buy the victim a new hat. 'Be glad 'tis only a hat you'll buy,' he said, 'and not a coffin.' That was a rare penalty for Tait, who was golden like Tommy, so lucky that when he dropped a hunting knife while wading in the bay, he found the knife by stepping on it – its blade sticking straight up between two of his toes. He grew up to be a gentleman golfer and soldier. After winning the Amateur Championship in 1896 and '98 and getting shot in the leg during the Boer War in 1899, Freddie Tait rushed back into battle a month later and was shot in the heart. He was thirty.

By then Prince Leopold had slipped on wet stairs at the yacht club in Cannes, France, cracking his knee and dying in a haze of blood and morphine. He too was thirty. Two years after that, Tom's son-in-law, James Hunter, died in Georgia aged thirty-seven. Lizzie brought her husband's body and her four surviving children back home to St Andrews where she helped look after Tom.

Davie Strath saw his money-match prospects dry up after Tommy died. Strath became greenkeeper at North Berwick, then fled to Oz to preserve his health. 'Oz' was what Scots called Australia, where warm January afternoons were thought to save consumptives' lives. Davie had begun coughing blood by the time he booked his passage to Melbourne, a trip that took eighty-four days. His throat closed on the way and he died speechless in 1879, three years before a German scientist identified the tubercule bacillus.

Jack Morris, Tommy's paraplegic brother, worked late in his father's workshop on the night of 21 February 1893. Jack, thirty-three years old, had been 'making golf balls up to a late hour', according to the *Citizen*, 'and on retiring to rest was in his usual health.' He died in his bed. 'It is understood death was caused by a spasm of the heart.' In fact Jack's heart may have stopped after his pulmonary artery ruptured, just as Tommy's had done.

'Tom has had his share of trial,' a friend wrote. 'His wife and children are dead, save two – Jimmy and his only daughter, a young widow.' Still Tom kept his chin aimed towards heaven. Being gloomy was a bit of a sin, he said, because it suggested that we know the Lord's business better than He does.

All Tom knew for certain was that the game he and Tommy loved, the game poor Jack, Prince Leopold, Lang Willie, Colonel Fairlie, Lord Eglinton, Willie Park, Davie Strath and countless others all loved was thriving. There had been only seven golf societies in Britain in 1800 and twenty-five in 1860, but there were sixty in 1880 and 357 in 1890. By 1900 there would be 2,330.

In the autumn of 1895, twenty years after Tommy died, Tom played in his last Open. He was seventy-four years old, a deadeye with the putter but too weak to muscle the ball from a heavy lie in one of his bunkers. Attended by a crowd that had more than its share of grey whiskers, he came in seventy shots behind winner J.H. Taylor from Devon, the same Johnny Taylor who had mistaken Tom for St Andrew thirty years before. And with that, Tom bowed out of the tournament he helped create. He had played in twenty-seven Open Championships including the first fourteen, winning four times and striking more than 5,000 shots in Open competition. Now he was content to light his pipe and watch younger men play, though he still served as starter when the tournament returned to St Andrews, giving each pairing a word of encouragement before nodding and saying, 'You may go now, gentlemen.' He also teed up the incoming R&A captain at each autumn's Driving-In ceremony. Unlike Tommy, he never chafed at serving other men. 'I've always tried – as my business it was – to make myself pleasant to them,' Tom said of his employers. 'And they've been awful pleasant to me.'

In 1898, Lizzie Morris died aged forty-five and was buried in the Morris plot in the cathedral cemetery. Her father mourned his only daughter, putting a black armband over his sleeve yet again. He doted on her children, his only grandchildren. And still he carried on, bunting a gutty around the links with provosts, professors and statesmen including a pair of future prime ministers, Arthur Balfour and H.H. Asquith. No visitor escaped his promotion of golf and of what he called 'my dear native town', or his many tales of Tommy's brilliance.

Even after his back bent under the weight of his years, Tom never lost his good humour. When a neighbour bought an expensive telescope, golf's G.O.M. took a look at the moon and said: 'Faith, sir, she's terrible full o' bunkers.' In 1902, the year Tom got a ride in the town's first automobile, the R&A commissioned a portrait of him by Sir George Reid, president of the Royal Scottish Academy. Tom duly reported to Reid's studio in Edinburgh, where he sat for the better part of a week. When the renowned artist asked him to strike a golfing pose, Tom stuck a hand in his pocket and stood frozen in place. Reid asked what he was doing. 'Waiting for the other man to begin,' Tom said. After Reid's portrait of him went up in the R&A clubhouse, where it still hangs today, an observer described Tom's reaction: 'He gazed upon it mutely for some time, and then remarked, "The cap's like mine."'

In 1906, the year Tom turned eighty-five, Jimmy Morris died at the age of fifty-two. A good player but never a great one, he had led the 1876 Open with two holes to go, but took nine swings on the Road Hole. He led at Prestwick in 1878 until Jamie Anderson pipped him with help from an ace at the penultimate hole, where Anderson's ball struck a hill behind the green and rolled back into the cup. Nine years later Jimmy matched Tommy's 77 on their home links and briefly shared the course record, but soon another golfer shot 74. After that he lived quietly, managing his father's shop. And after a grand funeral, with flags flying at half mast all over town, Jimmy joined his siblings and his mother in the Morris plot in the cathedral cemetery. And still Tom lived on.

In his last years, Tom wore a great black overcoat and leaned on a cane. He kept his shoes, heavy brown brogues, polished to a mirror shine. His walks on the links were now confined to the acres near his shop. A collie named Silver, his constant companion, would wait for hours outside the shop, then bound up when Tom came out and fall in step behind him as he fired up his pipe and set off towards town or teeing-ground.

Tom's visits to the cathedral churchyard were his hardest work. His rusty knees made it a chore to find sure footing in the grass. Like any man of eighty-five he was afraid of slipping. Sometimes he leaned on a gravestone. Even in summer the stones were cool to the touch. Here was Allan Robertson's head-high obelisk with its bust of Allan on top. Nearby lay Tom Kidd, the dapper long driver who used his ribbed cleeks to beat Tommy at the watery Open of 1873. Jamie Anderson was here too, in an unmarked grave. Tom was surely glad that Jamie's father, Auld Daw, had gone sooner and was therefore spared that knowledge. Auld Daw had often bragged of how he had put Jamie through college with coin from his ginger-beer cart. But, after winning the Open in 1877, '78 and '79, Jamie developed a thirst for fine whisky that became in time a thirst for whisky of any sort. He went into club-making, drank his meager profits, died poor and got a pauper's burial.

Tom made his way to the cemetery's south wall. By mid-morning the dew had evaporated. The turf was dry – good footing for his shiny brown shoes. Tom made his way between other families' plots to the Morris plot and to Tommy's monument. It was not far short of life-sized, set into the wall, now weathered with age, white paint chipping off the out-of-round ball at the statue's feet. This statue of Tommy had been addressing that ball for twenty-nine years, five years more than Tommy had lived.

Near the statue stood the white marker Tom still thought of as Wee Tom's stone. There were now five more names on it. Tommy would have been angry to see the careless line devoted to Meg (*Margaret Morris or Drennen, who died 11th Sept 1875)*, whose maiden name was Drinnen, not Drennen, and who died on 4 September. By the time the stone was carved, no one noticed the errors.

There was no room for more names on Wee Tom's stone. When Tom's time came, he would need a new marker. He knew that his time was near. Tom had lived to see the future through his squinted eyes. He had lived to see the year 1908, when men flew in aeroplanes and sent their voices through wires at lightning speed and he had read the ninetieth Psalm enough to see the words without opening his Bible. 'The days of our years are threescore years and ten; and if by reason of strength they be fourscore years, yet is their strength labour and sorrow; for it is soon cut off, and we fly away.'

One day a reporter followed him home. Tom invited the man in for tea. Leading him up the gravel path through the garden, Tom climbed a flight of stairs to his sitting room, overlooking the links. 'He lights a gas stove in his house, where he has stored lots of wood for clubs,' his guest wrote, 'thorn and apple and linden-wood for heads, hickory and ash for shafts. Sits in his armchair and lights his briar-root pipe. A large window looks out over the putting green on the first hole, the teeing-ground of the starting point, the rocks, the sea, of which he says he "never wearies". He'll still holler at local lads playing on the Home green: "Off that puttin' green!" with a roar like a wounded lion.'

Tom was amused at the way writers practically queued up to visit him, filling notebooks with what they must have hoped would be his last words. 'Let us look at him in his home,' Tulloch wrote in a magazine story. 'Above his mantelpiece there is a large frame containing photographs,' the largest of which showed his golfing sons, Tommy on one side and Jimmy on the other, with the course record they had briefly shared beneath: the magical number 77. 'The walls of Tom's sanctum are covered with photographs of famous golfers and great golf matches. His bedroom is similarly decked, and on his toilet-table and mantelpiece are heaps of golf balls. He always sleeps with the window open, and one morning he woke to find himself half-enveloped in snow.' Tulloch was already burnishing anecdotes for the biography he would publish within weeks of Tom's demise.

'His habits are very simple and on a Sunday night you will find him, after having seen him officiate as an elder of the town church, quietly reading his family Bible with the big print. And if you ask him, he will rise from its perusal to show you the famous trophy, the champion belt of red morocco with rich silver ornamentations, bearing golfing devices. This became the property of young Tommy through three annual consecutive wins.'

Tom never had to be asked to show off the Championship Belt. 'I have it in my house,' he told another writer. 'In my eyes it is absolutely priceless.'

Hefting the Belt became something of a rite of passage for visitors. He would guide their hands over its red leather and tarnished silver plates, pointing out the medal to the left of the buckle that read TOM MORRIS JR, CHAMPION GOLFER. Many were surprised at how heavy the Belt was. 'Heavy with memories,' Tom said.

He was often asked about the golfers of the old days. Allan Robertson was the 'cleverest little player', he said. 'Willie Park was a splendid driver and a splendid putter. I've been neither, yet I managed to beat him.' The Rook had his days Tom said, and Davie Strath would be more remembered had he not played his best when Tommy played better. Yet they were small beer compared to the one who must never be forgotten.

'I could cope with 'em all on the course,' said Tom. 'All but Tommy. He was the best the old game ever saw.'

After Tom retired as greenkeeper in 1903, the R&A kept him on full salary and renamed the Old Course's eighteenth hole after him. The boneyard Home Hole has officially been the Tom Morris Hole ever since, though hardly anyone calls it that. The club also made Tom an honorary member – a bit of an afterthought after forty years of service. Not that he would have dreamed of exercising the unspecified privileges of his honorary membership. Even as G.O.M. he was the same tradesman who had spent decades tapping on the club secretary's window. Tom would have felt as uneasy in the hushed corridors of the R&A clubhouse as the gentlemen would have felt seeing him there. He made life easier for everyone by spending his days 300 yards away, in a sunny corner of the members' lounge at the New Club.

Founded in 1902, the New Club incorporated a clutch of local golf societies including the Rose Club. Each chipped in £100 to buy a house beside the eighteenth fairway, which they turned it into their clubhouse. The New Club's members included merchants, professors and a former town provost as well as grocers, tailors, hatters, fishmongers and a confectioner. They had wanted to call themselves the Tom Morris Golf Club, but Tom said he would bolt if they did. Instead, he became the club's unofficial figurehead. Tom Morris spent long afternoons in a bright corner of the members' lounge, sitting in a leather chair by the window, watching golfers bump balls through the Valley of Sin to the Home green while the sun through the window warmed his bones. He would smile and nod when someone tapped his shoulder or squeezed his hand, but his memory was going; he greeted old friends as if meeting them for the first time.

On a Sunday in May 1908, Tom made his way from church to his usual seat by the window at the New

Club. From here he could see what he still called the Home Hole, with the R&A clubhouse to his right and the sea beyond. To his left the course bent towards the River Eden, as it had for centuries. His old enemies, the whins, were young again, bursting with spring blooms. Tom, feeling as though he was going to burst, climbed out of his chair and started for the toilet.

A short, dark corridor led from the members' lounge to the loo. There were two doors at the end of the corridor. The one on the right was the toilet door. The other opened onto a stone staircase to the cellar. Tom, coming from his seat in dazzling sun, fuddled and momentarily blind in the darkness, opened the door on the left and stepped into space.

# EPILOGUE

# *St Andrews Forever*

THE OPEN CHAMPIONSHIP has not been held at
Prestwick since 1925. The Prestwick links doubled in
size after the club bought land north of the old stone
wall and extended the course from twelve to eighteen
holes – the St Andrews standard – but in time the
tournament outgrew its birthplace. Today Prestwick
is quiet, the breeze off the Firth of Clyde skimming
shaggy dunes where the schoolboy Tommy Morris
ran. Goosedubs Swamp is long gone, drained and re-
turfed. The links' humps and hollows, blessedly free
of the whins in the Morrises' day, are choked with
whins planted later to make the course look more like
a 'classic links', which is to say more like St Andrews.
The only sign that the Open began here at Prestwick
is a cairn on the spot where the first teeing-ground
used to be. A plaque on the cairn gives the length of
Tom's opening hole, 578 yards, and the date of the
first Open, 17 October 1860. There is no mention of
Tommy's miracle three on this hole at the 1870 Open,

or his 1869 ace at the Station Hole, golf's first recorded hole-in-one, or his four consecutive Open victories on this course, but then it's a small plaque.

St Andrews is a different story. The town's golf heritage is all over the place, from Tommy's memorial in the cathedral cemetery to £90 hickory putters in the souvenir shop by the Home green to the £822-a-night Royal & Ancient Suite at the hulking Old Course Hotel to the golf-ball shaped mints in the tourist centre on Market Street. This is Provost Playfair's dream come true with a vengeance, the thousand-year-old town reborn as golf's capital. Where generations of religious pilgrims once came looking for St Andrew's kneecap, golfers now make pilgrimages to the Old Course. It wasn't the first course, but it is the most important, due largely to the work Tom Morris began here in 1864, when he brought his family home from Prestwick.

Tom took over a mangy links that wound along narrow footpaths through stands of whins, with putting-greens pocked by heather, crushed shells and bare dirt. He turned it into a course that was the envy of the world. As a player, he won four Opens and helped make the professional game respectable. Tom heard his supporters shout 'St Andrews forever' when he beat another town's champion and heard the same glad shout when Tommy won the Championship Belt. When Tommy surpassed him, he became his son's ally and playing partner, and after Tommy died he carried on for decades as the game's G.O.M., golf's living memory and its tireless publicist. No one ever did more for his sport or his native town.

The Royal & Ancient Golf Club of St Andrews has been the game's ruling body since 1897, when Tom ceded his role as the ultimate authority on balls that landed in beards or went down rabbit holes. Today the R&A oversees golf everywhere except in the USA and Mexico, where its younger cousin the USGA rules. Today there are fifty million golfers worldwide, playing on more than 30,000 courses, each of which can trace its lineage back to the course that Tom built.

Today he oversees the Old Course from a spot halfway up the west wall of the R&A clubhouse. A bronze bust there inscribed 'Tom Morris 1821–1908', shows the most famous St Andrean in a buttoned tweed jacket and full Mosaic beard, looking to his right, towards the first tee, as if to say, 'You may go now, gentlemen.' Golf's G.O.M. would be amazed to see the golfers queuing up to pay £120 to attack his old links with titanium drivers and anvil-shaped milled-aluminium putters. He might enjoy the golf-ball ads that show him as a ghost, gaping at a three-piece, 392-dimple polybutadiene ball, and he would surely love another wonder: a five-pound note with his picture on it, issued in 2004 by the Royal Bank of Scotland to mark the R&A's 250th anniversary. In the twenty-first century, the symbol of the R&A is not a red-jacketed gentleman or even a full member of the club, but the son of John Morris the weaver.

The Open returns to the Old Course every five years. The tournament Tom helped create, now run solely by the R&A, is golf's premier event. In all of sport, only the Olympics and football's World Cup draw more television viewers worldwide. The winner isn't merely the Champion Golfer of Scotland anymore; he is 'Champion Golfer of the Year'. First-place money has grown from £0 in the Open's first four years, when custody of the Belt was thought to be reward enough, to a year's custody of the Claret Jug and a cheque for £720,000.

The Open champion at St Andrews in 2000 and again in 2005 was Tiger Woods, a former junior-golf celebrity who turned professional at the age of twenty and soon reached a level of dominance unseen since Tommy's day. But Woods struggled after his 2005 Open title. He couldn't hit his driver in the fairway. Then came news that Woods' father, Earl, was dying of prostate cancer. Tiger pressed to win for his father, but only played worse. Earl Woods died two months before the 2006 Open Championship at Royal Liverpool Golf Club, Hoylake. This was the course that George Morris, Tom's brother, laid out in 1869, digging the holes with a penknife, the course where Tommy won the richest tournament in early golf history three years later. Hoylake is flat and hard with knee-high rough – no place for a crooked driver. During Open week in 2006, Woods left his driver in the bag and played four rounds that Old Tom would have applauded, hitting irons off the tees, tacking his way from point to point, bouncing approach shots onto the greens. He had a miracle shot of his own, a 205-yard four-iron that bounded into the cup for an eagle two. Later he holed a last putt for a two-stroke win and then, unexpectedly, burst into tears. 'I miss my Dad so much,' said Woods, 'and I wish he could have seen this one last time.'

Tom Morris had the joy of seeing all four of his son's Open victories and the sorrow of outliving all five of his children: Wee Tom, Lizzie, Jack, Jimmy and Tommy, the one everybody wanted to talk about.

Tom collected testimonials to Tommy's genius. There were many, but one will do here. In the early 1900s, William Doleman, who had been low amateur in Tommy's Opens, answered partisans of the Great Triumvirate – Harry Vardon, J.H. Taylor and James Braid – who claimed old-timers like Doleman romanticized Young Tom Morris. 'I know with whom lies the prejudice, and I leave all such to love their own darkness,' Doleman wrote. 'Some of these moderns are grand golfers, no doubt, but the more I think out these things, the more I am convinced of Tommy's surpassing greatness.'

Just inside the R&A clubhouse is a glass display case that holds the Claret Jug. The first name on the trophy is *Tom Morris Jr*, the latest is *Tiger Woods*. Between them are Vardon, Taylor, Braid, Bobby

Jones, Arnold Palmer, Jack Nicklaus and sixty-seven others, all members of the game's most exclusive fraternity. The Claret Jug may be the most important trophy in golf, but it is not alone in its display case. Above it hangs Tommy's Championship Belt. In 1908, Tom's grandchildren, following his wishes, gave the Belt to the R&A so that it could be seen by all who entered the clubhouse.

Moments after Tom went looking for the loo at the New Club on 24 May 1908, according to the *Citizen*, 'the noise of someone falling was heard ... Old Tom was found in an unconscious condition.' It was mercifully quick: he cracked his skull at the bottom of the stairs and never woke up. But perhaps Tom had time for a last blink of thought. An eighty-six-year-old man falling in the dark, he might have seen the links in the late-day sun that casts shadows over every bump and makes the land look like water. He might have seen his son again, a brave boy knocking in a putt to beat his Da and flinging his putter straight up. Whatever Tom believed his sins to be, he had lived the last thirty-three years of his life in Tommy's honour.

# Acknowledgments

One of the perks of writing a book is following leads that lead to friendships. Among the pleasures of working on *Tommy's Honour* was meeting Dr David Malcolm of St Andrews, whose intellect may be matched only by his warmth and generosity. 'Doc' Malcolm welcomed me into his life and his work, providing details of Tom and Tommy's lives as well as most of what I know about Margaret. He would not tell the story the same way I have (any mistakes are mine), but he has been a crucial resource, a kind host and a prized friend. I am also a fan of his wife, Ruth, who paints the world's most gorgeous mackerels.

Dr Bruce Durie of Strathclyde University in Glasgow wrote a clever 2003 novel called *The Murder of Young Tom Morris* – recommended reading for anyone who likes this book. Bruce shared his research with me: census entries, marriage and death records, train schedules from 1864. He put me up in his home and whipped up the best haggis I have ever had. Note to the Grand Ole Opry: Dr Durie is also a gifted country-western singer. Fond thanks to Bruce, with shout-outs to Adrienne and Jamie.

Golf fans know David Joy as the actor who plays Tom Morris in Titleist commercials with John Cleese. I'm glad to know David, whose one-man show as Old Tom is not to be missed (ditto his book *The Scrapbook of Old Tom Morris*), as a source of historic books, photos and artifacts. We used hickory clubs to knock balls around his garden, then talked for hours. I still owe him a Tennent's lager.

I owe thanks to many others in Scotland, England and America. Golf historian David Hamilton showed me around the R&A clubhouse and lent me a tie to wear inside. Peter Lewis, director of the British Golf Museum, shared his views on early professional golf and pointed me to the St Andrews University library (open until midnight!), where I spent many nights unspooling microfiche, poring over 135-year-old editions of the *St Andrews Citizen* and the *Fifeshire Journal*. The staff there were patient and helpful, as were the folks at the Mitchell Library in Glasgow, where I thumbed the crinkly pages of original copies of *The Field*. In Hoylake club historian Joe Pinnington played host to a round of golf at last year's Open venue and gave me the key to Royal Liverpool's library. At Prestwick Golf Club, Ian Bunch led me through his club's archives. Robert Fowler and Neil Malcolm provided helpful facts from the archives of Royal North Devon Golf Club and Stirling Golf Club, respectively. Director Rand Jerris and librarian Doug Stark welcomed me to the USGA Library in Far Hills, New Jersey, where the marvellous Patty Moran helped me chase 19th Century stories through the stacks.

Many thanks to Michael Doggart for publishing *Tommy's Honour*. I am also grateful to Tom Whiting for his sharp edit and to PFD's Jim Gill for his help with the proposal. In the US, Bill Shinker of Gotham Books got the ball rolling and Scott Waxman was crucial at every turn.

Almost 40 years ago my mother, Dr Patricia Cook of Indianapolis, took me to Pleasant Run Golf Course for my first round of golf. Her kindness and love of the game are still part of my life. Thanks, Mom.

Much of the spirit of this father-son story had its source in the generous soul of Art 'Lefty' Cook, minor-league pitcher, Hall of Fame father. Dad, I miss you every day.

On 19 December 1981, I went to a J Geils Band concert with the best thinker and writer I know. In 1986 she took me to Scotland – my first pilgrimage – and the seeds of this book were sown. Pamela Marin, whose memoir, *Motherland*, is a model of deep feeling and crystalline writing, is my in-house editor, partner and paramour. To her I owe the other great loves of